SECOND EDITION

Passing

the

CPE

College Placement Examination

Frank Pintozzi

Timothy Ransom

Elaine Hubbard

Kennesaw State College

CPC *CONTEMPORARY PUBLISHING COMPANY*

508 ST. MARYS STREET, RALEIGH, N.C. 27605—(919) 821-4566

ACKNOWLEDGEMENTS

A book is never written in isolation. Several people gave of their time and talents preparing this text. We grateful to our diligent typists. Carol Callahan, Sheila Coen, and Glen Owen. Not only did they decipher our handwriting, but they also made many suggestions about the manuscript. We extend our appreciation to Colleen Pintozzi for helping to prepare the reading section and to Harriet Gustafson for proofreading the math section.

We are also indebted to Dr. Joe Kelly, Director of the Instructional Resource Center at Kennesaw College, for helping us with technical aspects of preparing the manuscript. Last, but certainly not least, we acknowledge all our former students, whose needs and concerns have guided us in preparing this book.

The Authors

ISBN: 0-89892-086-8

PREFACE

Passing the College Placement Examination is designed for two groups of students: 1) those preparing for admission to Georgia colleges and universities and 2) those currently enrolled in Developmental Studies programs. Passing the College Placement Examination (CPE) in Mathematics, English, and/or Reading is a requirement for exiting from these programs.

This book is divided into three parts—Mathematics, English and Reading. Each part is self-contained to meet individual needs for passing one, two, or all three subtests of the College Placement Examination. In addition, each part includes: 1) general information on each test; 2) a diagnostic test to assess needs; 3) discussion of skills and strategies for passing each test; 4) several practice tests. Answers to all tests and exercises are in the back of the book. Also provided is a list of books for improving math, English, and reading proficiency.

We welcome comments and suggestions for making this book more useful. Please write to Tim Ransom for English, Frank Pintozzi for Reading, or Elaine Hubbard for Mathematics. Our address is

> Kennesaw State College
> Department of Developmental Studies
> P.O. Box 444
> Marietta, GA 30061

A WORD ABOUT TEST FORMAT

Starting in 1989, new forms of the CPE went into use. The new forms for both English and reading (but not mathematics) use four instead of five alternative answers. Our revision for the second edition reflects the new format. However, it was decided to retain the five-alternative format in half the English and reading tests. We cannot be sure that future forms of the test will not return to the longer format. Meanwhile, students who take the tests with five alternative answers should be especially well prepared to take the shorter form of the actual CPE.

The format of all the tests in mathematics remains unchanged, that is, with five alternative answers.

TABLE OF CONTENTS

READING

KEYS TO EXAMINATIONS

PREPARATION

for the

MATHEMATICS TEST

MATHEMATICS

Introduction to the Mathematics CPE

The math portion of the College Placement Exam (CPE) is a 40 item, 45 minute, multiple choice test developed by ACT. The exam covers basic topics from high school mathematics including arithmetic, elementary algebra, intermediate algebra, and plane geometry. It is designed to evaluate not only manipulative skills, but also mathematical reasoning ability. Each of the 40 questions has 5 choices, with only one choice being correct. Occasionally, one is the choices is "None of the above."

The topics included and the approximate portion of the test devoted to each topic are:

Arithmetic	17%
Elementary Algebra	25%
Intermediate Algebra	43%
Geometry	15%

The portion of the test devoted to each skill is:

Computational	80%
Reasoning	20%

The arithmetic portion includes operations on rational numbers, square roots, absolute value, exponents, scientific notation, percents, averages, ratio and proportion, graphs, and terminology. The elementary algebra portion includes evaluating and simplifying algebraic expressions, linear equations and inequalities, and properties of exponents. The intermediate algebra portion includes operations on polynomials, factoring, operations on rational expressions, radicals, radical equations, rational exponents, graphs of linear equations, slope, intercept, systems of equations, and counting principles. The geometry portion includes the Pythagorean theorem, parallel lines, similar triangles, and area and perimeter of basic geometric figures. In the sections following the diagnostic test, the major points in each area are summarized and illustrated with examples.

Test Preparation

Take the diagnostic test in this book and use the guide to analyze your performance. This guide will help you determine the areas in which you need to concentrate your review. Following the diagnostic test, most of the topics covered on the exam are reviewed briefly. Carefully read the review sections and work the examples in each section. Remember, mathematics is not a spectator sport. It is played with a pencil and paper. So pick up your pencil and work problems. For more extensive review, see the list of references in this book.

After studying the review sections, practice taking the exam under timed conditions. In this book there are three practice exams similar in format to the CPE. You should allow yourself forty—five minutes to take the exam. Then score the exam using the key provided. Complete solutions are also included to help you determine how to solve the problems you missed. Calculators are not allowed on the CPE so do the practice exam without the aid of a calculator.

On test day here are some things to do:
——Do arrive a few minutes early to give yourself time to relax before the test.
——Do bring 3 or 4 #2 pencils, sharpened. A dull pencil may mean a dull mind.
——Do bring a watch to help you budget your time.

On test day here are some things not to do:
——Do not bring a calculator. Calculators are not allowed.
——Do not write on the test. Do all work on the scratch paper provided.

Diagnostic Mathematics Test

1. $-3 + 12 =$
   A. -36
   B. -9
   C. 15
   D. -15
   E. 9

2. $9 - 2(5 - 3) =$
   A. 14
   B. -14
   C. 13
   D. 5
   E. -4

3. $(-.3)(1.2) =$
   A. $-.36$
   B. $.36$
   C. 3.6
   D. -3.6
   E. -36

4. $-\dfrac{1}{8} + \left[-\dfrac{1}{12} \right] =$
   A. $-\dfrac{5}{24}$
   B. $\dfrac{5}{24}$
   C. $\dfrac{1}{24}$
   D. $-\dfrac{1}{24}$
   E. $-\dfrac{1}{10}$

5. $\dfrac{3}{4} \div \left[-\dfrac{2}{3} \right] =$
   A. $\dfrac{9}{8}$
   B. $-\dfrac{9}{8}$
   C. $\dfrac{1}{2}$
   D. $-\dfrac{1}{2}$
   E. 1

6. The prime factors of 30 are
   A. 2 and 3
   B. 1, 2, 3, 5, 6, 10 and 30
   C. 2, 3, 5 and 6
   D. 3 and 5
   E. 2, 3 and 5

7. The least common multiple of 9 and 15 is
   A. 135
   B. 60
   C. 3
   D. 5
   E. 45

8. In a bread recipe, the ratio of milk to flour is 5 to 4. If 7 cups of flour are used, how many cups of milk are used?
   A. $5\dfrac{3}{5}$
   B. $3\dfrac{3}{4}$
   C. $8\dfrac{3}{4}$
   D. 3
   E. 8

9. On consecutive days the stock market changed 20, -1, 10, -5, and 4 points. What was the average change for the market?
   A. 28
   B. 8
   C. -8
   D. -5.6
   E. 5.6

10. $\dfrac{-3 - 2(5)}{3(-8) - 2} =$
    A. $\dfrac{25}{24}$
    B. $-\dfrac{25}{24}$
    C. $\dfrac{5}{8}$
    D. $-\dfrac{1}{2}$
    E. $\dfrac{1}{2}$

11. $9(x + 5) + 4(x - 2) =$
    A. $13x - 3$
    B. $5x + 38$
    C. $5x - 3$
    D. $13x + 53$
    E. $13x + 37$

12. $7a - 2(3a - 4) =$
    A. $a + 4$
    B. $a - 4$
    C. $a + 8$
    D. $a - 8$
    E. $13a - 8$

5

Diagnostic Mathematics Test

13. When $a = -2$ and $b = 2$, the value of $2ab - 3b$ is

    A. -48
    B. 48
    C. -11
    D. 14
    E. -14

14. $-3x^3(-2x^4 - 5x^2 + 7x) =$

    A. $6x^7 + 15x^5 - 21x^4$

    B. $-6x^7 + 15x^6 - 21x^3$

    C. $6x^7 - 15x^5 + 21x^4$

    D. $6x^{12} + 15x^6 - 21x^3$

    E.   None of the above

15. $(3x - 2)^2 =$

    A. $9x^2 + 12x + 4$
    B. $9x^2 - 12x + 4$
    C. $9x^2 + 4$
    D. $9x^2 - 4$
    E. $3x^2 - 4$

16. $(1 + 2x)(1 - 3x) =$

    A. $1 - x$
    B. $1 - 6x^2$
    C. $1 + x - 6x^2$
    D. $1 - x - 6x^2$
    E. $1 + 5x + 6x^2$

17. $16 - 9x^2 =$

    A. $(4 + 3x)^2$
    B. $(3x - 4)^2$
    C. $(3x + 4)(3x - 4)$
    D. $(4 + 3x)(4 - 3x)$
    E. $(4 + 9x)(4 - 9x)$

18. The greatest common monomial factor of $a^3b^2c^2 + a^2b^3c^2 - 2a^2b^2c^3$ is

    A. a^2b^2c
    B. $a^3b^3c^3$
    C. $a^2b^2c^2$
    D. a^3
    E. a^2b^2

19. One of the factors of $6x^2 - x - 12$ is

    A. $2x + 3$
    B. $2x - 3$
    C. $x + 2$
    D. $x - 3$
    E. $6x + 2$

20. The value of y satisfying $5y - 2 = 28 - y$ is

    A. 24
    B. 5
    C. $\dfrac{13}{2}$
    D. $\dfrac{13}{3}$
    E. -5

21. The solution of $10 - 3(2x - 1) = 1$ is $x =$

    A. 2
    B. 1
    C. -1
    D. $\dfrac{4}{7}$
    E. $\dfrac{5}{3}$

22. The solution to the inequality $3x - 6 \geq 2x + 7$ is

    A. $x \leq 13$
    B. $x \geq 13$
    C. $x \leq 1$
    D. $x \geq 1$
    E. $x \geq \dfrac{13}{5}$

Diagnostic Mathematics Test

23. The values of y satisfying $5 - 9y \le 2 - 8y$ are

A. $y \ge 3$
B. $y \le 3$
C. $y \le -3$
D. $y \ge -3$
E. $y \le \frac{7}{17}$

24. The solution(s) of $x^2 + 16 = 8x$ is (are) $x =$

A. 4 or -4
B. 4 only
C. -4 only
D. 2 or 826
E. 2 only

25. The solutions of $y^2 - 3y - 28 = 0$ are $y =$

A. -7 or 4
B. 7 or -4
C. 2 or -14
D. -2 or 14
E. 14 only

26. $(-2x^2 y)^3 =$

A. $-8x^6 y^3$
B. $-8x^8 y^3$
C. $6x^8 y^3$
D. $-6x^6 y^3$
E. $-6x^9 y^3$

27. $(2x^3 y^6)(-3xy^4) =$

A. $6x^3 y^{10}$
B. $-6x^3 y^{24}$
C. $-x^3 y^{10}$
D. $-6x^4 y^{10}$
E. $-x^4 y^{10}$

28. $\dfrac{y^{12}}{y^3} =$

A. y^9
B. y^4
C. $\dfrac{1}{y^4}$
D. $\dfrac{1}{y^9}$
E. y^{15}

29. $\dfrac{1}{x^5} \cdot \dfrac{1}{x^3} =$

A. $\dfrac{1}{x^{15}}$
B. x^{15}
C. x^8
D. x^8
E. $\dfrac{1}{x^8}$

30. The sum of three consecutive odd integers is 117. If x represents the smallest integer, the equation which determines the value of the smallest integer is

A. $x + 2x + 3x = 117$
B. $x + (x + 1) + (x + 2) = 117$
C. $3x = 117$
D. $3x + 1 = 117$
E. $x + (x + 2) + (x + 4) = 117$

31. Simplify $\dfrac{4 - t^2}{t^2 - 4t + 4} =$

A. $\dfrac{1}{t - 2}$
B. $\dfrac{-1}{t - 2}$
C. $\dfrac{1}{4t}$
D. $\dfrac{-1}{4t}$
E. $-\dfrac{2 + t}{t - 2}$

7

32. The quotient,

$$\frac{x^2 - 9}{4x + 12} \div \frac{x - 3}{6} =$$

   A. $\quad \dfrac{(x - 3)^2}{24}$

   B. $\quad \dfrac{x + 3}{4x + 2}$

   C. $\quad \dfrac{3}{2}$

   D. $\quad \dfrac{3(x - 3)}{2(x + 3)}$

   E. $\quad \dfrac{(x - 3)^2}{24}$

33. The product,

$$\frac{x^2 - 9}{x^2} \cdot \frac{x^2 - 3x}{x^2 + x - 12} =$$

   A. $\quad \dfrac{-3x(x + 3)}{x + 4}$

   B. $\quad \dfrac{3x + 9}{12}$

   C. $\quad \dfrac{(x - 3)^2}{x(x + 4)}$

   D. $\quad \dfrac{(x + 3)(x - 3)}{x(x + 4)}$

   E. $\quad \dfrac{27}{12}$

34. $(-27)^{\frac{2}{3}} =$

   A. 9
   B. −9
   C. 18
   D. −18
   E. −6

35. $\sqrt{16x^{16}} =$

   A. $2x^4$
   B. $2x^2$
   C. $4x^4$
   D. $4x^8$
   E. $2x^8$

36. $\sqrt{12b^7} =$

   A. $6\sqrt{b^7}$
   B. $6b^2\sqrt{b^3}$
   C. $3b^3\sqrt{2b}$
   D. $2b^3\sqrt{3b}$
   E. $2b^2\sqrt{2b}$

37. In the solution to the system of equations
$$x + 3y = 19$$
$$x - y = -1,$$
the value of x is

   A. 4
   B. 3
   C. $\dfrac{9}{2}$
   D. 5
   E. −5

38. The graph of the equation $y = 3x - 2$ is

39. The slope of the graph of the equation
$5x - y = -6$ is

A. -5
B. 5
C. -6
D. 6
E. $\dfrac{6}{5}$

40. The y—intercept of the graph of the equation
$2x + 3y = 9$ is

A. $(0, 3)$
B. $(0, 9)$
C. $\left[0, \dfrac{9}{2}\right]$
D. $(0, -3)$
E. $(0, -9)$

41. For $x > 0$, $\dfrac{1}{x} + \dfrac{2}{x + 2} =$

A. $\dfrac{3}{x + 2}$
B. $\dfrac{2x + 2}{x(x + 2)}$
C. $\dfrac{3x + 2}{x(x + 2)}$
D. 2
E. $\dfrac{4}{x + 2}$

42. A car salesperson receives a base salary, b, and a commission of d dollars for each car sold. If c cars are sold the total salary, s, is

A. $s = b(c + d)$
B. $s = c + bd$
C. $s = d + cb$
D. $s = c(b + d)$
E. $s = b + cd$

43. A salesperson must call on 5 customers. How many ways can this be done?

A. 1
B. 60
C. 20
D. 5
E. 120

44. For $x \neq 1$, $\dfrac{x}{x - 1} - \dfrac{x - 2}{x - 1} =$

A. $\dfrac{-2}{x - 1}$
B. $\dfrac{2}{x - 1}$
C. 2
D. -3
E. $\dfrac{2x + 2}{x - 1}$

45. For $\dfrac{3}{x} = \dfrac{x}{12}$, $x =$

A. 6 only
B. -6 only
C. 2 or -2
D. 0 only
E. 6 or -6

46. If an engine requires 48 liters of gasoline in one week, how many liters are required in 10 days?

A. 58
B. 70
C. 480
D. 33.6
E. 68.57

47. A president, vice president, and treasurer are to be selected from 6 people. How many ways can a slate of officers be chosen?

A. 1
B. 6
C. 30
D. 60
E. 120

48. A card is to be selected from a deck of 52 cards, then a coin is tossed. One possible outcome is a 4 of diamonds and a head, written (4D, H). How many outcomes are possible?

A. 8
B. 13
C. 26
D. 52
E. 104

49. What value of y satisfies

$\sqrt{5 - 2y} = 7$?

A. -1
B. 1
C. 22
D. -22
E. 6

50. A solution of 40% acid is to be mixed with a solution of 25% acid to produce 10 liters of 34% acid solution. If x represents the number of liters of 40% solution and y the number of liters of 25% acid, one equation is $x + y = 10$. The other equation is

A. $.4x + .25y = 34$
B. $.25x + .4y = 34$
C. $40x + 25y = 34$
D. $.25x + .4y = 3.4$
E. $.4x + .25y = 3.4$

51.

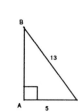

The length of $\overline{AB}$ is

A. 18
B. $\sqrt{194}$
C. 144
D. 12
E. 8

52. How long is a guy wire reaching from the top of a 10—foot pole to a point 8 feet from the base of the pole?

A. $4\sqrt{13}$
B. 6
C. $2\sqrt{41}$
D. 18
E. 2

53. The area of a square with side, x, is 7. What is the area of a square with side $2x$?

A. 14
B. 49
C. 98
D. 196
E. 28

54.

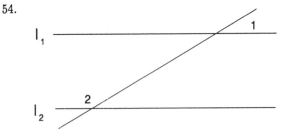

What is the sum of the measures of $\angle 1$ and $\angle 2$?

A. 90°
B. 270°
C. 360°
D. 45°
E. 180°

55.

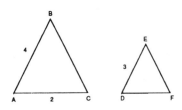

In the figure, the measures of $\angle A$ and $\angle D$ are equal and the measures of $\angle C$ and $\angle F$ are equal. What is the length of $\overline{DF}$?

A. 1
B. 2
C. $\dfrac{3}{8}$
D. 3
E. 1.5

56.

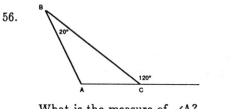

What is the measure of ∠A?

A. $40°$

B. $100°$

C. $140°$

D. $120°$

E. $80°$

57.

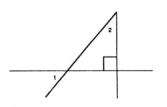

If the measure of ∠2 is $35°$, then the measure of ∠1 is

A. $55°$

B. $35°$

C. $145°$

D. $45°$

E. $65°$

58.

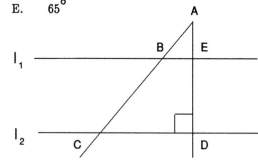

In the diagram, l_1 and l_2 are parallel, $\overline{AB} = 2$, $\overline{BE} = 1$, and $\overline{CD} = 2$. What is the length of $\overline{AC}$?

A. 4

B. $2\sqrt{2}$

C. 3

D. $\sqrt{13}$

E. 5

59.

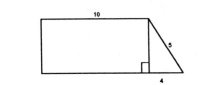

What is the area of the rectangle?

A. 6

B. 50

C. 40

D. 30

E. 19

60. What is the perimeter of a rectangle with length, 9, and width $\frac{1}{3}$ of the length?

A. 18.67

B. 12

C. 9.33

D. 24

E. 27

Diagnostic Mathematics Test Evaluation

To evaluate the result of the diagnostic test:

1. Check your responses using the key.
2. In the chart below, circle the number of each problem you did correctly.

3. Count the number of correct problems in each box and enter the total in the space provided.
4. Use the chart to determine which section in the book to review.

Circle the number of each problem you did correctly.	Number Correct
1 2 3 4 5 6 7 8 9 10	
11 12 13 14 15 16 17 18 19 20 21 22 23 24 25 26 27 28 29 30	
31 32 33 34 35 36 37 38 39 40 41 42 43 44 45 46 47 48 49 50	
51 52 53 54 55 56 57 58 59 60	

	Rating	Review
7—10 5—6	Good Fair	Arithmetic Section
14—20 10—13	Good Fair	Elementary Algebra Section
14—20 10—13	Good Fair	Intermediate Algebra Section
7—10 5—6	Good Fair	Geometry Section

1. $-3 + 12 = 9$

2. $9 - 2(5 - 3) = 9 - 2(2) =$
   $9 - 4 = 5$

3. $(-.3)(1.2) = -.36$

4. $-\dfrac{1}{8} + \left[-\dfrac{1}{12}\right] =$
   $\dfrac{-3}{24} + \dfrac{-2}{24} = \dfrac{-5}{24}$

5. $\dfrac{3}{4} \div \left[-\dfrac{2}{3}\right] = \dfrac{3}{4}\left[-\dfrac{3}{2}\right] = -\dfrac{9}{8}$

6. The factors of 30 are 1, 2, 3, 5, 6, 10, 15 and 30 but only 2, 3, and 5 are prime.

7. The lease common multiple of 9 and 15 is 45.

8. $\dfrac{5}{4} = \dfrac{x}{7}$ or $x = \dfrac{35}{4} = 8\dfrac{3}{4}$

9. $\dfrac{20 + (-1) + 10 + (-5) + 4}{5}$
   $= \dfrac{28}{5} = 5.6$

10. $\dfrac{-3 - 2(5)}{3(-8) - 2} =$
    $\dfrac{-3 - 10}{-24 - 2} = \dfrac{-13}{-26} = \dfrac{1}{2}$

11. $9(x + 5) + 4(x - 2) =$
    $9x + 45 + 4x - 8 = 13x + 37$

12. $7a - 2(3a - 4) =$
    $7a - 6a + 8 = a + 8$

13. $2ab - 3b = 2(-2)(2) - 3(2) =$
    $-8 - 6 = -14$

14. $-3x^3(-2x^4 - 5x^2 + 7x) =$
    $6x^7 + 15x^5 - 21x^4$

15. $(3x - 2)^2 = (3x - 2)(3x - 2) =$
    $9x^2 - 6x - 6x + 4 = 9x^2 - 12x + 4$

16. $(1 + 2x)(1 - 3x) =$
    $1 - 3x + 2x - 6x^2 =$
    $1 - x - 6x^2$

17. $16 - 9x^2 = (4 + 3x)(4 - 3x)$

18. $a^3b^2c^2 + a^2b^3c^2 - 2a^2b^2c^3 =$
    $a^2b^2c^2(a + b - 2c)$. The greatest common monomial factor is $a^2b^2c^2$.

19. $6x^2 - x - 12 = (2x - 3)(3x + 4)$

20. $5y - 2 = 28 - y$
    $6y = 30$
    $y = 5$

21. $10 - 3(2x - 1) = 1$
    $10 - 6x + 3 = 1$
    $-6x + 13 = 1$
    $-6x = -12$
    $x = 2$

22. $3x - 6 \geq 2x + 7$
    $x \geq 13$

23. $5 - 9y \leq 2 - 8y$
    $-y \leq -3$
    $y \geq 3$

24. $x^2 + 16 = 8x$
    $x^2 - 8x + 16 = 0$
    $(x - 4)^2 = 0$
    $x - 4 = 0$
    $x = 4$

25. $y^2 - 3y - 28 = 0$
    $(y - 7)(y + 4) = 0$
    $y - 7 = 0$ or $y + 4 = 0$
    $y = 7$ or $y = -4$

26. $(-2x^2y)^3 = (-2)^3x^6y^3 =$
    $-8x^6y^3$

27. $(2x^3y^6)(-3xy^4) = -6x^4y^{10}$

28. $\dfrac{y^{12}}{y^3} = y^{12 - 3} = y^9$

29. $\dfrac{1}{x^5} \cdot \dfrac{1}{x^3} = \dfrac{1}{x^8}$

30. x = first integer
$x + 2$ = second integer
$x + 2 + 2$ = third integer
$x + (x + 2) + (x + 4) = 117$

31. $\dfrac{4 - t^2}{t^2 - 4t + 4} =$

$\dfrac{(2 + t)(2 - t)}{(t - 2)(t - 2)} = -\dfrac{2 + t}{t - 2}$

32. $\dfrac{x^2 - 9}{4x + 12} \div \dfrac{x - 3}{6} =$

$\dfrac{x^2 - 9}{4x + 12} \cdot \dfrac{6}{x - 3} =$

$\dfrac{(x + 3)(x - 3)}{4(x + 3)} \cdot \dfrac{6}{x - 3} = \dfrac{3}{2}$

33. $\dfrac{x^2 - 9}{x^2} \cdot \dfrac{x^2 - 3x}{x^2 + x - 12} =$

$\dfrac{(x + 3)(x - 3)}{x^2} \cdot \dfrac{x(x - 3)}{(x + 4)(x - 3)} =$

$\dfrac{(x + 3)(x - 3)}{x(x + 4)}$

34. $(-27)^{\frac{2}{3}} = \left[\sqrt[3]{-27}\right]^2 =$
$(-3)^2 = 9$

35. $\sqrt{16x^{16}} = 4x^8$

36. $\sqrt{12b^7} = \sqrt{4b^6}\sqrt{3b} =$
$2b^3\sqrt{3b}$

37. $x + 3y = 19$
$x - y = -1$
Multiply the second equation by 3.
$\quad x + 3y = 19$
$\quad 3x - 3y = -3$
$\quad\quad 4x \quad = 16$
$\quad\quad\ x \quad = 4$

38. The y—intercept is $(0, -2)$ and the slope is 3 or $\dfrac{3}{1}$.

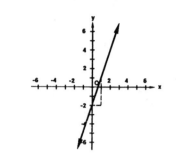

39. Solve for y.
$5x - y = -6$
$-y = -5x - 6$
$y = 5x + 6$
The slope is 5.

40. Solve for y.
$2x + 3y = 9$
$3y = -2x + 9$
$y = -\dfrac{2}{3}x + 3$
The y intercept is $(0, 3)$

41. $\dfrac{1}{x} + \dfrac{2}{x + 2} =$

$\dfrac{x + 2}{x(x + 2)} + \dfrac{2x}{x(x + 2)} = \dfrac{3x + 2}{x(x + 2)}$

42. $s = b + cd$

43. $5 \cdot 4 \cdot 3 \cdot 2 \cdot 1 = 120$ ways

44. $\dfrac{x}{x - 1} - \dfrac{x - 2}{x - 1} =$

$\dfrac{x - x + 2}{x - 1} = \dfrac{2}{x - 1}$

45. $\dfrac{3}{x} = \dfrac{x}{12}$
Multiply by $12x$.
$12x \cdot \dfrac{3}{x} = 12x \cdot \dfrac{x}{12}$
$36 = x^2$
$\pm 6 = x$

46. $\dfrac{48}{7} \cdot 10 = 68.57$

47. $6 \cdot 5 \cdot 4 = 120$ ways

48. $52 \cdot 2 = 104$ outcomes

49. $\sqrt{5 - 2y} = 7$
$5 - 2y = 49$
$-2y = 44$
$y = -22$

50. $.40x + .25y = .34(10)$
or $.4x + .25y = 3.4$

51. $5^2 + b^2 = 13^2$
$25 + b^2 = 169$
$b^2 = 144$
$b = 12$

52. $c^2 = 8^2 + 10^2$
$c^2 = 64 + 100$
$c^2 = 164$
$c = \sqrt{164} = \sqrt{4}\sqrt{41} = 2\sqrt{41}$

53. The length of a side of the smaller square is $\sqrt{7}$
and of the larger is $2\sqrt{7}$. Then
$A = \left[2\sqrt{7}\right]^2 = 4 \cdot 7 = 28$

54. $m\angle 1 + m\angle 2 = 180°$

55. Since the triangles are similar,
$\frac{3}{4} = \frac{x}{2}$ or $x = \frac{3}{2} = 1.5$.
The length of $\overline{DF}$ is $\frac{3}{2}$ or 1.5.

56. $m\angle A + 20° = 120°$
$m\angle A = 100°$

57. $m\angle 1 + 35° = 90°$
$m\angle 1 = 55°$

58. Since the triangles are similar,
$\frac{x}{2} = \frac{2}{1}$ or $x = 4$.
The length of $\overline{AC}$ is 4.

59. The width, w, is given by
$w^2 + 4^2 = 5^2$
$w^2 + 16 = 25$
$w^2 = 9$
$w = 3$
The area is $(10)(3)$ or 30.

60. The width is 3.
$P = 2l + 2w = 2(9) + 2(3)$
$= 18 + 6 = 24$

Chapter 1: Arithmetic

Operations on Real Numbers

Integers

This section includes addition, subtraction, multiplication, and division of positive and negative integers.

In addition, when the numbers are combined, the answer has the sign of the larger number (disregarding the sign).

Example 1: Addition
$10 + (-7) = 3$
$-3 + (-2) = -5$
$9 + (-15) = -6$

In subtraction, add the opposite of the subtrahend.

Example 2: Subtraction
$-6 - (-3) = -6 + 3 = -3$
$-5 - 3 = -5 + (-3) = -8$

In multiplication and division, the answer is positive if both numbers have the same sign and is negative if the two numbers have different signs.

Example 3:
Multiplication
$(-5)(-2) = 10$
$(-12)(5) = -60$
Division
$\frac{20}{(-4)} = -5$
$-36 \div (-12) = 3$

Fractions and decimals

Here, operations of addition, subtraction, multiplication, and division are included as well as conversion of fractions to decimals or decimals to fractions.

Addition or subtraction of fractions requires a common denominator.

Example 4: Subtraction

$$\frac{3}{4} - \frac{5}{6} = \frac{9}{12} - \frac{10}{12} = \frac{-1}{12}$$

To divide fractions, invert the divisor and multiply.

Example 5: Division

$$\frac{5}{12} \div \frac{7}{9} = \frac{5}{12} \cdot \frac{9}{7} = \frac{15}{28}$$

Example 6: The product of 2.13 and .7 is 1.491.

Order of operations

When more than one operation is included, operations within parentheses are performed first. Next multiplication and division operations are performed. This is followed by addition and subtraction.

Example 7: $5 - 2(7 - 10) =$
$5 - 2(-3) = 5 + 6 = 11$

Example 8: $4 + 6 \div 2 - 3 \cdot 5 =$
$4 + 3 - 15 = -8$

Example 9:
$$\frac{5 + 3(-2)}{3 - 2(5)} = \frac{5 - 6}{3 - 10} = \frac{-1}{-7} = \frac{1}{7}$$

Properties of real numbers

There are several terms and definitions necessary for understanding the questions on the exam.

1. A number is prime if it is not divisible by any number other than itself and 1.

2. A number, n, is a factor of b if b/n is an integer.

3. A number, n, is a multiple of b and c if n/b and n/c are integers. The number, n, is the least common multiple for numbers b and c if n is the smallest multiple of b and c.

4. The greatest common factor of b and c is the largest factor of b and c. This is also called the greatest common divisor.

Example 1: For the numbers 12 and 18, the greatest common factor is 6 and the least common multiple is 36.

Example 2: The factors of 60 are 1, 2, 3, 4, 5, 6, 10, 12, 15, 20, 30, and 60. The prime factors are 2, 3, and 5.

17

Applications

On the CPE, an understanding of practical applications of arithmetic as well as reasoning ability in arithmetic is necessary.

Averages and percents

To find the average of n numbers, add the numbers and divide by n.

Example 1: The average of 5, −10, 12, and −19 is

$$\frac{5 + (-10) + 12 + (-19)}{4} = \frac{-12}{4} = -3$$

To convert a percent to a decimal, move the decimal two places to the left. To convert a decimal to a percent, move the decimal two places to the right.

Example 2: $45\% = .45$ and $.035 = 3.5\%$

To determine what percent b is of c, divide b by c and convert the result to a percent.

Example 3: What percent of 80 is 25? Since $\frac{25}{80} = .3125$, the percent is 31.25%

To find a certain percent of a number, convert the percent to a decimal and multiply by the number.

Example 4: If an exam has 45 problems and 20% are word problems, how many word problems are there? Since $20\% = .2$, there are $.2(45)$ or 9 word problems.

Graphs

The interpretation of data reported by a bar, line, or circle graph is included in this area.

Example 5: The sales per day are shown in the graph. What is the average daily sales for the week?

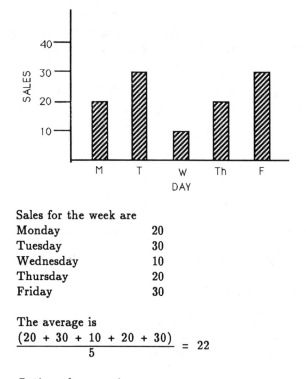

Sales for the week are

Monday	20
Tuesday	30
Wednesday	10
Thursday	20
Friday	30

The average is
$$\frac{(20 + 30 + 10 + 20 + 30)}{5} = 22$$

Ratio and proportion

Example 6: If it takes 4 hours for 9 people to do a job, how long does it take for 8 people to do the job?

Since $\frac{8}{9} = \frac{4}{x}$, $x = 4.5$. It takes 4.5 hours for 8 people to do the job.

Chapter 2: Elementary Algebra

Operations on Algebraic Expressions

Evaluation

To evaluate an expression involving one or more variables, substitute the given values of the variables into the expression. It is important to use the correct order of operations in completing the arithmetic.

Example 1: Evaluate $-x^2 + 2x - 3$ when $x = -3$.

$-x^2 + 2x - 3$

$= -1(-3)^2 + 2(-3) - 3$

$= -1(9) - 6 - 3 = -9 - 6 - 3 = -18$

Example 2: Evaluate $ab - 4a + 3b$ when $a = 2$ and $b = 0$.

$ab - 4a + 3b = 2 \cdot 0 - 4 \cdot 2 + 3 \cdot 0$

$= 0 - 8 + 0 = -8$

Removing parentheses and simplification

To simplify an algebraic expression, remove parentheses and combine like terms. Terms are alike if they involve the same variable and the same exponent. They are combined by combining the coefficients. Parentheses are removed using the distributive property.

Distributive Property: For real numbers a, b, and c,
$a(b + c) = ab + ac$ and
$a(b - c) = ab - ac$.

Example 3: $(2x^2 - 7x + 1) + (3x^2 + x - 2)$

$= 5x^2 - 6x - 1$

Example 4: $x + 2y + 3(x - y) - 2(x + y)$

$= x + 2y + 3x - 3y - 2x - 2y = 2x - 3y$

Multiplication of polynomials

Multiplication of polynomials also requires the use of the distributive property.

Example 5: $(2x + 3)(3x - 1) = 6x^2 - 2x + 9x - 3$

$= 6x^2 + 7x - 3$

Example 6: $(2x^2 + 1)(3 - x) = 6x^2 - 2x^3 + 3 - x$

$= -2x^3 + 6x^2 - x + 3$

Example 7: $(x + 2)^2 = (x + 2)(x + 2)$
$= x^2 + 2x + 2x + 4 = x^2 + 4x + 4$

Factorization of polynomials

The exam includes problems on identifying a common monomial factor as well as factoring trinomials.

To factor, first look for the greatest common monomial factor and use the distributive property to write the polynomial as a product. Second, check to see if the factors can be factored further.

Example 8: $2x^3 + x^2y - x^2 = x^2(2x + y - 1)$

Example 9: $x^2 - 9 = (x + 3)(x - 3)$

Example 10: $x^2 - x - 12 = (x + 3)(x - 4)$

Example 11: $2x^2 - 10x + 12 = 2(x^2 - 5x + 6)$
$= 2(x - 2)(x - 3)$

Equations and inequalities

The CPE includes solving basic equations and inequalities involving one variable, as well as formulating and solving word problems.

Linear equations

A linear equation in one variable is a statement of equality involving a single variable with 1 as the greatest exponent. There are two major principles in solving linear equations.

1. The same quantity may be added to both sides of an equation.

2. Both sides of an equation may be multiplied (or divided) by the same nonzero quantity.

These principles are used to isolate the variable in an equation and thus arrive at the solution. The proposed solution of an equation should always be checked by substituting back into the equation.

Example 1:
$$3x - 7 = 8 - 2x$$
$$5x = 15$$
$$x = 3$$

Example 2: Solve $2 - (x + 3) = 7$.
$$2x - x - 3 = 7$$
$$x - 3 = 7$$
$$x = 10$$

Applications

It is important to be able to formulate verbal information into an algebraic expression or equation. Some problems will ask only for the equation or expression to be formulated, while others will require a complete solution to the equation. Here are some hints on how to approach these problems.

1.   Read the problem carefully.
2.   Define the variable.
3.   Formulate the equation.
4.   Solve the equation.
5.   Interpret the solution to the equation.

Example 3: If two times a number is subtracted from 20 the result is 26. What is the original number? Let x = the original number. The equation is
$$20 - 2x = 26$$
$$-2x = 6$$
$$x = -3$$
The original number is -3.

Example 4: A mouse trap salesman receives a salary of d dollars per week plus a commission of c dollars per mouse trap he sells. If he sells n traps, what is his weekly income, I?
$$I = d + cn$$

Linear inequalities

Linear inequalities in one variable are similar to linear equations with the equal sign replaced with an inequality symbol. Inequalities are solved in the same manner as equations except for one important point.

If both sides of an inequality are multiplied (or divided) by a negative quantity, the direction of the inequality must be reversed.

Example 5: Solve $4 - 3x < 16$.
$$-3x < 12$$
$$x > -4$$

The solution of an inequality is often shown graphically on a number line. An open dot is used for $<$ or $>$ to indicate the end point is not included in the solution and a closed dot is used for $\leq$ or $\geq$ to indicate the end point is included in the solution.

Example 6: The graph of $-3 \leq x \leq 2$ is

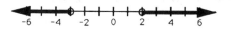

and the graph of $x < -3$ or $x > 2$ is

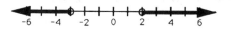

Second degree equations

A second degree equation in one variable involves a single variable with 2 as the greatest exponent. A second degree (or quadratic) equation may be written in standard form:
$$ax^2 + bx + c = 0, \quad a \neq 0.$$

It is advisable to know at least two methods for solving second degree equations. For either method, the equation should be written in standard form. The first method, and usually easier, is factoring. If possible, factor the polynomial. Set each factor equal to 0 and solve for the variable.

Example 7: Find the solution to
$x^2 + 5x - 6 = 0, x > 0.$
$$(x + 6)(x - 1) = 0$$
$$x + 6 = 0 \quad \text{or} \quad x - 1 = 0$$
$$x = -6 \quad \text{or} \quad x = 1$$

Since $x > 0$, the solution is $x = 1$.

Example 8: Find the solutions to
$x(x - 1) = 2.$
$$x^2 - x = 2$$
$$x^2 - x - 2 = 0$$
$$(x - 2)(x + 1) = 0$$
$$x - 2 = 0 \quad \text{or} \quad x + 1 = 0$$
$$x = 2 \quad \text{or} \quad x = -1$$

If the polynomial cannot be factored, use the quadratic formula to give the solutions. The formula works for any quadratic equation.

The quadratic formula is
$$x = \frac{-b \pm \sqrt{b^2 - 4ac}}{2a}$$

Example 9: Find the solutions to
$$x^2 + 3x + 1 = 0.$$

Since the trinomial will not factor, use the quadratic formula with $a = 1$, $b = 3$, and $c = 1$.

$$x = \frac{-3 \pm \sqrt{9 - 4}}{2}$$

$$= \frac{-3 \pm \sqrt{5}}{2}$$

Exponents

A positive integer exponent indicates the number of times the base is used as a factor. A negative exponent is defined by

$$a^{-n} = \frac{1}{a^n}$$

where $n > 0$.

Example 1: $5^3 = 5 \cdot 5 \cdot 5 = 125$

$$(-4)^{-3} = \frac{1}{(-4)^3} = -\frac{1}{64}$$

There are several properties of exponents which are used in simplifying exponential expressions.

1. $a^n \cdot a^m = a^{n+m}$

2. $\dfrac{a^n}{a^m} = a^{n-m}$

3. $(ab)^n = a^n b^n$

4. $\left[a^m\right]^n = a^{nm}$

Example 2:

$$x^3 \cdot x^7 = x^{10}$$

$$\frac{x^5}{x^3} = x^2$$

$$\frac{x^3}{x^5} = \frac{1}{x^2}$$

$$\left[x^3\right]^4 = x^{12}$$

Example 3: $\dfrac{1}{x^2} \cdot \dfrac{1}{x^4} = \dfrac{1}{x^6}$

Example 4: $\dfrac{6x^4 y^3}{15xy^5} = \dfrac{2x^3}{5y^2}$

Scientific notation

Scientific notation is used to write a number as the product of a number between 1 and 10 times 10 raised to an integer exponent.

Example 5: $3210000 = 3.21 \times 10^6$

$$0.00056 = 5.6 \times 10^{-4}$$

Chapter 3: Intermediate Algebra

Rational expressions

A rational expression is the quotient of polynomials. Operations involving rational expressions are similar to operations with fractions.

Simplification

To simplify, or reduce, a rational expression both the numerator and denominator should be factored completely and the common factors cancelled.

Example 1:

$$\frac{2x + 6}{x^2 + 5x + 6} = \frac{2(x + 3)}{(x + 3)(x + 2)}$$
$$= \frac{2}{x + 2}$$

Addition and subtraction

In addition and subtraction, the rational expressions must have a common denominator. Then the numerators are combined and simplified. Finally, if possible, the fraction is reduced.

Example 2:

$$\frac{1}{x} + \frac{3}{x + 3} = \frac{x + 3}{x(x + 3)} + \frac{3x}{x(x + 3)}$$
$$= \frac{4x + 3}{x(x + 3)}$$

Example 3:

$$\frac{2}{x - 2} - \frac{1}{x - 3} = \frac{2(x - 3) - (x - 2)}{(x - 2)(x - 3)}$$
$$\frac{2x - 6 - x + 2}{(x - 2)(x - 3)} = \frac{x - 4}{(x - 2)(x - 3)}$$

Multiplication and division

To multiply rational expressions, the numerator and denominator must be factored completely and factors common to both numerator and denominator cancelled. As in arithmetic, to divide, invert the divisor and multiply.

Example 4:

$$\frac{x}{x + 1} \cdot \frac{x^2 + 2x + 1}{x^2} = \frac{x}{x + 1} \cdot \frac{(x + 1)^2}{x^2}$$
$$= \frac{x + 1}{x}$$

Example 5:

$$\frac{x + 3}{2x - 4} \div \frac{x + 3}{x^2 - 4} = \frac{x + 3}{2x - 4} \cdot \frac{x^2 - 4}{x + 3}$$
$$= \frac{x + 3}{2(x - 2)} \cdot \frac{(x + 2)(x - 2)}{x + 3} = \frac{x + 2}{2}$$

Equations

When an equation involves a fraction or rational expression, the process of solving the equation is simplified by first multiplying both sides of the equation by the least common multiple of the denominators. This eliminates all fractions, making the subsequent computations easier.

Example 6:

$$\frac{x}{2} + \frac{x}{5} = \frac{1}{2}$$
$$10 \cdot \frac{x}{2} + 10 \cdot \frac{x}{5} = 10 \cdot \frac{1}{2}$$
$$5x + 2x = 5$$
$$7x = 5$$
$$x = \frac{5}{7}$$

Example 7:

$$\frac{12}{x + 2} = 4$$
$$(x + 2) \cdot \frac{12}{x + 2} = (x + 2) \cdot 4$$
$$12 = 4x + 8$$
$$4 = 4x$$
$$1 = x$$

Example 8:

$$\frac{3}{x} = \frac{x}{27}$$
$$27x \cdot \frac{3}{x} = 27x \cdot \frac{x}{27}$$
$$81 = x^2$$
$$\pm 9 = x$$

Rational exponents and radicals

A radical, $\sqrt[n]{a}$, is the number, b, where $b^n = a$. Note, for even n and $a < 0$, $\sqrt[n]{a}$ is not a real number.

A rational exponent is defined in terms of a radical.

$$a^{m/n} = (\sqrt[n]{a})^m$$

Example 1:

$$36^{1/2} = \sqrt{36} = 6$$

Example 2:

$$27^{2/3} = \left[\sqrt[3]{27}\right]^2 = 3^2 = 9$$

Simplification

Two major properties of radicals are used in simplifying radical expressions.

If a and b are positive, then

1. $\sqrt{ab} = \sqrt{a}\sqrt{b}$

2. $\dfrac{\sqrt{a}}{\sqrt{b}} = \sqrt{\dfrac{a}{b}}$

A radical expression is simplified when the expression under the radical does not have a perfect square factor.

Example 3:

$$\sqrt{x^7}\sqrt{x^4} = \sqrt{x^{11}} = \sqrt{x^{10}}\sqrt{x}$$
$$= x^5\sqrt{x}$$

Example 4: $\dfrac{\sqrt{x^9}}{\sqrt{x^3}} = \sqrt{x^6} = x^3$

Example 5: $\sqrt{50x^7} = \sqrt{25x^6}\sqrt{2x}$
$= 5x^3\sqrt{2x}$

Radical equations

To solve an equation with a variable under the square root, isolate the radical and square both sides of the equation to eliminate the radical. Then solve the resulting equation. Remember to check the answer by substitution.

Example 6:

$$\sqrt{3x - 4} = 3$$
$$3x - 4 = 9$$
$$3x = 13$$
$$x = \frac{13}{3}$$

<u>Graphs in the plane</u>

The CPE includes locating points in the plane and sketching the graphs of simple equations.

Cartesian plane and distance formula

Example 1: In the graph below, the coordinates of A, B, C, and D are (2, 0), (−1, 3), (−3, −1), and (1, −3) respectively.

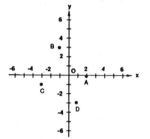

The distance between two points (x_1, y_1) and (x_2, y_2) is given by

$$d = \sqrt{(x_2 - x_1)^2 + (y_2 - y_1)^2}$$

Example 2: The distance between (−2, 5) and (−1, 3) is

$$d = \sqrt{\left[-1 - (-2)\right]^2 + (3 - 5)^2}$$
$$= \sqrt{(-1 + 2)^2 + (3 - 5)^2}$$
$$= \sqrt{(1)^2 + (-2)^2} = \sqrt{1 + 4} = \sqrt{5}$$

Graphs of linear equations

A linear equation may be written in the form $y = mx + b$ where m and b are constants. The graph may be drawn by determining values (x, y) which satisfy the equation and plotting these points in the plane. For a linear equation, these points should be colinear and the graph a straight line.

Another, often quicker, way to draw the graph is to use the slope and y—intercept. First, write the equation in the form $y = mx + b$. The point where the graph crosses the y—axis is called the y—intercept. The coordinates are $(0, b)$. The slope of the line, rise/run, is m. Express the slope as a fraction, $m = \dfrac{n}{d}$. Locate the y—intercept on the graph and from the y—intercept move up n units and over d units. The graph passes through these two points.

Example 3: Graph $y = -2x + 1$.

The y—intercept is $(0, 1)$ and the slope is -2 or $\dfrac{-2}{1}$.

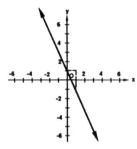

Example 4: Determine the slope and y—intercept of $3x - 4y = 16$.
Solve for y.

$$3x - 4y = 16$$
$$-4y = -3x + 16$$
$$y = \frac{3x}{4} - 4$$

The slope is $\dfrac{3}{4}$ and the y—intercept is $(0, -4)$.

Systems of equations

The solution to a system of linear equations is the point where the graphs intersect. A system of equations can be solved by several methods, one of which is the addition method. In this method one or both equations are multiplied by appropriate numbers, so that adding the equations together eliminates a variable. The resulting equation is solved and the number is substituted back into one of the original equations to obtain the value of the other variable.

Example 5:
$$2a + 3b = 4$$
$$3a + b = -1$$
Multiply the second equation by -3.
$$2a + 3b = 4$$
$$\underline{-9a - 3b = 3}$$
$$-7a = 7$$
$$a = -1$$
Substitute $a = -1$ into the second equation.
$$3a + b = -1$$
$$3(-1) + b = -1$$
$$b = 2$$
The solution is $a = -1$ and $b = 2$.

Applications

Many applications lead to systems of equations. The student should be able to formulate and solve a system of equations. The exam may ask for only the equations to be set up, for only the value of one of the variables of the solution, or for the entire solution. Read the problem carefully.

Example 6: A collection of nickels and dimes is worth 65 cents. If there are 10 coins and x represents the number of nickels and y the number of dimes, what are the equations?
$$x + y = 10$$
$$5x + 10y = 65$$

Counting principle

If events E_1, E_2,..., E_n, can occur in a_1, a_2,..., a_n, ways, then the number of ways E_1, followed by E_2,..., followed by E_n can occur is $a_1 \cdot a_2 \cdot ... \cdot a_n$.

Example 1: A football uniform can be made of 2 types of helmets, 4 styles of jerseys, and 2 colors for pants. How many uniforms are possible? There are $2 \cdot 4 \cdot 2$ or 16 possible uniforms.

Chapter 4: Geometry

Triangles

There are some basic properties of triangles necessary for the CPE.

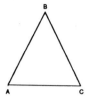

In the triangle above the vertices are labeled A, B, and C. The sides are usually referred to as $\overline{AB}$, $\overline{BC}$, and $\overline{AC}$. The angles are referred to as ∠BAC (or ∠A), ∠ABC (or ∠B), and ∠ACB (or ∠C). Notice, when 3 letters are used to name an angle, the vertex of the angle is the letter in the middle.

Properties

The sum of the measures of the angles of a triangle is always 180°.

Example 1: Find the measure of ∠ABC when $m∠BAC = 20^{\circ}$ and $m∠ACB = 30^{\circ}$. Since the sum of the angles is 180°,
$20^{\circ} + 30^{\circ} + m∠ABC = 180^{\circ}$ or $m∠ABC = 130^{\circ}$.

Triangles are similar if the corresponding angles are equal. If triangles ABC and DEF are similar, then the corresponding sides are proportional.

Example 2: Find the length of $\overline{AB}$.

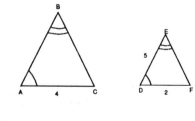

$\dfrac{\overline{AB}}{5} = \dfrac{4}{2}$ or $\overline{AB} = 10$.

The exterior angle of a triangle is equal to the sum of the remote interior angles.

Example 3: In the triangle below, what is the measure of ∠ABC?

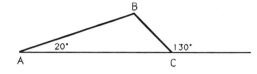

The sum of the remote interior angles is equal to the exterior angle. Therefore, $130^{\circ} = 20^{\circ} + m∠ABC$ or $m∠ABC = 110^{\circ}$.

Right triangles

In a right triangle, two of the sides are perpendicular to each other; that is, they form a 90° angle. These two sides are called the legs of the triangle. The other side is called the hypotenuse. The Pythagorean theorem gives the relationship of the lengths of the sides of a right triangle. If a and b represent the lengths of the legs and c the length of the hypotenuse, then

$$a^2 + b^2 = c^2.$$

Example 4: In the triangle below, what is the length, a, of $\overline{AB}$?

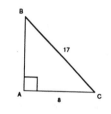

$a^2 + 8^2 = 17^2$
$a^2 + 64 = 289$
$a^2 = 225$
$a = 15$

Parallel lines

Parallel lines never intersect. A straight line crossing two parallel lines is called a transversal line.

Alternate interior angles are equal. Corresponding angles are equal. The sum of interior angles on the same side of the transversal is $180°$.

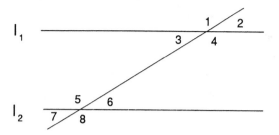

Example 5: Angles 3 and 6 are alternate interior angles and have equal measure. Angles 1 and 5 are corresponding angles and have equal measure. The sum of the measures of angles 4 and 6 is $180°$ since angles 4 and 6 are interior angles on the same side of the transversal.

Example 6: Which of the following angles shown in the diagram have equal measures and which have measures with sum $180°$?

1 and 5	equal
2 and 6	equal
3 and 6	equal
3 and 5	sum $180°$
5 and 7	sum $180°$
1 and 2	sum $180°$

Area and perimeter formulas

It is necessary to be familiar with some basic area and perimeter formulas and how to apply these formulas. In the following, A represents area, P perimeter, and C circumference.

Square with side, s

$$A = s^2$$
$$P = 4s$$

Rectangle with length, l, and width, w.

$$A = lw$$
$$P = 2l + 2w$$

Triangle with base, b, and height, h.

$$A = \frac{1}{2}bh$$

Circle with radius, r.

$$A = \pi r^2$$
$$C = 2\pi r$$

Example 7: What is the perimeter of a square with area 49? Since the area is 49, $s = 7$ and $P = 4(7) = 28$.

Example 8: What is the area of a triangle with base 7 and height 4?
$$A = \frac{1}{2}(7)(4) = 14$$

Example 9: Find the area of a circle with diameter 10. Since the radius is $\frac{10}{2}$ or 5, $A = 25\pi$.

PRACTICE

MATHEMATICS

TESTS

Practice Mathematics Test I

1. If 3 pounds of potatoes cost $1.20, what is the cost of 5 pounds?

   A. $6.00
   B. $2.40
   C. $4.80
   D. $2.00
   E. $1.80

2. For all x, $x^2 + 3x - 5 + 2x - 4x^2 =$

   A. $-3x^2 + 5x - 5$
   B. $3x^2$
   C. $-3x^2$
   D. $-4x^2 + 5x - 5$
   E. $3x^2 - 5x + 5$

3. $(-2)^5 =$

   A. -10
   B. -32
   C. 10
   D. 32
   E. 16

4. For all x, $(x - 3)^2 =$

   A. $x^2 + 9$
   B. $x^2 - 9$
   C. $x^2 - 6x - 9$
   D. $x^2 + 6x + 9$
   E. $x^2 - 6x + 9$

5. For all x and y, $(2x^2 y)^3 =$

   A. $6x^6 y^3$
   B. $8x^8 y^3$
   C. $8x^6 y$
   D. $8x^6 y^3$
   E. $6x^6 y$

6. If $f(x) = x^2 - 3x - 1$, then $f(-2) =$

   A. 1
   B. -11
   C. 9
   D. -3
   E. 23

7. The point with coordinates $(-2, 3)$ is

8. The solution of the inequality

   $4 - 3x \leq x - 6$ is

   A. $x \geq \dfrac{5}{2}$
   B. $x \leq \dfrac{5}{2}$
   C. $x \geq 5$
   D. $x \geq 1$
   E. $x \leq 5$

9. The least common multiple of 6, 8, and 12 is

   A. 3
   B. 24
   C. 2
   D. 48
   E. 576

10. For all x, $2(x - 3) - 4(x + 2) =$

    A. $-2x + 2$
    B. $-2x - 1$
    C. $-2x - 14$
    D. $2x - 14$
    E. None of the above

11. In the solution of the system of equations $3x + y = 4$ and $5x + y = 10$, the value of y is

    A. 3
    B. 1
    C. 5
    D. 7
    E. -5

12. If the figure below, AC is 5 units long and CD is 3 units long. What is the perimeter of rectangle ABCD?

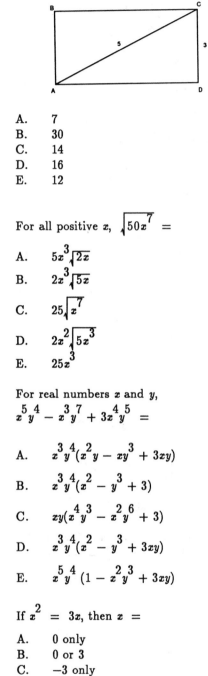

- A. 7
- B. 30
- C. 14
- D. 16
- E. 12

13. For all positive x, $\sqrt{50x^7}$ =

- A. $5x^3\sqrt{2x}$
- B. $2x^3\sqrt{5x}$
- C. $25\sqrt{x^7}$
- D. $2x^2\sqrt{5x^3}$
- E. $25x^3$

14. For real numbers x and y,
$$x^5y^4 - x^3y^7 + 3x^4y^5 =$$

- A. $x^3y^4(x^2y - xy^3 + 3xy)$
- B. $x^3y^4(x^2 - y^3 + 3)$
- C. $xy(x^4y^3 - x^2y^6 + 3)$
- D. $x^3y^4(x^2 - y^3 + 3xy)$
- E. $x^5y^4(1 - x^2y^3 + 3xy)$

15. If $x^2 = 3x$, then $x =$

- A. 0 only
- B. 0 or 3
- C. −3 only
- D. 0 or −3
- E. 3 only

16. $(x^5y^7)(xy^3) =$

- A. x^6y^{10}
- B. x^5y^{10}
- C. x^6y^4
- D. x^4y^4
- E. x^5y^{21}

17. For before tax salary, s, if 35% is withheld for taxes, the expression for the take home salary, t, is

- A. $t = .35s$
- B. $t = s/.35$
- C. $t = 1.35s$
- D. $t = s - 35$
- E. $t = .65s$

18. $|-7| + |-2| - |3| =$

- A. 12
- B. −6
- C. −12
- D. 6
- E. 2

19. If $\dfrac{x}{2} + \dfrac{1}{3} = \dfrac{5}{6}$ then $x =$

- A. $\dfrac{10}{3}$
- B. $\dfrac{4}{3}$
- C. −1
- D. 1
- E. 0

20. In the figure below, the measure of ∠BCD is 100° and the measure of ∠ABC is 40°. The measure of ∠BAC is

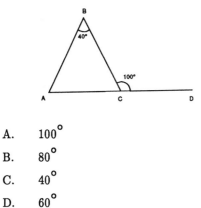

   A.   100°

   B.   80°

   C.   40°

   D.   60°

   E.   120°

21. In the figure below, lines l_1 and l_2 are parallel. If $\overline{AC}$ is 2 units long, $\overline{BC}$ is 3 units long, and $\overline{CE}$ is 4 units long, how long is $\overline{CD}$?

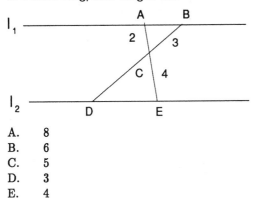

   A.   8
   B.   6
   C.   5
   D.   3
   E.   4

22. Which of the following is the graph of $y = x$?

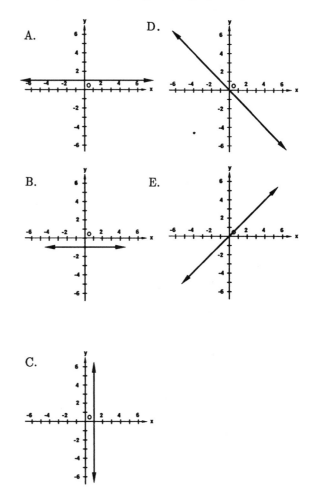

23. An orchestra always plays one of 10 Bach symphonies, followed by one of 8 Mozart symphonies, followed by one of 3 modern works. How many programs can it play?

   A.   21
   B.   720
   C.   7980
   D.   1330
   E.   240

24. $\dfrac{1.2 - 3(2.7)}{.23} =$

   A.   3
   B.   −3
   C.   −30
   D.   30
   E.   −.3

25. For $a = -2$ and $b = 3$, the value of $5ab + 3b - a$ is

    A. -23
    B. -19
    C. 37
    D. 41
    E. 23

26. $\dfrac{a^{12}}{a^4} =$

    A. a^8
    B. a^3
    C. 8
    D. 3
    E. a^{16}

27. $(x + 5)(2x + 3) =$

    A. $2x^2 + 13x + 15$
    B. $3x + 8$
    C. $2x^2 + 10x + 15$
    D. $x^2 + 8x + 15$
    E. $x^2 + 13x + 8$

28. $\sqrt{12}\sqrt{3} =$

    A. $\sqrt{15}$
    B. 18
    C. 3
    D. 2
    E. 6

29. For $x \neq \pm 1$, $\dfrac{1}{x - 1} - \dfrac{1}{x + 1} =$

    A. $\dfrac{2}{x^2 - 1}$
    B. 0
    C. $\dfrac{1}{x}$
    D. $\dfrac{2x + 1}{x^2 - 1}$
    E. $\dfrac{2}{x}$

30. If $\sqrt{3 - x} = 2$, then $x =$

    A. -1
    B. 1
    C. 4
    D. -4
    E. 5

31. The slope of the graph of $x - 2y = 6$ is

    A. 1
    B. -2
    C. $\dfrac{1}{2}$
    D. $-\dfrac{1}{2}$
    E. 6

32. If the diameter of a circle is 6 units long, what is the area of the circle?

    A. 9π
    B. 36π
    C. 3π
    D. 6π
    E. 12π

33. For $x \neq -2$ and $x \neq -1$, $\dfrac{x + 2}{x^2 + 3x + 2} =$

    A. $x + 1$
    B. $\dfrac{1}{3x}$
    C. $\dfrac{1}{x^2 + 3}$
    D. $\dfrac{1}{x + 1}$
    E. $\dfrac{1}{x + 3}$

34. One factor of $3a^2 - 5ab - 2b^2$ is

    A. $(3a - b)$
    B. $(3a + b)$
    C. $(a - 2b)$
    D. $(3a + 2b)$
    E. $(a - b)$

34

35. $(-8)^{\frac{2}{3}} =$
    A. $\frac{16}{3}$
    B. $-\frac{16}{3}$
    C. -2
    D. -4
    E. 4

36. If $x + \frac{1}{x} = 2$, then $x =$
    A. -1 only
    B. 1 or -1
    C. 1 only
    D. 2 only
    E. 2 or -2

37. A collection of nickels and dimes is worth $1.15. If there are 16 coins and n represents the number of nickels and d represents the number of dimes, then one equation is $n + d = 16$. The other equation is
    A. $5n + 10d = 1.15$
    B. $10n + 5d = 1.15$
    C. $10n + 5d = 115$
    D. $n + d = 115$
    E. $5n + 10d = 115$

38. If $x + 3 = 10 - 3(x - 1)$, then $x =$
    A. $\frac{5}{3}$
    B. $-\frac{5}{3}$
    C. 1
    D. $-\frac{5}{2}$
    E. $\frac{5}{2}$

39. The interest on $360 at 7% for 5 months is
    A. $25.00
    B. $2.10
    C. $21.00
    D. $10.50
    E. $105.00

40. $-\frac{2}{3} \div \frac{5}{9} =$
    A. $\frac{10}{27}$
    B. $-\frac{10}{27}$
    C. $-\frac{6}{5}$
    D. $\frac{6}{5}$
    E. $-\frac{1}{9}$

1. The largest prime factor of 24 is

   A. 24
   B. 12
   C. 8
   D. 3
   E. 2

2. The y— intercept of the graph of
   $5x + 2y - 10 = 0$ is

   A. (0, 5)
   B. (0, −5)
   C. (0, 10)
   D. (0, −10)
   E. (0, 2)

3. The graph below shows the percentage of
   voters in an election. In which group(s) did
   more than half vote?

   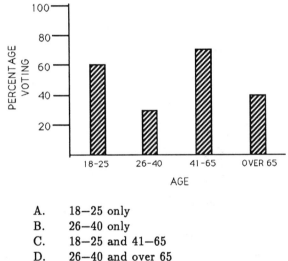

   A. 18—25 only
   B. 26—40 only
   C. 18—25 and 41—65
   D. 26—40 and over 65
   E. 41—65 and over 65

4. The solution of $2x - 5 = 7$ is $x =$

   A. 1
   B. 0
   C. 6
   D 10
   E. None of the above

5. For $x \neq 0$ and $x \neq -1$, $\dfrac{1}{x} + \dfrac{1}{x+1} =$

   A. $\dfrac{2}{x+1}$

   B. $\dfrac{2}{2x+1}$

   C. 1

   D. $\dfrac{2}{x}$

   E. $\dfrac{2x+1}{x(x+1)}$

6. What is the greatest common divisor of 12, 24,
   and 30?

   A. 2
   B. 6
   C. 120
   D. 12
   E. 30

7. For all x, $12x^2 - x - 6 =$

   A. $(4x - 3)(3x + 2)$
   B. $(4x + 3)(3x - 2)$
   C. $12(x - 3)(x + 3)$
   D. $(6x + 3)(2x - 2)$
   E. $(6x - 3)(2x + 2)$

8. The cost of renting a car is $30.00 plus 20
   cents per mile. If the cost of renting is C and
   m is the number of miles the car is driven,
   then

   A. $C = 20m + 30$
   B. $C = 30m + 20$
   C. $C = .2m + 30$
   D. $C = 30m + .2$
   E. $C = (30 + .2)m$

9. For $b = 3$ and $h = 5$, the value of
   $\dfrac{1}{2}bh$ is

   A. 15
   B. 7.5
   C. 30
   D. 4
   E. $\sqrt{15}$

10. $(2x^5 y^2)(3x^2 y) =$

A. $6x^{10} y^2$

B $6x^7 y^3$

C. $5x^7 y^3$

D. $5x^{10} y^2$

E. $6x^7 y^2$

11. If $2x^2 + 3x - 1 = 0$, then $x =$

A. $\dfrac{-3 \pm \sqrt{17}}{4}$

B. -1 or $-\dfrac{1}{2}$

C. $-\dfrac{1}{2}$ or -1

D. $\dfrac{1}{2}$ or -1

E. $\dfrac{3 \pm \sqrt{17}}{2}$

12. If the cost per pound of apples, pears, and grapes is a, p, and g respectively, then which expression states the cost of 2 pounds of apples and 3 pounds of pears equals the cost of 5 pounds of grapes?

A. $a + p = g$

B. $2a + 3p = g$

C. $a + p = 5$

D. $6ap = 5g$

E. $2a + 3p = 5g$

13. For all x, $(2x - 1)^2 =$

A. $4x^2 + 1$

B. $4x^2 - 1$

C. $4x^2 + 4x + 1$

D. $4x^2 - 4x + 1$

E. $4x^2 + 4x - 1$

14. The value of $-x^2 + 4$ when $x = -3$ is

A. 13

B. 1

C. -5

D. -1

E. -2

15. For positive x and y, $\sqrt{9x^9 y^{12}} =$

A. $3x^4 y^6 \sqrt{x}$

B. $3x^3 y^6$

C. $3x^3 y^3 \sqrt{y^3}$

D. $3x^4 y^6$

E. $4.5x^4 y^6 \sqrt{x}$

16. The product, $\dfrac{x^2 - x}{x^2 + x - 2} \cdot \dfrac{x + 2}{x}$, is

A. $\dfrac{x^2 - 1}{x^2}$

B. $\dfrac{(x - 1)(x + 2)}{(x - 2)(x + 1)}$

C. $\dfrac{-x}{x - 1}$

D. 1

E. $\dfrac{-x + 2}{x - 2}$

17. $.0000532 =$

A. 5.32×10^{-4}

B. 5.32×10^{-5}

C. 5.32×10^{-6}

D. 5.32×10^{4}

E. 5.32×10^{5}

18. For $x > 0$, $\dfrac{\sqrt[4]{27x^{11}}}{\sqrt{3x^5}} =$

A. $3x^2 \sqrt{x}$

B. $9x^3$

C. $3x^2 \sqrt[4]{x}$

D. $9x^2 \sqrt{x}$

E. $3x^3$

19. In the triangle below, $\overline{AB}$ is 10 units and $\overline{BC}$ is 6 units. What is the altitude (height) of triangle ABD?

A. 4
B. $\sqrt{136}$
C. 16
D. 10
E. 8

20. $a + b - (2a - 3b) + (a - 2b) =$

A. $-4b$
B. $4a - 4b$
C. $6b$
D. $2b$
E. $-2a - 4b$

21. $\frac{1}{2} + \frac{1}{3} =$

A. $\frac{1}{5}$
B. $\frac{2}{5}$
C. $\frac{1}{6}$
D. $\frac{5}{6}$
E. $\frac{1}{3}$

22. In the figure below, the measures of $\angle A$ and $\angle D$ are equal and the measures of $\angle C$ and $\angle F$ are equal. If $\overline{AB}$ is 40 units, $\overline{BC}$ is 30 units, and $\overline{DE}$ is 24 units, how long is $\overline{EF}$?

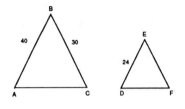

A. 18
B. 14
C. 24
D. 30
E. 50

23. $(.021)(3.2) =$

A. .672
B. .0672
C. 6.72
D. 67.2
E. .00672

24. The product, $(x + 1)(x^2 + 3)$, is

A. $x^3 + x + 3$
B. $x^3 + x^2 + 3x + 3$
C. $x^2 + 4x + 3$
D. $2x^2 + 3x + 3$
E. $x^2 + 3x + 3$

25. Three less than twice a number is -5. What is the number?

A. -1
B. 4
C. -4
D. $\frac{7}{3}$
E. $\frac{1}{2}$

26. $25 - x^2 =$

A. $(x + 5)(x - 5)$
B. $(5x - x)^2$
C. $(5x + x)^2$
D. $5(5 - x)$
E. $(5 + x)(5 - x)$

27. The graph of the solutions of $-1 \leq x - 2 \leq 3$ is

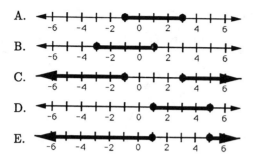

A.
B.
C.
D.
E.

28. What is the solution of the following system of equations?

$$x + 3y = 2$$
$$3x - 2y = 1$$

A. $x = \dfrac{7}{11}, y = \dfrac{5}{11}$

B. $x = \dfrac{13}{11}, y = \dfrac{3}{11}$

C. $x = \dfrac{3}{11}, y = \dfrac{19}{33}$

D. $x = 2, y = -\dfrac{1}{2}$

E. None of the above

29. The graph of the equation $2x - 3y = 9$ is

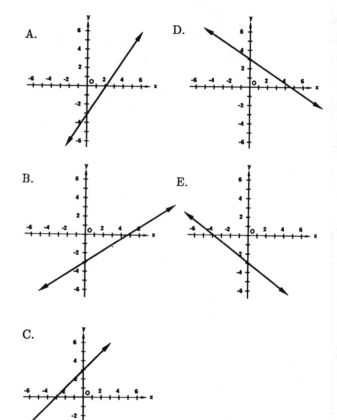

A.
B.
C.
D.
E.

30. The low temperatures for January 3–8 are given below. What is the average low temperature for January 3–8?

Date	Low Temperature
3	12°
4	-3°
5	-10°
6	-5°
7	25°
8	20°

A. 12.5°

B. 6.5°

C. 7.8°

D. 25°

E. -10°

31. For all real numbers x,
$x(x-3) - 4(x-3) =$

A. $x^2 - 7x + 12$

B. $x - 4$

C. $x^2 - 7x - 12$

D. $x - 3$

E. $x^2 - 4x - 6$

32. An $18m$ board is cut in 3 pieces. The second piece is twice as long as the first and the third is $3m$ longer than the second. If x represents the length of the first piece, then which equation determines the length of the first piece?

A. $x + (x+2) + (x+3) = 18$

B. $x + 2x + (x+3) = 18$

C. $x + (x+2) + (x+5) = 18$

D. $x + (x+2) + (2x+3) = 18$

E. $x + 2x + (2x+3) = 18$

33. $\left[3x^3\right]^2 =$

A. $6x^6$

B. $9x^9$

C. $3x^6$

D. $6x^9$

E. $9x^6$

34. If $\dfrac{4}{x-2} = 3$, then $x =$

A. 2

B. -2

C. $-\dfrac{2}{3}$

D. $\dfrac{10}{3}$

E. $\dfrac{2}{3}$

35. The solution of $2x^2 + 5x = 3$, $x > 0$ is

A. -1

B. 3

C. $\dfrac{1}{2}$

D. 1

E. -3

36. In the triangle below what is the length of $\overline{AB}$?

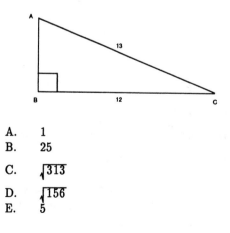

A. 1

B. 25

C. $\sqrt{313}$

D. $\sqrt{156}$

E. 5

37. For $x,\ y \neq 0$, $\dfrac{x^2}{4y^5} \cdot \dfrac{2y^2}{x^2} =$

   A. $2y^3$

   B. $\dfrac{x}{2y^3}$

   C. $\dfrac{1}{2y^3}$

   D. $\dfrac{1}{4y^4}$

   E. $4y^{2.5}$

38. A car travels 72 miles in 1 hour and 20 minutes. The average speed is

   A. 60 mph
   B. 54 mph
   C. 90 mph
   D. 65 mph
   E. 62 mph

39. In the figure below, lines l_1 and l_2 are parallel.

   What is is the sum of the measures of $\angle 1$ and $\angle 2$?

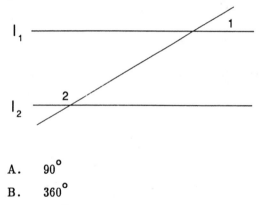

   A. 90°

   B. 360°

   C. 270°

   D. 180°

   E. 100°

40. If the length of a rectangle, l, is decreased by 4 and the width, w, is doubled, then the area is

   A. $(w + 2)(l - 4)$

   B. $\dfrac{lw}{2}$

   C. $\dfrac{l}{4}(w + 2)$

   D. $2w(4 - l)$

   E. $2w(l - 4)$

1. For all x, $(x + 3)(x - 5) =$
   - A. $x^2 + 2x - 15$
   - B. $x^2 - 2x - 15$
   - C. $x^2 - 2x - 2$
   - D. $x - 2$
   - E. $x - 15$

2. A ball is chosen from a box containing one red ball, one white ball, and one blue ball. Next a die is thrown. One possible outcome is a red ball and a 3, written (R, 3). How many outcomes are possible?
   - A. 18
   - B. 9
   - C. 36
   - D. 3
   - E. 6

3. If $5x - 3 = 4 - 2x$, then $x =$
   - A. $\frac{1}{3}$
   - B. $\frac{1}{7}$
   - C. $\frac{7}{3}$
   - D. 1
   - E. -1

4. $\frac{1}{6} - \frac{5}{14} + \frac{4}{21} =$
   - A. 42
   - B. $\frac{1}{42}$
   - C. $\frac{3}{23}$
   - D. $\frac{15}{21}$
   - E. 0

5. For all a and b, $a + 5b - 3a + 10b =$
   - A. $-2a + 15b$
   - B. $-2a - 5b$
   - C. $4a + 15b$
   - D. $4a - 5b$
   - E. $6a + 7b$

6. $50 \div 200 =$
   - A. 25
   - B. 2.5
   - C. .25
   - D. .4
   - E. 4

7. If $\dfrac{1}{x + 2} = 10$, then $x =$
   - A. 8
   - B. $-\frac{19}{10}$
   - C. $\frac{19}{10}$
   - D. 3
   - E. -2

8. Which of the following is the graph of the equation $y = -x + 2$?

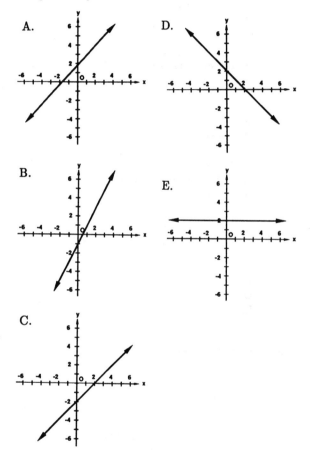

9. For all x and y, $y(x + y) - x(x - y) =$
   - A. $y^2 - x^2$
   - B. $x^2 - y^2$
   - C. $xy - x^2$
   - D. $y^2 + 2xy - x^2$
   - E. $-x^2 + xy + 2y$

10. $13.2 - 4.03 =$
    A. 2.71
    B   27.1
    C. −2.71
    D. −9.17
    E. 9.17

11. For all x, $(x^2 + 3x) + (x^2 - 4x + 3) =$
    A. $x^2 - x + 3$
    B. $2x^2 - x + 3$
    C. $2x^2 + 2x$
    D. $7x - 3$
    E. $-x + 3$

12. Which number is prime?
    A. 21
    B. 39
    C. 17
    D. 35
    E. 52

13. What is the solution of the pair of equations given below?
    $$2n + 3d = 4$$
    $$n + 2d = 1$$
    A. $n = 5, d = -2$
    B. $n = -2, d = 5$
    C. $n = 11, d = -5$
    D. $n = -1, d = 1$
    E. $n = -1, d = -2$

14. In which quadrants does the graph of $y = x^2$ lie?

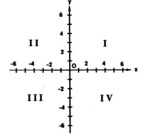

    A. I and II only
    B. III and IV only
    C. I and IV only
    D. I only
    E. IV only

15. If five pizzas are to be divided equally among eleven people, what fractional part does each person receive?
    A. $\dfrac{6}{5}$
    B. $\dfrac{5}{6}$
    C. $\dfrac{5}{16}$
    D. $\dfrac{5}{11}$
    E. $\dfrac{11}{5}$

16. In $\triangle ABC$, what is the length of $\overline{BC}$?

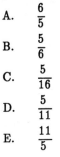

    A. 1
    B. 9
    C. 3
    D. $\sqrt{3}$
    E. $\sqrt{41}$

17. If $4 - 3(5) = 2(2 - 5) - x$, then $x =$
    A. −11
    B. 1
    C. 5
    D. −5
    E. 10

18. If $c = 2$, then $2 - 5c - 1 =$
    A. 11
    B. −9
    C. 9
    D. 13
    E. −22

19. For nonzero x and y, $\dfrac{x^4 y^3}{x^6 y^2} =$

  A. $x^2 y$

  B. $\dfrac{x^2}{y}$

  C. $x^{10} y^5$

  D. $\dfrac{y}{x^2}$

  E. $\dfrac{1}{x^{10} y^5}$

20. If the area of a square is 36, what is the perimeter?

  A. 144
  B. 36
  C. 18
  D. 48
  E. 24

21. In the figure below, if l_1 and l_2 are parallel, which pair of angles is supplementary (the sum of their measures is $180°$)?

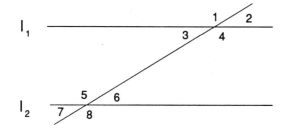

  A. $\angle 1$ and $\angle 4$
  B. $\angle 1$ and $\angle 5$
  C. $\angle 3$ and $\angle 6$
  D. $\angle 4$ and $\angle 6$
  E. $\angle 3$ and $\angle 7$

22. Which expression describes all values of t that solve $12 < 2t - 6$?

  A. $t < 9$
  B. $t > 9$
  C. $t > 6$
  D. $t < 6$
  E. $t > 3$

23. The cost of developing a roll of film is s cents plus a charge of r cents for each print. If there are p prints, the cost, C, of developing a roll is

  A. $C = s + r + p$
  B. $C = s(r + p)$
  C. $C = s + rp$
  D. $C = srp$
  E. $C = (s + r)p$

24. For all x, $(x - 2)(3 - x) =$

  A. -6
  B. $-x^2 - 6$
  C. $x^2 + 6$
  D. $x^2 - 5x + 6$
  E. $-x^2 + 5x - 6$

25. What is the area of rectangle ABCD?

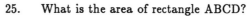
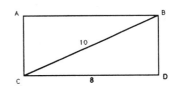

  A. 48
  B. 28
  C. 40
  D. 80
  E. 40

26. For all x, $x + 2y - 3(x - y) + 2y =$

  A. $-2x + y$
  B. $-2x + 7y$
  C. $-2x + 3y$
  D. $4x + y$
  E. $4x + 7y$

27. For all x, $(2x + 1)(x^2 - 3) =$

  A. $2x^3 + x^2 - 6x - 3$
  B. $2x^3 - 2x - 3$
  C. $2x^3 - 5x - 3$
  D. $2x^2 - 2x - 3$
  E. $2x^2 - 5x - 3$

28. For all a and b, $ab^2 - 3a^2b + ab =$

    A. $ab(b - 3a)$

    B. $a^2b^2(a - 3b)$

    C. $a(b^2 - 3b + 1)$

    D. $b(a - 3a^2 + 1)$

    E. $ab(b - 3a + 1)$

29. For nonzero x and y, $\dfrac{x^3}{5y^2} \cdot \dfrac{10y^5}{2x^6} =$

    A. $\dfrac{y^3}{x^3}$

    B. $\dfrac{x^3}{y^3}$

    C. $\dfrac{10x^9}{7y^7}$

    D. $\dfrac{10x^9}{7y^9}$

    E. $\dfrac{y^8}{x^8}$

30. For $x \neq 0$, $3 + \dfrac{4}{x} =$

    A. $\dfrac{7}{x}$

    B. $\dfrac{3x + 4}{x}$

    C. $\dfrac{4}{3x}$

    D. $\dfrac{4}{3 + x}$

    E. $\dfrac{7}{1 + x}$

31. If $\sqrt{1 - x} = 3$, then $x =$

    A. 9
    B. 2
    C. -8
    D. 8
    E. -2

32. For all x, $(3x^2 - x + 5) - (3x^2 + 2x - 4) =$

    A. $x^2 - 3x + 9$
    B. $x + 1$
    C. $x^2 + x + 1$
    D. $-3x + 1$
    E. $-3x + 9$

33. For all positive x, $\dfrac{x^2 + 6x + 5}{x + 5} =$

    A. $x + 6$
    B. $7x$
    C. $x + 1$
    D. $x^2 + 6$
    E. $x + 5$

34. What is the greatest common monomial factor of $4b^2 + 8b^3 + 2b^4$?

    A. $2b^4$
    B. $8b^3$
    C. $8b^4$
    D. $2b^2$
    E. $2b$

35. For nonzero x, $\dfrac{1}{x^9} \cdot \dfrac{1}{x^7} =$

    A. $\dfrac{1}{x^{63}}$

    B. $\dfrac{1}{x^2}$

    C. x^{16}

    D. $\dfrac{1}{x^{16}}$

    E. $-x^{16}$

36. For all positive y, $\sqrt{y^7}\sqrt{y^8} =$

    A. y^{15}
    B. y^{28}
    C. y^6
    D. $y\sqrt{y^7}$
    E. $y^7\sqrt{y}$

37. An alloy weighing 40 ounces, contains 15% gold. How many ounces of gold does it contain?

    A.   6
    B.   26.6
    C.   25
    D.   34
    E.   2.66

38. For all x, $(x + 1)(x - 5) =$

    A. $x - 4$
    B. $x^2 - 5$
    C. $x^2 - 6x - 5$
    D. $x^2 - 4x - 4$
    E. $x^2 - 4x - 5$

39. For $x < -2$, $\dfrac{1}{x} + \dfrac{2}{x + 2} =$

    A. $\dfrac{4}{x + 2}$
    B. $\dfrac{3}{x + 2}$
    C. $\dfrac{3x + 2}{x(x + 2)}$
    D. $\dfrac{3}{x(x + 2)}$
    E. $\dfrac{3}{2x + 2}$

40. For integers m, n, and p, if $mp = 6n$ where $p > 3$ is prime, then m must be a multiple of

    A.   3
    B.   5
    C.   12
    D.   4
    E.   7

47

Practice Mathematics Test 4

1. One pound of nuts costs $1.60. How many pounds can be purchased for $6.00?

   A. 3.75
   B. 2.67
   C. 4
   D. 9.6
   E. 4.4

2. The solution to $2x^2 + 3x - 9 = 0$, $x > 0$, lies between what two consecutive integers?

   A. -4 and -3
   B. -3 and -2
   C. 1 and 2
   D. 0 and 1
   E. 2 and 3

3. For $x, y \neq 0$, $\dfrac{x^3}{y^2} \cdot \dfrac{xy^4}{x^3 y^5} = ?$

   A. $\dfrac{1}{y^6}$

   B. $\dfrac{1}{y^3}$

   C. $\dfrac{x}{y^6}$

   D. $\dfrac{x}{y^3}$

   E. xy^3

4. $\dfrac{(3 \cdot 10^3)(4 \cdot 10^{-2})}{2 \cdot 10^4} = ?$

   A. .006
   B. .06
   C. 6000
   D. 600
   E. 60

5. The volume of a right circular cylinder is given by $V = \pi r^2 h$ where h is the height of the cylinder and r is the radius of the base. If the height of a cylinder is 4 inches and the diameter of the base is 6 inches, what is the volume of the cylinder?

   A. 96π
   B. 48π
   C. 24π
   D. 144π
   E. 36π

6. If $f(x) = x^2 + 1$ and the domain of f is $\{-1, 1, 2\}$, what is the range of f?

   A. $\{2, 5\}$
   B. $\{1, 4\}$
   C. $\{0, 2, 5\}$
   D. $\{0, 2, 3\}$
   E. None of the above

7. If $x = -1$, $y = 3$, and $z = 2$, then $xy^z = ?$

   A. 8
   B. -8
   C. 9
   D. -9
   E. -6

8. For $x > 0$, $\sqrt{50x} + \sqrt{18x} = ?$

   A. $5\sqrt{8x}$
   B. $8\sqrt{2x}$
   C. $5\sqrt{2x}$
   D. $2\sqrt{17x}$
   E. $\sqrt{68x}$

9. What is the equation of line ℓ?

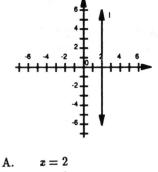

 A. $x = 2$
 B. $y = 2$
 C. $x = -2$
 D. $y = -2$
 E. $y = 2x$

10. If n is an integer, which expression must be an even integer?

 A. $2n + 1$
 B. $2n - 1$
 C. $n + 1$
 D. $2n^2$
 E. n^2

11. What is the value of y in the solution of the system of equations below?

$$x + 3y = 4$$
$$2x - 2y = 1$$

 A. $11/8$
 B. $7/8$
 C. $-7/8$
 D. $-11/8$
 E. 1

12. Which of the following is a factor of $4x^2 + 22x - 42$?

 A. $(2x + 3)$
 B. $(2x - 3)$
 C. $(x - 7)$
 D. $(2x - 7)$
 E. $(x + 3)$

13. The cost of a pound of cheddar cheese is one less than two thirds the cost of a pound of Swiss cheese. If c is the cost per pound of Swiss cheese, then which expression describes the cost of cheddar cheese?

 A. $1 - \dfrac{2}{3}c$
 B. $\dfrac{2}{3}(1 - c)$
 C. $\dfrac{2}{3}(c - 1)$
 D. $\dfrac{2}{3}c - 1$
 E. $(1 - \dfrac{2}{3})c$

14. For $x, y > 0$, $\sqrt{32x^9 y^6} = ?$

 A. $16x^4 y^3 \sqrt{x}$
 B. $16x^3 y^3$
 C. $4x^3 y^3 \sqrt{2}$
 D. $4x^4 y^3 \sqrt{2x}$
 E. $2x^3 y^3 \sqrt{8}$

15. In triangle ABC, the measure of angle A is x, the measure of angle B is $x + 60°$, and the measure of angle C is $2x$. What is the measure of angle A?

 A. $30°$
 B. $60°$
 C. $90°$
 D. $75°$
 E. $45°$

16. Which product(s) is (are) divisible by 12?

 I. $42 \cdot 10$
 II. $30 \cdot 35$
 III. $13 \cdot 23$

 A. I only
 B. I and II
 C. II only
 D. II and III
 E. III only

17. For $x > 0$, $\dfrac{1}{x + 3} - \dfrac{1}{x + 2}$ = ?

    A. $\dfrac{5}{(x + 3)(x + 2)}$

    B. $\dfrac{-1}{(x + 3)(x + 2)}$

    C. $\dfrac{1}{(x + 3)(x + 2)}$

    D. $\dfrac{-x + 3}{x + 3}$

    E. 0

18. For $x > 0$, $x^{3/4}$ = ?

    A. $\sqrt[4]{x^3}$

    B. $\sqrt[3]{x^4}$

    C. $x^3\sqrt{x}$

    D. $\dfrac{3}{4}x$

    E. $x^{-4/3}$

19. Which points(s) has (have) the property that the product of the coordinates is less than zero?

    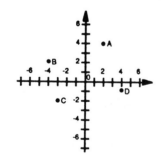

    A. B only
    B. D only
    C. B and D
    D. C only
    E. C and D

20. If $x = -1$, what is the value of $-x^3 + x^2 + x + 1$?

    A. 2
    B. 0
    C. 4
    D. -2
    E. -4

21. For all x and y, $(2x^5y^2)^3$ = ?

    A. $2x^{15}y^6$

    B. $8x^{125}y^8$

    C. $6x^{15}y^6$

    D. $8x^{15}y^6$

    E. $6x^{15}y^8$

22. The points $(2,1)$ and $(-1,4)$ determine a line. Which of the following is another point on the line?

    A. $(1,5)$
    B. $(-3,0)$
    C. $(0,3)$
    D. $(1,-4)$
    E. $(1,4)$

23. Triangle ABC is similar to triangle RST. Which of the following must be true?

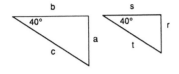

    A. $a + b = c$
    B. $a + b = r + s$
    C. $r + s = t$
    D. $\dfrac{b}{s} = \dfrac{a}{r}$
    E. $\dfrac{a}{b} = \dfrac{s}{r}$

24. A bank determined the following information about their accounts. What percent of the accounts is below $1000?

Number of accounts	Size of account in dollars
100	0 – 499
150	500 – 999
600	1000 – 1999
900	2000 – 4999
250	5000 – 10,000

    A.   42.5
    B.   12.5
    C.   87.5
    D.   57.5
    E.   25

25. $4 - 2(3 - 5) + 7 = ?$

    A.   15
    B.   3
    C.   7
    D.   11
    E.   1

26. Which of the following expressions is the complete factorization of $18 - 50x^2$?

    A. $2(9 - 25x^2)$
    B. $2(5x + 3)(5x - 3)$
    C. $2(3 + 5x)(3 - 5x)$
    D. $2(25x^2 - 9)$
    E. $(3 - 2x)(6 + 25x)$

27. What are the solutions to the equation
$$\frac{x + 4}{x} = \frac{x}{2} ?$$

    A.   4 and −1
    B.   −4 and 1
    C.   4 and −2
    D.   −4 and 2
    E.   2 and −2

28. The length of a rectangle is 12 feet. The width is one more than half the length. What is the area of the rectangle in square feet?

    A.   38
    B.   60
    C.   156
    D.   72
    E.   84

29. Which of the following represents the graph of $y = 2$?

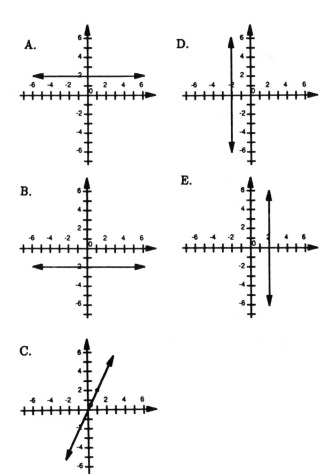

A.

B.

C.

D.

E.

30. What is the solution to the equation

$$(x + 2)(x - 1) - x(x + 3) = 7 ?$$

A. 9/4
B. −9/4
C. −3
D. 9/2
E. −9/2

31. For $a,b \neq 0$, $\dfrac{a^4 b^3 - a^3 b^4 - ab^2}{ab^2} = ?$

A. $a^4 b^3 - a^3 b^4 - 1$

B. $a^3 b - a^2 b^2 - 1$

C. $a^3 b - a^2 b^2$

D. $a^4 b^3 - a^3 b^4$

E. $a^3 b - a^3 b^4 - ab^2$

32. If $f(x) = \sqrt{2x + 1}$, then $f(12) = ?$

A. $\sqrt{26}$
B. $\sqrt{24} + 1$
C. 25
D. −5
E. 5

33. For $x > 0$, $\sqrt{6x^6} \sqrt{15x^5} = ?$

A. $3x^{15} \sqrt{10}$

B. $45x^5 \sqrt{x}$

C. $3x^5 \sqrt{10x}$

D. $x^5 \sqrt{21x}$

E. None of the above

34. The area of a square is 36. What is the perimeter?

A. 144
B. 12
C. 24
D. 26
E. 6

35. If $\dfrac{z}{3} - \dfrac{z+2}{6} = -2$, then $z = ?$

   A. 0
   B. −4
   C. −14
   D. 14
   E. −10

36. What is the y—intercept of the linear equation $8z + y + 2 = 0$?

   A. (−2,0)
   B. (0,8)
   C. (2,0)
   D. (0,2)
   E. (0,−2)

37. For all z, $z^2 - 6z - 72 = ?$

   A. $(z - 12)(z + 6)$
   B. $(z + 12)(z - 6)$
   C. $(z + 9)(z - 8)$
   D. $(z - 9)(z + 8)$
   E. $(z - 18)(z + 4)$

38. If $az - b = c$, then $z = ?$

   A. $b + c - a$
   B. $c - b - a$
   C. $\dfrac{b}{a} + c$
   D. $\dfrac{b - c}{a}$
   E. $\dfrac{b + c}{a}$

39. For $z \neq 0$, the equation
$$\frac{z+2}{z} - \frac{z}{2} = 1$$
is equivalent to which of the following equations?

   A. $z^2 - 2z - 3 = 0$
   B. $z^2 - 2 = 0$
   C. $z^2 - 4 = 0$
   D. $z^2 - 2z - 1 = 0$
   E. $z = 1$

40. Which of the following describes the solutions of the inequality $1 - 2z < 5$?

   A. $z < -2$
   B. $z > -2$
   C. $z < -3$
   D. $z > -3$
   E. $z < 6$

28. The number $\sqrt{82}$ lies between what two consecutive integers?

    A. 81 and 83
    B. 9 and 10
    C. 8 and 9
    D. 10 and 11
    E. 41 and 42

29. For $b \neq 0$, $a^4 \cdot \dfrac{a^2 b^3}{b^{-2}} = ?$

    A. $a^6 b^5$
    B. $a^6 b$
    C. $a^2 b$
    D. $a^2 b^5$
    E. a^6

30. If one person ate 1/3 of a pizza and another ate 1/4 of the pizza, what portion of the pizza remains?

    A. 5/7
    B. 7/12
    C. 5/12
    D. 2/7
    E. 6/7

31. What is the solution of the following system of equations?

    $$3x + y = 3$$
    $$2x + 2y = 5$$

    A. $x = -2$ and $y = 9$
    B. $x = -11/4$ and $y = 9$
    C. $x = 0$ and $y = 3$
    D. $x = 1/4$ and $y = 9/4$
    E. $x = 1$ and $y = 0$

32. The value of x which satisfies the equation

    $$\frac{x}{x + 1} - \frac{1}{x} = 1$$

    is $x = ?$

    A. 2
    B. $-1/2$
    C. -2
    D. $1/2$
    E. None of the above

33. For $a > 0$, $\sqrt{a} + 5\sqrt{a} = ?$

    A. $5\sqrt{a}$
    B. $5\sqrt{2a}$
    C. $6\sqrt{2a}$
    D. $6\sqrt{a}$
    E. $5a$

34. The formula for converting degrees Celsius to degrees Farenheit is $F = 1.8C + 32$. If the temperature is $86°$ Farenheit, what is the temperature in degrees Celsius?

    A. $186.8°$
    B. $65.5°$
    C. $52.2°$
    D. $30°$
    E. $35°$

35. The solution of the equation

    $$2x - 4(x - 3) = 3 - (-7)$$

    is $x = ?$

    A. 11
    B. -11
    C. 1
    D. -1
    E. 8

36. For $z = 3$, $z^z + z = ?$

    A. 30
    B. 12
    C. 81
    D. 9
    E. 27

37. The complete factorization of $6a^2 + 15a - 9$ is

    A. $3(2a - 3)(a + 1)$
    B. $3(2a - 1)(a + 3)$
    C. $(2a - 1)(3a + 9)$
    D. $(6a - 3)(a + 3)$
    E. $3(2a + 1)(a - 3)$

38. $-3 - (-2 - 5) = ?$

    A. -10
    B. 0
    C. -6
    D. -4
    E. 4

39. For $c > 0$, $\sqrt{6c}\sqrt{15c} =$

    A. $10c\sqrt{3}$
    B. $3c\sqrt{10}$
    C. $3\sqrt{10c}$
    D. $10\sqrt{3c}$
    E. $\sqrt{21c}$

40. Which point has the smallest y coordinate?

    A. A
    B. B
    C. C
    D. D
    E. E

PRACTICE

MATHEMATICS

TESTS

SOLUTIONS

Practice Mathematics Test I Solutions

1. Let x = cost of 5 pounds of potatoes. Then
$$\frac{1.20}{3} = \frac{x}{5}$$
$$.4 = \frac{x}{5}$$
$$2 = x$$
The cost is $2.00.

2. Like terms are x^2, $-4x^2$ and $3x$, $2x$.
Combining and writing in descending powers of x gives
$$x^2 + 3x - 5 + 2x - 4x^2$$
$$= -3x^2 + 5x - 5$$

3. $(-2)^5 = (-2)(-2)(-2)(-2)(-2)$
$$= -32$$

4. $(x - 3)^2 = (x-3)(x-3)$
$$= x^2 - 3x - 3x + 9$$
$$= x^2 - 6x + 9$$

5. $\left[2x^2y\right]^3 = 2^3 \left[x^2\right]^3 y^3$
$$= 8x^6 y^3$$

6. Since $f(x) = x^2 - 3x - 1$,
$$f(-2) = (-2)^2 - 3(-2) - 1$$
$$= 4 + 6 - 1$$
$$= 9$$

7. To locate $(-2, 3)$, move left 2 units and up 3 units.

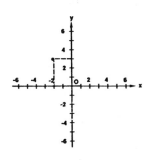

8. $$4 - 3x \leq x - 6$$
$$4 - 3x - x \leq x - 6 - x$$
$$4 - 4x \leq -6$$
$$4 - 4x - 4 \leq -6 - 4$$
$$-4x \leq -10$$
$$\frac{-4x}{-4} \geq \frac{-10}{-4}$$
$$x \geq \frac{5}{2}$$

9. The factors of 6, 8 and 12 are
$$6 = 2 \cdot 3$$
$$8 = 2 \cdot 2 \cdot 2$$
$$12 = 2 \cdot 2 \cdot 3$$
The least common multiple is
$$2 \cdot 2 \cdot 2 \cdot 3 \text{ or } 24.$$

10. $2(x - 3) - 4(x + 2)$
$$= 2x - 6 - 4x - 8$$
$$= -2x - 14$$

11. To solve $\quad 3x + y = 4$
$$5x + y = 10$$
multiply the second equation by -1 and add.
$$3x + y = 4$$
$$\underline{-5x - y = -10}$$
$$-2x = -6$$
$$x = 3$$

Substitute $x = 3$ into the first equation.
$$3x + y = 4$$
$$3(3) + y = 4$$
$$9 + y = 4$$
$$y = -5$$

12. Use the Pythagorem theorem to determine the length, l, of $\overline{AD}$.
$$l^2 + 3^2 = 5^2$$
$$l^2 + 9 = 25$$
$$l^2 = 16$$
$$l = 4$$
The perimeter is
$$P = 2l + 2w$$
$$= 2(4) + 2(3)$$
$$= 8 + 6 = 14$$

13. $\sqrt{50x^7} = \sqrt{25x^6}\sqrt{2x}$
$$= 5x^3\sqrt{2x}$$

14. The greatest common monomial factor

is $x^3 y^4$ thus

$x^5 y^4 - x^3 y^7 + 3x^4 y^5$

$= x^3 y^4 (x^2 - y^3 + 3xy)$

15. Solve by factoring

$x^2 = 3x$

$x^2 - 3x = 0$

$x(x - 3) = 0$

$x = 0$ or $x - 3 = 0$

$x = 3$

The solutions are $x = 0$ or $x = 3$.

16. $(x^5 y^7)(xy^3) = x^6 y^{10}$

17. Tax $= .35s$

$t =$ take home salary

$=$ before tax salary $-$ tax

$= s - .35s = .65s$

18. $|-7| + |-2| - |3| = 7 + 2 - 3 = 6$

19. $\dfrac{x}{2} + \dfrac{1}{3} = \dfrac{5}{6}$

Multiply both sides of the equation by 6.

$\dfrac{6}{1} \cdot \dfrac{x}{2} + \dfrac{6}{1} \cdot \dfrac{1}{3} = \dfrac{6}{1} \cdot \dfrac{5}{6}$

$3x + 2 = 5$

$3x + 2 - 2 = 5 - 2$

$3x = 3$

$x = 1$

20. Since $\angle ACB$ and $\angle BCD$ are supplementary angles,

$m\angle ACB + m\angle BCD = 180°$

$m\angle ACB + 100° = 180°$

$m\angle ACB = 80°$

The sum of the measures of the angles in a triangle is $180°$, so

$m\angle BAC + m\angle ACB + m\angle ABC = 180°$

$m\angle BAC + 80° + 40° = 180°$

$m\angle BAC + 120° = 180°$

$m\angle BAC = 60°$

21. Since $\triangle ABC$ and $\triangle CDE$ are similar (their angles are equal),

$\dfrac{\overline{CE}}{\overline{AC}} = \dfrac{\overline{CD}}{\overline{BC}}$

$\dfrac{4}{2} = \dfrac{\overline{CD}}{3}$

$2 = \dfrac{\overline{CD}}{3}$

$6 = \overline{CD}$

22. For $y = x$, the slope is 1 and the y-intercept is $(0, 0)$.

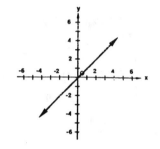

23. The number of programs is

$10 \cdot 8 \cdot 3 = 240$

24. $\dfrac{1.2 - 3(2.7)}{.23} = \dfrac{1.2 - 8.1}{.23}$

$= \dfrac{-6.9}{.23} = -30$

25. For $a = -2$ and $b = 3$,

$5ab + 3b - a$

$= 5(-2)(3) + 3(3) - (-2)$

$= -30 + 9 + 2 = -19$

26. $\dfrac{a^{12}}{a^4} = a^8$

27. $(x + 5)(2x + 3)$

$= 2x^2 + 3x + 10x + 15$

$= 2x^2 + 13x + 15$

28. $\sqrt{12}\sqrt{3} = \sqrt{36} = 6$

29. The lowest common denomimator is $(x - 1)(x + 1)$, so

$$\frac{1}{x - 1} - \frac{1}{x + 1}$$

$$= \frac{x + 1}{(x - 1)(x + 1)} - \frac{x - 1}{(x - 1)(x + 1)}$$

$$= \frac{x + 1 - x + 1}{(x - 1)(x + 1)}$$

$$= \frac{2}{(x - 1)(x + 1)} = \frac{2}{x^2 - 1}$$

30. $\sqrt{3 - x} = 2$
    $3 - x = 4$
    $-x = 1$
    $x = -1$

31. To find the slope, isolate y, then the slope is the coefficient of x.

$x - 2y = 6$
$-2y = -x + 6$
$y = \frac{1}{2}x - 3$

The slope is $\frac{1}{2}$.

32. Since the diameter is 6, the radius is 3. Then the area is

$A = \pi r^2 = \pi(3)^2 = 9\pi$

33. $\frac{x + 2}{x^2 + 3x + 2} = \frac{x + 2}{(x + 2)(x + 1)}$

$= \frac{1}{x + 1}$

34. $3a^2 - 5ab - 2b^2 = (3a + b)(a - 2b)$

35. $(-8)^{2/3} = \left[\sqrt[3]{-8}\right]^2 = (-2)^2 = 4$

36. Multiply both sides of the equation by x and solve by factoring.

$x + \frac{1}{x} = 2$

$x \cdot x + x \cdot \frac{1}{x} = 2x$

$x^2 + 1 = 2x$

$x^2 - 2x + 1 = 0$

$(x - 1)^2 = 0$

$x - 1 = 0$

$x = 1$

37. The value (in cents) of the nickels is $5n$ and the value of the dimes is $10d$. The equation is $5n + 10d = 115$.

38. $x + 3 = 10 - 3(x - 1)$
    $x + 3 = 10 - 3x + 3$
    $x + 3 = -3x + 13$
    $x + 3 + 3x = -3x + 13 + 3x$
    $4x + 3 = 13$
    $4x + 3 - 3 = 13 - 3$
    $4x = 10$
    $x = \frac{10}{4} = \frac{5}{2}$

39. Use the formula $I = Prt$, where $P = 360$, $r = .07$, and $t = \frac{5}{12}$ (the time in years). Then

$I = (360)(.07)\left[\frac{5}{12}\right] = \$10.50$

40. $-\frac{2}{3} \div \frac{5}{9} = \frac{-2}{3} \cdot \frac{9}{5} = -\frac{6}{5}$

Practice Mathematics Test 2 Solutions

1. The factors of 24 are 1, 2, 3, 4, 6, 8, 12, and 24. Of these factors only 2 and 3 are prime. The largest prime factor is 3.

2. Solve the equation for y. Then the constant term is the second coordinate of the y-intercept.
$$5x + 2y - 10 = 0$$
$$2y = -5x + 10$$
$$y = -\frac{5}{2}x + 5$$

   The y-intercept is $(0, 5)$

3. In the 18-25 group, 60% voted and in the 41-65 group, 70% voted. In the other groups less than 50% voted.

4. $2x - 5 = 7$
   $2x - 5 + 5 = 7 + 5$
   $2x = 12$
   $x = 6$

5. The lowest common denominator is $x(x + 1)$.
$$\frac{1}{x} + \frac{1}{x+1} = \frac{x+1}{x(x+1)} + \frac{x}{x(x+1)}$$
$$= \frac{2x+1}{x(x+1)}$$

6. The greatest common divisor is 6.

7. $12x^2 - x - 6 = (4x - 3)(3x + 2)$

8. The cost is 30 plus .20 times m or $C = .2m + 30$.

9. For $b = 3$ and $h = 5$,
$$\frac{1}{2}bh = \frac{1}{2}(3)(5) = \frac{15}{2} = 7.5$$

10. $(2x^5y^2)(3x^2y) = 6x^7y^3$

11. Use the quadratic equation with $a = 2$, $b = 3$, and $c = -1$. Then
$$x = \frac{-b \pm \sqrt{b^2 - 4ac}}{2a}$$
$$= \frac{-3 \pm \sqrt{3^2 - 4(2)(-1)}}{2(2)}$$
$$= \frac{-3 \pm \sqrt{17}}{4}$$

12. $2a + 3p = 5g$

13. $(2x - 1)^2 = (2x - 1)(2x - 1)$
$$= 4x^2 - 2x - 2x + 1$$
$$= 4x^2 - 4x + 1$$

14. When $x = -3$,
$$-x^2 + 4 = -(-3)^2 + 4$$
$$= -9 + 4 = -5$$

15. $\sqrt{9x^9y^{12}} = \sqrt{9x^8y^{12}}\sqrt{x} = 3x^4y^6\sqrt{x}$

16. $\frac{x^2 - x}{x^2 + x - 2} \cdot \frac{x + 2}{x}$
$$= \frac{x(x - 1)}{(x + 2)(x - 1)} \cdot \frac{x + 2}{x} = 1$$

17. $.0000532 = 5.32 \times 10^{-5}$

18. $\frac{\sqrt[4]{27x^{11}}}{\sqrt{3x^5}} = \sqrt{9x^6} = 3x^3$

19. Use the Pythagoream theorem with h representing height.
$$6^2 + h^2 = 10^2$$
$$36 + h^2 = 100$$
$$h^2 = 64$$
$$h = 8$$

20. $a + b - (2a - 3b) + (a - 2b) =$
$$= a + b - 2a + 3b + a - 2b = 2b$$

21. $\frac{1}{2} + \frac{1}{3} = \frac{3}{6} + \frac{2}{6} = \frac{5}{6}$

22. Since the triangles are similar,
$$\frac{24}{40} = \frac{EF}{30} \text{ and } EF = 18.$$

23. $(.021)(3.2) = .0672$

24. $(x + 1)(x^2 + 3) = x^3 + 3x + x^2 + 3$
$$= x^3 + x^2 + 3x + 3$$

Practice Mathematics Test 2 Solutions

25. Let x represent the number, then
$2x - 3 = -5$.
$2x = -2$
$x = -1$
The number is -1.

26. $25 - x^2 = (5 + x)(5 - x)$

27. $-1 \leq x - 2 \leq 3$
$-1 + 2 \leq x - 2 + 2 \leq 3 + 2$
$1 \leq x \leq 5$

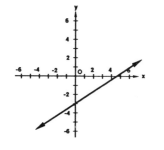

28. Multiply the first equation by -3 and add.
$$\begin{array}{r} -3x - 9y = -6 \\ 3x - 2y = 1 \\ \hline -11y = -5 \\ y = \dfrac{5}{11} \end{array}$$

Substitute $y = \dfrac{5}{11}$ into the first equation.
$$x + 3y = 2$$
$$x + 3 \cdot \dfrac{5}{11} = 2$$
$$x = \dfrac{7}{11}$$

29. Solve for y.
$2x - 3y = 9$
$-3y = -2x + 9$
$y = \dfrac{2}{3}x - 3$

The slope is $\dfrac{2}{3}$ and the y-intercpt is $(0, -3)$.

30. Average $=$
$$\dfrac{12 + (-3) + (-10) + (-5) + 25 + 20}{6}$$
$$= \dfrac{39}{6} = 6.5$$

31. $x(x - 3) - 4(x - 3) =$
$= x^2 - 3x - 4x + 12$
$= x^2 - 7x + 12$

32. Since $x = $ length of the first piece,
$2x = $ length of the second piece and
$2x + 3 = $ length of the third piece.
The equation is $x + 2x + (2x + 3) = 18$

33. $\left[3x^3\right]^2 = 9x^6$

34. Multiply both sides by $x - 2$.
$$\dfrac{4}{x - 2} = 3$$
$$\dfrac{(x - 2)}{1} \cdot \dfrac{4}{x - 2} = 3(x - 2)$$
$$4 = 3x - 6$$
$$10 = 3x$$
$$\dfrac{10}{3} = x$$

35. Solve by factoring.
$2x^2 + 5x = 3$
$2x^2 + 5x - 3 = 0$
$(2x - 1)(x + 3) = 0$
$2x - 1 = 0$ or $x + 3 = 0$
$x = \dfrac{1}{2}$ or $x = -3$

Since $x > 0$, the solution is $x = \dfrac{1}{2}$.

36. Use the Pythagorem theorem with l
representating the length of $\overline{AB}$.
$l^2 + 12^2 = 13^2$
$l^2 + 144 = 169$
$l^2 = 25$
$l = 5$

37. $\dfrac{x^2}{4y^5} \cdot \dfrac{2y^2}{x^2} = \dfrac{1}{2y^3}$

38. Since $d = 72$ and time, t, in hours is $1\dfrac{1}{3}$, use
the formula $r = d/t$,
$r = 72 \div 1\dfrac{1}{3} = 72 \div \dfrac{4}{3}$
$= \dfrac{72}{1} \cdot \dfrac{3}{4} = 54$ mph

39. Since $\angle 1$ and $\angle 2$ are supplementary angles,
$m\angle 1 + m\angle 2 = 180^\circ$.

40. Since the length is decreased by 4, the new length is $l-4$. The new width is $2w$. The area is $2w(l-4)$.

Practice Mathematics Test 3 Solutions

1. $(x + 3)(x - 5) = x^2 - 5x + 3x - 15$
   $= x^2 - 2x - 15$

2. There are $3 \cdot 6$ or 18 possible outcomes.

3. $5x - 3 = 4 - 2x$
   $5x - 3 + 3 + 2x = 4 - 2x + 3 + 2x$
   $7x = 7$
   $x = 1$

4. $\dfrac{1}{6} - \dfrac{5}{14} + \dfrac{4}{21} = \dfrac{7}{42} - \dfrac{15}{42} + \dfrac{8}{42}$
   $= \dfrac{0}{42} = 0$

5. $a + 5b - 3a + 10b = -2a + 15b$

6. $50 \div 200 = .25$

7. Multiply both sides by $(x + 2)$.
   $(x + 2) \cdot \dfrac{1}{x + 2} = 10(x + 2)$
   $1 = 10x + 20$
   $-19 = 10x$
   $-\dfrac{19}{10} = x$

8. For $y = -x + 2$, the slope is -1 or $\dfrac{-1}{1}$ and the y–intercept is $(0, 2)$.

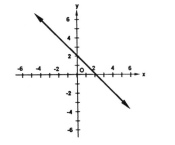

9. $y(x + y) - x(x - y)$
   $= xy + y^2 - x^2 + xy = y^2 + 2xy - x^2$

10. $13.2 - 4.03 = 9.17$

11. For all x, $(x^2 + 3x) + (x^2 - 4x + 3) =$
    $= 2x^2 - x + 3$

12. The number 17 is only divisible by itself and 1, so 17 is prime.

13. $2n + 3d = 4$
    $n + 2d = 1$
    Multiply the second equation by -2.
    $2n + 3d = 4$
    $\underline{-2n - 4d = -2}$
    $-d = 2$
    $d = -2$
    Substitute $d = -2$ into the second equation.
    $n + 2d = 1$
    $n + 2(-2) = 1$
    $n - 4 = 1$
    $n = 5$

14. Since $y = x^2 \geq 0$, the graph is in quadrants I and II only.

15. Each person receives $\dfrac{5}{11}$.

16. Let $b = $ length of $\overline{BC}$.
    $4^2 + b^2 = 5^2$
    $16 + b^2 = 25$
    $b^2 = 9$
    $b = 3$

17. $4 - 3(5) = 2(2 - 5) - x,$
    $4 - 15 = 2(-3) - x$
    $-11 = -6 - x$
    $-5 = -x$
    $5 = x$

18. $2 - 5c - 1 = 2 - 5(2) - 1$
    $= 2 - 10 - 1$
    $= -9$

19. $\dfrac{x^4 y^3}{x^6 y^2} = \dfrac{y}{x^2}$

20. A side has length 6. The perimeter is $4(6)$ or 24.

21. Only angles 4 and 6 are supplementary. The other pairs are equal.

22. $12 < 2t - 6$
    $18 < 2t$
    $9 < t$

23. $C = s + rp$

Practice Mathematics Test 3 Solutions

24. $(x - 2)(3 - x) = 3x - x^2 - 6 + 2x$
    $= -x^2 + 5x - 6$

25. The length is 8. If w represents the width then
$$8^2 + w^2 = 10^2$$
$$64 + w^2 = 100$$
$$w^2 = 36$$
$$w = 6$$
The area is A $= lw = 6(8) = 48$.

26. $x + 2y - 3(x - y) + 2y =$
    $x + 2y - 3x + 3y + 2y =$
    $-2x + 7y$

27. $(2x + 1)(x^2 - 3) = 2x^3 - 6x + x^2 - 3$
    $= 2x^3 + x^2 - 6x - 3$

28. $ab^2 - 3a^2b + ab = ab(b - 3a + 1)$

29. $\dfrac{x^3}{5y^2} \cdot \dfrac{10y^5}{2x^6} = \dfrac{y^3}{x^3}$

30. $3 + \dfrac{4}{x} = \dfrac{3}{1} + \dfrac{4}{x} = \dfrac{3x}{x} + \dfrac{4}{x}$
    $= \dfrac{3x + 4}{x}$

31. $\sqrt{1 - x} = 3$
    $1 - x = 9$
    $-x = 8$
    $x = -8$

32. $(3x^2 - x + 5) - (3x^2 + 2x - 4) =$
    $3x^2 - x + 5 - 3x^2 - 2x + 4 =$
    $-3x + 9$

33. $\dfrac{x^2 + 6x + 5}{x + 5} = \dfrac{(x + 5)(x + 1)}{x + 5}$
    $= x + 1$

34. $4b^2 + 8b^3 + 2b^4 = 2b^2(2 + 4b + b^2)$

    The greatest common monomial factor is $2b^2$.

35. $\dfrac{1}{x^9} \cdot \dfrac{1}{x^7} = \dfrac{1}{x^{16}}$

36. $\sqrt{y^7} \sqrt{y^8} = \sqrt{y^{15}} = \sqrt{y^{14}} \sqrt{y} = y^7 \sqrt{y}$

37. The number of ounces of gold is .15(40) or 6.

38. $(x + 1)(x - 5) = x^2 - 5x + x - 5$
    $= x^2 - 4x - 5$

39. $\dfrac{1}{x} + \dfrac{2}{x + 2} = \dfrac{x + 2}{x(x + 2)} + \dfrac{2x}{x(x + 2)}$
    $= \dfrac{3x + 2}{(x + 2)}$

40. The number m is divisible by 6; therefore it is a multiple of 3 and 2.

Practice Mathematics Test 4 Solutions

1. $\dfrac{6.00}{1.60} = 3.75$ pounds

2. $2z^2 + 3z - 9 = 0$
$(2z - 3)(z + 3) = 0$
$2z - 3 = 0$ or $z + 3 = 0$
$2z = 3$ or $z = -3$
$z = 3/2$

3. $\dfrac{z^3}{y^2} \cdot \dfrac{zy^4}{x^3y^5} = \dfrac{x^4y^4}{x^3y^7} = \dfrac{x}{y^3}$

4. $\dfrac{(3 \cdot 10^3)(4 \cdot 10^{-2})}{2 \cdot 10^4} = \dfrac{12 \cdot 10}{2 \cdot 10^4}$
$= 6 \cdot 10^{-3} = .006$

5. Since the diameter is 6, $r = 3$. For $r = 3$ and $h = 4$, $V = \pi(3^2)(4) = 36\pi$.

6. Since $f(-1) = (-1)^2 + 1 = 2$,
$f(1) = 1^2 + 1 = 2$,
and $f(2) = 2^2 + 1 = 5$,
the range is $\{2,5\}$.

7. $xy^z = (-1)(3^2) = (-1)(9) = -9$

8. $\sqrt{50x} + \sqrt{18x} = \sqrt{25 \cdot 2x} + \sqrt{9 \cdot 2x}$
$= 5\sqrt{2x} + 3\sqrt{2x} = 8\sqrt{2x}$.

9. A vertical line two units to the right of the y-axis is $x = 2$.

10. Since $2n^2$ has a factor 2, it is even.

11. $z + 3y = 4$
$2z - 2y = 1$

Multiply both sides of the first equation by -2.
$$\begin{aligned} -2z - 6y &= -8 \\ 2z - 2y &= 1 \\ \hline -8y &= -7 \\ y &= 7/8 \end{aligned}$$

12. $4z^2 + 22z - 42$
$= 2(2z^2 + 11z - 21)$
$= 2(2z - 3)(z + 7)$.
The factors are 2, $(2z - 3)$, and $(z + 7)$.

13. One less than two thirds of c is $\dfrac{2}{3}c - 1$.

14. $\sqrt{32x^9y^6} = \sqrt{16x^8y^6}\sqrt{2x}$
$= 4x^4y^3\sqrt{2x}$

15. Since the sum of the measures of the angles of a triangle is $180°$,
$$\begin{aligned} x + (x + 60) + 2x &= 180 \\ 4x + 60 &= 180 \\ 4x &= 120 \\ x &= 30 \end{aligned}$$
Angle A is $30°$.

16. The prime factorization of 12 is $2^2 \cdot 3$.
The product $42 \cdot 10 = 2^2 \cdot 3 \cdot 7 \cdot 5$ is divisible by $2^2 \cdot 3$.
The product $30 \cdot 35 = 2 \cdot 3 \cdot 5^2 \cdot 7$ is not divisible by $2^2 \cdot 3$.
The product $13 \cdot 23$ is not divisible by $2^2 \cdot 3$ since 13 and 23 are prime.

Practice Mathematics Test 4 Solutions

17. $\dfrac{1}{x+3} - \dfrac{1}{x+2}$

$= \dfrac{x+2}{(x+3)(x+2)} - \dfrac{x+3}{(x+3)(x+2)}$

$= \dfrac{x+2-x-3}{(x+3)(x+2)} = \dfrac{-1}{(x+3)(x+2)}.$

18. $x^{3/4} = (x^3)^{1/4} = \sqrt[4]{x^3}$

19. Since the coordinates of the points B and D have opposite signs, the product of the coordinates is less than zero.

20. $-x^3 + x^2 + x + 1$

$= -(-1)^3 + (-1)^2 + (-1) + 1$

$= 1 + 1 - 1 + 1 = 2.$

21. $(2x^5y^2)^3 = 2^3 x^{15} y^6 = 8x^{15}y^6.$

22. The slope of the line is

$$m = \dfrac{4-1}{-1-2} = \dfrac{3}{-3} = -1$$

and the equation is given by

$$\begin{aligned} y - 1 &= -1(x-2) \\ y - 1 &= -x + 2 \\ y &= -x + 3 \end{aligned}$$

Another point on the line is $(0,3)$ since the equation is satisfied when $x = 0$ and $y = 3$.

23. Corresponding sides of similar triangles are proportional. Thus $\dfrac{b}{s} = \dfrac{a}{r}$.

24. The total number of accounts is 2000 and the number below $1000 is 250. The percentage is $\dfrac{250}{2000} \cdot 100 = 12.5.$

25. $4 - 2(3-5) + 7 = 4 - 2(-2) + 7$
$= 4 + 4 + 7 = 15.$

26. $18 - 50x^2$

$= 2(9 - 25x^2) = 2(3 + 5x)(3 - 5x)$

27. $$\dfrac{x+4}{x} = \dfrac{x}{2}$$

$$\dfrac{2x}{1} \cdot \dfrac{x+4}{x} = \dfrac{2x}{1} \cdot \dfrac{x}{2}$$

$$2(x+4) = x^2$$

$$2x + 8 = x^2$$

$$0 = x^2 - 2x - 8$$

$$0 = (x-4)(x+2)$$

$$x - 4 = 0 \quad \text{or} \quad x + 2 = 0$$

$$x = 4 \quad \text{or} \quad x = -2$$

The solutions are 4 and −2.

28. The width is $1 + \dfrac{1}{2} \cdot 12 = 1 + 6 = 7$ and the area $A = \ell w = (12)(7) = 84.$

29. The graph of $y = 2$ is a horizontal line with y–intercept at $(0,2)$.

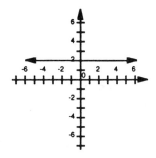

Practice Mathematics Test 4 Solutions

30.
$$(x + 2)(x - 1) - x(x + 3) = 7$$
$$x^2 + 2x - x - 2 - x^2 - 3x = 7$$
$$-2x - 2 = 7$$
$$-2x = 9$$
$$x = -9/2.$$

31.
$$\frac{a^4 b^3 - a^3 b^4 - ab^2}{ab^2}$$
$$= \frac{ab^2(a^3 b - a^2 b^2 - 1)}{ab^2}$$
$$= a^3 b - a^2 b^2 - 1.$$

32.
$$f(12) = \sqrt{2(12) + 1}$$
$$= \sqrt{24 + 1} = \sqrt{25} = 5$$

33.
$$\sqrt{6x^6}\sqrt{15x^5} = \sqrt{90x^{11}} =$$
$$\sqrt{9x^{10}}\sqrt{10x} = 3x^5\sqrt{10x}$$

34. Since the area is 36, the length of one side of the square is 6. The perimeter is
$$p = 4s = (4)(6) = 24.$$

35.
$$\frac{x}{3} - \frac{x + 2}{6} = -2$$
$$\frac{6}{1} \cdot \frac{x}{3} - \frac{6}{1} \cdot \frac{x + 2}{6} = (-2)(6)$$
$$2x - (x + 2) = -12$$
$$2x - x - 2 = -12$$
$$x - 2 = -12$$
$$x = -10$$

36. The y–intercept occurs when $x = 0$. From $8x + y + 2 = 0$, we obtain
$$(8)(0) + y + 2 = 0$$
$$y + 2 = 0$$
$$y = -2.$$
The y–intercept is $(0, -2)$.

37. $x^2 - 6x - 72 = (x - 12)(x + 6)$.

38.
$$ax - b = c$$
$$ax = b + c$$
$$x = \frac{b + c}{a}.$$

39.
$$\frac{x + 2}{x} - \frac{x}{2} = 1$$
$$\frac{2x}{1} \cdot \frac{x + 2}{x} - \frac{2x}{1} \cdot \frac{x}{2} = (2x)(1)$$
$$2(x + 2) - x^2 = 2x$$
$$2x + 4 - x^2 = 2x$$
$$0 = x^2 - 4$$

40.
$$1 - 2x < 5$$
$$-2x < 4$$
$$x > -2.$$

1.
$$2x + y = 3$$
$$x - y = 6$$
$$\overline{}$$
$$3x = 9$$
$$x = 3$$

Substitute $x = 3$ into the equation
$$2x + y = 3.$$
$$2(3) + y = 3$$
$$6 + y = 3$$
$$y = -3$$

2. $\sqrt{75} + \sqrt{27} = \sqrt{25 \cdot 3} + \sqrt{9 \cdot 3}$
$= 5\sqrt{3} + 3\sqrt{3} = 8\sqrt{3}$.

3. $3x + 2 - 5x + 6 = 22$
$-2x + 8 = 22$
$-2x = 14$
$x = -7$.

4. $m\angle A + 82^\circ = 114^\circ$
$m\angle A = 32^\circ$

5. $\sqrt{x^{16}} = x^8$

6. For $a = 3$, $b = 0$, and $c = -1$, we have
$$a^b c^a = 3^0 (-1)^3 = 1(-1) = -1.$$

7. $\dfrac{1}{x} - \dfrac{3}{x+2} = 0$

Multiply both sides of the equation by $x(x+2)$.

$$\frac{x(x+2)}{1} \cdot \frac{1}{x} - \frac{x(x+2)}{1} \cdot \frac{3}{x+2} = 0 \cdot x(x+2)$$
$$x + 2 - 3x = 0$$
$$-2x = -2$$
$$x = 1$$

8.
$$2x^2 + 5x = 3$$
$$2x^2 + 5x - 3 = 0$$
$$(2x - 1)(x + 3) = 0$$
$$2x - 1 = 0 \quad \text{or} \quad x + 3 = 0$$
$$2x = 1 \quad \text{or} \quad x = -3$$
$$x = 1/2 \quad \text{or} \quad x = -3.$$

The smaller solution is -3.

9. $3(x - 1)(2x - 1)$
$= 3(2x^2 - x - 2x + 1)$
$= 6x^2 - 9x + 3$

10. Since n is the smaller odd integer, the next odd integer must be $n + 2$. Therefore the equation is
$$(n + 2)^2 - n^2 = 56.$$

11. $2x^2 + 11x - 30 = (2x + 15)(x - 2)$

12. $3 - 7(2 - 4) - (-3)(2)$
$= 3 - 7(-2) - (-6)$
$= 3 + 14 + 6 = 23$

13. The graph of $y = -2x/3 + 1$ is a line with y-intercept at $(0,1)$ and slope of $-2/3$.

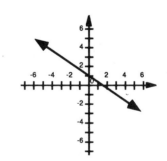

14. $$\frac{6x^3 + 8x^2y^2 + 2x}{2x}$$

$$= \frac{2x(3x^2 + 4xy^2 + 1)}{2x}$$

$$= 3x^2 + 4xy^2 + 1$$

15. The first letter can be chosen in **3** ways. For each of these **3** ways, there are **4** ways of choosing the second letter. Finally, for each of the (4)(3) ways of choosing the first two letters, there are **3** ways of choosing the third letter. The number of codes is therefore (3)(4)(3) = **36**.

16. $\sqrt{1 - 2x} = 7$
$1 - 2x = 49$
$-2x = 48$
$x = -24$.

17. $x^2 + 3 = 7$
$x^2 = 4$
$x = \pm 2$.

The graph is

18. Since the traingles are similar, corresponding sides are proportional. Therefore

$$\frac{14}{24} = \frac{x}{18}$$

$$\frac{18}{1} \cdot \frac{14}{24} = x$$

$$10.5 = x$$

19. If $x = 3$ and $y = -3$, then

$$x^y = 3^{-3} = \frac{1}{3^3} = \frac{1}{27},$$

$$y^x = (-3)^3 = -27,$$

$$xy = (-3)(3) = -9,$$

$$x + y = 3 - 3 = 0,$$

$$x/y = 3/(-3) = -1.$$

The largest of these numbers is x^y.

20. Combining like terms gives

$$(t^5 + 3t^3 + 4) + (t^3 - 3t + 1) - (t^3 - 2t)$$

$$= t^5 + 3t^3 + 4 + t^3 - 3t + 1 - t^3 + 2t$$

$$= t^5 + 3t^3 - t + 5$$

21. The length is

$$\sqrt{(-1 - 2)^2 + (5 - 1)^2}$$

$$= \sqrt{(-3)^2 + 4^2}$$

$$= \sqrt{9 + 16} = \sqrt{25} = 5.$$

22. The sides are proportional.

$$\frac{9}{6} = \frac{x}{5}$$

$$\frac{5}{1} \cdot \frac{9}{6} = x$$

$$7.5 = x.$$

23. $(2/3 - 3/4 + 1/2) \div 2$

$$= (8/12 - 9/12 + 6/12) \div 2$$

$$= \frac{5}{12} \div \frac{2}{1} = \frac{5}{12} \cdot \frac{1}{2} = \frac{5}{24}$$

Practice Mathematics Test 5 Solutions

24. Since the diameter is 12, the radius r is 6. Therefore the area is
$$A = \pi r^2 = \pi(6^2) = 36\pi.$$

25. Let z be the number of 30¢ stamps purchased.
$$.25z + .30z + .50z = 14.70$$
$$1.05z = 14.70$$
$$z = 14.$$

26. $\triangle ABD$ is a right triangle. Use the Pythagorean theorem to determine the length of the side $\overline{BD}$.
$$z^2 + 2^2 = 3^2$$
$$z^2 + 4 = 9$$
$$z^2 = 5$$
$$z = \sqrt{5}$$

27.
$$-3 \leq 2z - 1 \leq 5$$
$$-2 \leq 2z \leq 6$$
$$-1 \leq z \leq 3$$

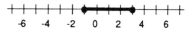

28. Since $81 < 82 < 100$, we have $\sqrt{81} < \sqrt{82} < \sqrt{100}$ and therefore $9 < \sqrt{82} < 10$.

29. $a^4 \cdot \dfrac{a^2 b^3}{b^{-2}} = a^4 \cdot a^2 b^3 \cdot b^2 = a^6 b^5.$

30. The portion that remains is
$$1 - \frac{1}{3} - \frac{1}{4} = \frac{12}{12} - \frac{4}{12} - \frac{3}{12} = \frac{5}{12}.$$

31.
$$3z + y = 3$$
$$2z + 2y = 5$$
Multiply the first equation by -2.
$$-6z - 2y = -6$$
$$2z + 2y = 5$$
$$\overline{}$$
$$-4z = -1$$
$$z = 1/4.$$
Substitute $z = 1/4$ into the first equation.
$$3z + y = 3$$
$$3(1/4) + y = 3$$
$$3/4 + y = 3$$
$$y = 9/4.$$
The solution is $z = 1/4$ and $y = 9/4$.

32. $$\frac{z}{z+1} - \frac{1}{z} = 1$$
Multiply both sides of the equation by $z(z+1)$.
$$\frac{z(z+1)}{1} \cdot \frac{z}{z+1} - \frac{z(z+1)}{1} \cdot \frac{1}{z} = z(z+1).$$
$$z^2 - (z+1) = z(z+1)$$
$$z^2 - z - 1 = z^2 + z$$
$$-1 = 2z$$
$$-1/2 = z.$$

33. $\sqrt{a} + 5\sqrt{a} = (1+5)\sqrt{a} = 6\sqrt{a}.$

34.
$$F = 1.8C + 32$$
$$86 = 1.8C + 32$$
$$54 = 1.8C$$
$$30 = C.$$

35.
$$2z - 4(z - 3) = 3 - (-7)$$
$$2z - 4z + 12 = 3 + 7$$
$$-2z + 12 = 10$$
$$-2z = -2$$
$$z = 1$$

36. For $z = 3$,
$$z^z + z = 3^3 + 3 = 27 + 3 = 30.$$

37. $6a^2 + 15a - 9$
$$= 3(2a^2 + 5a - 3)$$
$$= 3(2a - 1)(a + 3)$$

38. $-3 - (-2 - 5) = -3 - (-7)$
$$= -3 + 7 = 4$$

39. $\sqrt{6c}\sqrt{15c} = \sqrt{90c^2}$
$$= \sqrt{9c^2} \cdot \sqrt{10} = 3c\sqrt{10}.$$

40. The point with the smallest y-coordinate is B.

PREPARATION
for the
ENGLISH TEST

English

INTRODUCTION: PREPARING FOR THE ENGLISH TEST

The English portion of the CPE includes 40 items and takes 45 minutes. It measures your understanding of both rhetorical skills and conventions of standard written English (SWE). Standard written English is the level of usage generally found in contemporary books, newspapers, magazines, and other publications. It reflects what educated users of the language currently accept as appropriate or correct in writing and careful speech.

The CPE does not, however, measure your ability to have memorized rules of grammar and mechanics. Instead, it requires that you analyze the kinds of prose writing you are likely to write and read in college.

The format is multiple choice. The test presents several sections which are underlined and numbered. Accompanying each underlined section are four or five options. In most cases the first option is to make no change in the underlined section. The other options are possible substitutes, only one of which is correct or more appropriate. Sometimes omitting the underlined section is an option. Other times an item may ask you to select an addition to the passage or to make a judgment about the passage as a whole.

Correctness, according to current conventions of SWE, may not be the only criterion you use in choosing answers. You will also have to consider which option is most effective in a particular rhetorical context.

You will not be allowed to use a dictionary or any other reference works during the exam.

To help you determine your strengths and weaknesses in the two major areas covered on the test, this book provides a diagnostic and seven practice tests, which you can take and score on your own. Answer keys are at the end of the book. Alongside each answer is at least one number in parentheses which corresponds to a particular kind of problem or error.

The test covers the following material. The numbers used in the answer keys correspond to those below:

RHETORICAL SKILLS (50%)

1. Coherence/Transitions

2. Development/Relevant detail

3. Logic (Shifts in tense and person, Clear pronoun reference)

4. Diction/Style

CONVENTIONS OF SWE (50%)

5. Sentence Fragments

6. Run-ons/Comma Splices

7. Sentence Structure

8. Subject-Verb Agreement

9. Pronoun-Antecedent Agreement

10. Pronoun Case

11. Other Inflected Forms (Verbs, Adjectives, Adverbs, Nouns)

12. Punctuation (Commas, Semicolons, Colons)

13. Apostrophes

After you score each practice test, note the kind of problem or error illustrated in each item you miss. Then turn to the Error Log which follows the Diagnostic Test. Here you can record the kinds of mistakes you make in each practice test and their frequency. If you fill in this log after each practice test, you will have an indication of the areas you need to study the most.

Even though this summary may seem to include a great deal of material, the exam does not include certain material you might expect. For example, it does not cover spelling and capitalization. If you thoroughly familiarize yourself with what the exam covers and concentrate on recognizing those kinds of problems and errors, and how to correct or replace them, you should be in a strong position to do well on the exam.

The next five chapters should help you review the material covered on the exam. They do not, however, cover the material exhaustively. Consult a current English handbook for additional explanations, illustrations, and practice exercises. You will find a brief list of such titles at the end of this book.

The passing score may vary from institution to institution. To find out the score you will need to pass the English CPE, ask your instructor, or a person in the testing or counseling office at your institution.

Diagnostic English Test

Take the following test before you study the material in this book. Score the test yourself, using the answer key in the back of the book. Pay particular attention to the type of errors you make. Fill in the Error Log which follows this test so you know which material in the book you especially need to study. Follow the same procedure as you take the additional practice tests at the end of the English section of the book.

Directions: In each of the passages which follow, certain portions are underlined and numbered. Most of these underlined sections contain errors and inappropriate expressions. You are asked to compare each with the four alternative passages in the answer column. If you consider the original version best, blacken the first choice. Otherwise, blacken the letter of the alternative you think best. If an item contains a question or statement to be completed, select the alternative which best answers the question or completes the statement.

PASSAGE ONE

President <u>Truman's victory,</u>
1
<u>coming as it did</u> after wide-
1
spread predictions to the

contrary, confounded many po-

litical experts in 1948. Truman

<u>had a bigger belief in himself</u>
2
than in the gloomy forecasts of

defeat. <u>In a defiant attitude,</u>
3
President Truman persisted in

taking his case to the people

on a whistlestop campaign tour

<u>that remains unsurpassed today.</u>
4
The nation <u>was being led</u>, it
5
seemed, by an ordinary man,

1A. No change
 B. Truman's victory, coming like it did
 C. Truman's victory coming as it did
 D. Truman's victory which came as it did
 E. Truman's victory that came as it did

2A. No change
 B. had a belief in hisself
 C. believed more in hisself
 D. believed more in himself
 E. believed most greatly in himself

3A. No change
 B. With defiance in mind
 C. Defiantly
 D. Taking a defiant position
 E. Being defiant

4A. No change
 B. that remains unsurpassed still today.
 C. which remains unsurpassed still today.
 D. which remains unsurpassed in this day and time.
 E. remaining unsurpassed these days

5A. No change
 B. having been led
 C. having been lead
 D. which was led
 E. was being lead

83

much as the voters themselfs were.
                                6
Consequently, the President won
            7
the trust and admiration of many.

One of the most famous photographs

in American politics show a
                      8
beaming President with a newspaper
                  8
whose headline reads, "Dewey
  8
Defeats Truman."

However, scandal and a
   9
stalemated Korean War ended the

popularity of the Truman

administration. When Truman left

the White House in 1953, he has
                              10
had the lowest popularity rating
 10
of any incumbent, before or since.

Time has largely reversed the

negative perceptions of his

contemporaries. Historians today

rank Truman among the six or eight

greatest presidents. Ordinary

Americans as well remember him

fondly as a decisive outspoken
               11
chief executive who presided over

one of the most difficult periods

in U.S. history.

6A. No change
 B. much like the voters
    themselves
 C. much like the voters
    theirselves
 D. much like the voters
    themselves were
 E. much as the voters
    theirselves were

7A. No change
 B. Nevertheless
 C. However
 D. On the other hand
 E. As a result of this

8A. No change
 B. show a beaming President
    with a newspaper who's
 C. show a beaming President
    with a newspaper which
 D. shows a beaming President
    with a newspaper whose
 E. demonstrates a beaming
    President with a newspaper
    whose

9A. No change
 B. Furthermore
 C. Moreover
 D. Therefore
 E. But

10A. No change
 B. use to have
 C. used to have
 D. had
 E. has

11A. No change
 B. decisive plus
 C. decisive, and
 D. decisive;
 E. decisive,

84

PASSAGE TWO

Although Underground Atlanta

began in the middle <u>1960s, it was</u>
$\quad\quad\quad\quad\quad\quad\quad\quad$ 12

not until the mid-1970s that the

entertainment center finally

collapsed. Only a few die-hard

businesses survived <u>to the end.</u>
$\quad\quad\quad\quad\quad\quad\quad$ 13
<u>Mostly</u> fast-food eateries and T-
13

shirt shops. <u>But at it's peak,</u>
$\quad\quad\quad\quad\quad\quad\quad$ 14

Underground was renowned all over

the country. Tourists <u>would</u>
$\quad\quad\quad\quad\quad\quad\quad$ 15
<u>typically ask</u> the whereabouts of
15

Underground and end up infusing

thousands of dollars into the

downtown economy. Underground,

actually an area beneath viaducts

built after the <u>Civil War, was</u>
$\quad\quad\quad\quad\quad\quad\quad$ 16
<u>also suppose</u> to spur interest in
16

history. More found it easier to

<u>believe, however,</u> that Underground
$\quad\quad\quad\quad\quad$ 17

was above all dedicated to making

money.

With the rebirth of Under-

ground in 1989, city leaders

looked to a promising future for

all of downtown Atlanta. Indeed,

the first few months of business

for Underground led merchants and

12A. No change
B. 1960's; it was
C. 1960s. It was
D. 1960s it was
E. 1960s, for it was

13A. No change
B. to the end, mostly
C. to the end; mostly
D. to the end, most
E. to the end. Most

14A. No change
B. Even at it's peak
C. Even at its peak
D. But at its peak
E. Although at its peak

15A. No change
B. typically ask
C. were typically asking
D. would typically request
E. were typically
requesting

16A. No change
B. Civil War was also
suppose
C. Civil War; was also
suppose
D. Civil War; was also
supposed
E. Civil War, was also
supposed

17A. No change
B. believe; however,
C. believe, however;
D. believe, therefore,
E. believe; therefore,

85

politicians to celebrate its

success. This time, in planning

the all-new Underground, <u>steps</u>
                          18
<u>were taken by the city's business</u>
                18
<u>and political communities</u> to avert
        18
the problems with crime and the

perception of crime that had

caused the demise of the original

Underground. This second

<u>incarnation they</u> were convinced,
      19
would be a magnet to draw

local suburbanites and

conventioneers alike to a

revitalized downtown. [20]

PASSAGE THREE

Anyone following current

events in the late 1980s <u>could not</u>
                              21
help <u>themselves</u> but be amazed by
      21
the sweeping tide of change in

eastern Europe. Some observers

characterized it as perhaps the

<u>importantest</u> of the post-World War
    22
II period. As recently as 1980,

most Westerners could not have

predicted that such widespread

social, political, and economic

changes would occur by the end of

the decade.

18A. No change
  B. steps had been made by the city's political and business communities
  C. the city's political and business communities took steps
  D. steps were being taken by the city's political and business communities
  E. they took steps

19A. No change
  B. incarnation, everybody
  C. incarnation. They
  D. incarnation, they
  E. incarnation; they

20. The next paragraph of the passage could logically focus on

  A. Mayor Young's popularity among Atlanta business people.
  B. Mayor Jackson's lack of popularity among Atlanta business people.
  C. the disappointments of the Fairlie-Poplar project.
  D. any one of the above.
  E. none of the above.

21A. No change
  B. could not help himself
  C. could not help
  D. couldn't help themselves
  E. could not help theirselves

22A. No change
  B. most maximum
  C. maximum
  D. most important
  E. more important

English Error Log

Directions: As you score each practice English test, note the types of errors you make. Next to each answer in the answer keys is at least one number which corresponds to one of the errors on this log. Alongside each type of error, make a mark in the appropriate box for each error of that type you make on each test. Monitor the errors you tend to make repeatedly, and work on avoiding them in the future.

	Diagnostic Test	Test 1	Test 2	Test 3
1. Coherence/Transitions				
2. Development/Relevance				
3. Logic (Tense/Person Shifts, Pronoun Reference)				
4. Diction/Style				
5. Sentence Fragments				
6. Run-ons/Comma Splices				
7. Sentence Structure				
8. Subject-Verb Agreement				
9. Pronoun-Antecedent Agreement				
10. Pronoun Case				
11. Other Inflected Forms (Verbs, Nouns, Adverbs, Adjectives)				
12. Punctuation (Commas, Semicolons, Colons)				
13. Apostrophes				

English Error Log
(CONTINUED)

	Test 4	Test 5	Test 6	Test 7
1. Coherence/Transitions				
2. Development/Relevance				
3. Logic (Tense/Person Shifts, Pronoun Reference)				
4. Diction/Style				
5. Sentence Fragments				
6. Run-ons/Comma Splices				
7. Sentence Structure				
8. Subject-Verb Agreement				
9. Pronoun-Antecedent Agreement				
10. Pronoun Case				
11. Other Inflected Forms (Verbs, Nouns, Adverbs, Adjectives)				
12. Punctuation (Commas, Semicolons, Colons)				
13. Apostrophes				

PART I:
RHETORICAL SKILLS

Chapter 5: Organization, Development, and Logic

A. COHERENCE

Writing is <u>coherent</u> when ideas are presented in a logical order. In addition, effective <u>transitions</u> between ideas improve the coherence of writing. Some common transitional words and phrases are listed below:

in addition	thus
for example	consequently
for instance	as a result
moreover	nevertheless
furthermore	nonetheless
however	on the other hand
therefore	finally

Coordinate conjunctions, of course, may often join ideas and set up an equal relationship between them:

and, or, nor, for, so, yet, but

Example: Craig wiped his feet on the mat, for he knew his roommate had just washed the floor.

Subordinate conjunctions <u>subordinate</u> one idea to another: The idea introduced by the subordinate conjunction is less complete, and therefore less important, than the other.

although	unless	when	even though
before	because	why	though
after	while	how	that
until	where	as	so that
once	since	if	as if

Example: <u>Although</u> the deadline is fast approaching, Mr. Dithers has received very few applications for Bumstead's old job.

On the CPE, pay attention to whether transitional expressions link ideas <u>logically</u>. Every transitional word or phrase has meaning, which must fit between the two ideas the writer wants to bridge. For example, the following transitional word makes no sense where it is used:

Roxanne tried desperately to question me. <u>However</u>, she persisted well into the night.

Keep in mind that transitions may be important between paragraphs as well as between sentences.

B. DEVELOPMENT

A paragraph is well developed if it contains adequate <u>details</u> to support the main idea. Details must be <u>relevant</u>; that is, they must pertain to the point of the paragraph. Irrelevant details weaken paragraph <u>unity</u>.

As you take the exam, evaluate sentences to make sure they relate to the central idea of the paragraph.

C. CLEAR PRONOUN REFERENCE

Vague or ambiguous pronoun reference may also weaken the logic of writing. Generally, pronouns have <u>antecedents</u>, that is, nouns or other pronouns they replace or refer to. Pronoun reference is unclear or ambiguous when the reader is not sure of the antecedent of a pronoun.

Example: Smith told Murphy that his injury might force him to leave the game. (Is the injury Smith's or Murphy's ?)

D. SHIFTS IN PERSON

Watch for passages in which the writer shifts from third-person to second-person references (or vice versa).

Example: First-year college <u>students</u> soon discover how important study habits are in <u>their</u> courses. The first lesson you learn is that daily notetaking in class is often indispensable.

To be logically consistent, the writer should continue using third-person references (students, their) once he/she has started, and not change to second-person (you) references.

E. SHIFTS IN VERB TENSE

As a general rule, writers should be consistent in their use of verb tense in a piece of writing. That is, if a writer begins writing in the present tense, he/she should not change to another tense unless a shift can be logically justified. The following passage contains logical shifts in verb tense:

Divorce statistics in the 1980s <u>continue</u> to climb, though not as dramatically as they <u>did</u> in the 1970s. At the turn of the century, the divorce rate <u>was</u> so low that one might think practically every married couple <u>were</u> blissfully happy.

Below is a passage of an <u>illogical</u> shift in verb tense:

Kevin <u>enjoys</u> working the nightshift because he <u>can be</u> by himself and even <u>relax</u> when business <u>was getting</u> slack.

Revised: Kevin enjoys working the night shift because he can be by himself and even relax when business <u>gets</u> slack.

Chapter 6: Diction and Style

A. DICTION AND TONE

Diction means a writer's <u>choice of words</u>. Choosing words depends on a number of factors, including the writer's purpose, the intended audience, the writer's tone, and the connotations of words.

If a writer's main purpose is to amuse the audience, explaining why he/she will never ride The Great Scream Machine at Six Flags, he/she may feel much freer to use informal, casual, even colloquial language. That is, the diction may resemble that of spoken conversation.

On the other hand, if the writer seeks to inform the reader of the serious ramifications of mandatory drug-testing on the job, his/her word choice is likely to be more formal, careful and less conversational.

<u>Tone</u> refers to the writer's attitude toward both the subject and the intended audience. Words like <u>sarcastic</u>, <u>ironic</u>, <u>insulting</u>, <u>flippant</u>, and <u>angry</u> may be used to describe tone. Diction plays an important role in setting the tone of a piece of writing.

<u>Consistency</u> and <u>appropriateness</u> are keys to recognizing diction problems. As you evaluate passages on the CPE, ask yourself whether the writer is shifting from one level of diction to another. Consider the mix of diction in the passage below:

> Dear Dean McGinty:
>
> Having received your letter of May 2 and given much thought to your nominating me to the Executive Council, I would definitely like to respond by hollering at the top of my lungs, "Wow! Let me at it! It's just the kind of job I've always been crazy about!" So even though a lot of my buddies say this job stinks to high heaven, man, you can bet I'm grabbing it in a flash. Is it OK if I get at it pronto?

Not only does the diction lapse into very informal, colloquial usage (after beginning on a fairly formal note), but given the intended audience — a college dean — the colloquial diction is most <u>inappropriate</u>, even if it were used throughout the piece.

Notice also how the exclamation marks affect the tone of the writing, making it over-charged emotionally, even hysterical.

In addition, many words have <u>connotations</u> which may affect the tone of writing. A connotation is an implied or suggested meaning. Be careful of words connoting certain things to your audience that you may not intend or be aware of.

Example: Professor Finch discussed his relations with international students very casually.

The writer may simply have meant to convey how relaxed the professor was in his discussion. However, for some readers, the phrase "very carefully" might connote a certain insensitivity and flippancy, as if Professor Finch did not take international students or his relations with them very seriously.

To convey the writer's intended meaning, the sentence might be revised:

> Discussing his relations with international students, Professor Finch was very relaxed.

Connotative meanings are not generally found in dictionaries. The writer and reader usually rely on context — that is, the surrounding words — to guide them in deciding if an expression carries any connotation.

Whenever possible, make your choice of words vivid and specific. Avoid vague, overused words:

> The woman I met in the elevator seems nice.

> Sean did a nice job on my car.

> We had a nice time at Stone Mountain.

Words like nice, great, and good (three of the most popular but empty words in the language) simply indicate approval. Such words are weak because they have so many meanings, none of them very clear or specific.

B. WORDINESS

Writing becomes wordy when a writer uses more words than he/she needs. A writer should use as few words as possible to convey an idea. If the point can be made in six words, then the good writer uses six words, not ten or twenty. Economy of expression is certainly a virtue in writing. Readers, after all, resent their time being taken up reading unnecessary words.

A frequent source of wordiness, as well as awkwardness, is the passive voice, in which the doer of the action is not the grammatical subject of the verb, but rather the object of a preposition.

Example: Little Frankie was taken to the park by Helen.

Most sentences in the passive voice can be changed to the active voice:

> Helen took little Frankie to the park.

The revised sentence gains strength through its directness and economy of expression.

The passive voice may be preferred if the doer of the action is unknown.

Example: The heiress was murdered in her sleep last night.

Below are two examples of wordy expressions:

> It is my opinion that...
> It can be seen that...

Related to wordiness is the problem of redundancy, which is needless repetition. The common expression period of time, for example, is redundant because a period, by definition, is a span of time. Hence, time is built into the meaning of period.

Example: The lawyer asked that his client not spend a long <u>period</u> of <u>time</u> in custody.

By eliminating the redundancy in the sentence above, the writer also cuts some wordiness, as follows:

The lawyer asked that his client not spend a long time in custody.

<u>or</u>

The lawyer asked that his client not spend a long period in custody.

The sentences below contain redundancies:

The gang <u>circled</u> <u>around</u> the parking lot for twenty minutes.

The <u>reason</u> some winners act embarrassed is <u>because</u> they are surprised by their success.

A special kind of redundancy is the <u>double</u> <u>negative</u>, in which a clause contains more than one negative word.

Example: He has<u>n't</u> got <u>no</u> money in the bank.

Corrected, the sentence reads:

He has <u>no</u> money in the bank.

<u>or</u>

He has<u>n't</u> any money in the bank.

Besides words like <u>not</u> and <u>no</u>, words like <u>hardly</u>, <u>barely</u> and <u>scarcely</u> are negative. The following sentence, then, contains a double negative:

The runners did not have hardly any time to warm up.

Revised: The runners had hardly any time to warm up.

C. AWKWARDNESS

One of the most difficult weaknesses to generalize about is <u>awkwardness</u>. Often the awkward expression is grammatically correct. Yet it chugs along clumsily instead of tripping off the tongue. It may sound like a group of words <u>forced</u> together, rather artificially. Such expressions lack fluency or a sense of idiom.

Non-native speakers of a language, as they try to learn that language, often end up constructing very awkward expressions. The words may well be recognizable, but the way they are <u>combined</u> may puzzle a native speaker who hears or reads the combination.

Consider the following example:

Precipitation is falling at this time.

No doubt this is an English sentence made up of English words. But the combination of these words is very odd and may even be difficult for some to understand, especially when the same idea is usually expressed as:

It's raining now.

The second sentence is much better than the first because the first is awkward, unidiomatic, and lacking fluency. The second is more direct, for using fewer and simpler words.

Sentences may also become awkward when prepositions are used incorrectly. For example, slight word changes involving prepositions can affect meaning considerably:

The attorneys agreed to the judge's deciding the case.

The attorneys agreed with the judge's decision in the case.

Consider how the meaning of conform changes slightly, according to the preposition it is used with:

All Freddie's classmates eagerly conform with their role models in the senior class.

Few of Freddie's classmates conform to all the rules of the school.

D. CLICHES

Cliche is a French word for a trite, or over-used and wornout, expression. Good writers generally avoid cliches because they smack of intellectual laziness. Instead of coming up with their own fresh, insightful ways of expressing ideas, less accomplished writers lean on cliches. Trite expressions are, in a sense, pre-fab, ready-made ideas, down to the last word. To understand this characteristic of cliches, see how easy it is to complete the following trite expressions:

It's always darkest _____.

Every cloud has a _____.

The more, the _____

To snatch victory _____

PART II:
CONVENTIONS OF STANDARD WRITTEN ENGLISH
(SWE)

Chapter 7: Sentence Structure

A. FRAGMENTS

In general, writers use complete sentences. Any group of words that <u>looks</u> <u>like</u> a sentence (beginning with a capital letter and ending with a period) but does <u>not</u> express a complete thought is called a sentence fragment.

A word group expresses a complete thought if it contains at least <u>one independent clause</u>. A clause always contains a <u>verb</u> with a <u>subject</u>.

Example: I spent the summer in Scotland.

"I" is the subject of the verb "spent." Try to locate the subject only <u>after</u> you have found the verb by asking yourself the question <u>Who</u>? or <u>What</u>? before the <u>verb</u>.

As soon as a clause is introduced by a <u>subordinate</u> <u>conjunction</u> or a <u>relative</u> <u>pronoun</u>, the clause becomes <u>dependent</u> and does not express a complete thought. It cannot stand alone. It must be connected to an independent clause.

Example: While I spent the summer in Scotland, my wife took an art history
         course in Florence.

See Chapter 5 for a list of subordinate conjunctions.

<u>Relative pronouns</u> are

who(ever)	what(ever)	that
whom(ever)	which	

Example: The man <u>who rang my doorbell</u> is selling vacuum cleaners.

A <u>phrase</u> is a meaningful word group which lacks a verb and subject. The function of a phrase is to <u>modify</u> some part of a sentence. Phrases, therefore, cannot stand alone as if they were sentences. Here are examples of phrases:

Waiting in line for over an hour in front of the theater
(4 phrases)
To earn her respect as the newest executive in the department
(3 phrases)
Played repeatedly during the darkest hours of British resistance
(3 phrases)

B. RUN-ONS AND COMMA SPLICES

In a sense, these two problems are "cousins." A run-on sentence (or fused sentence) occurs when a writer joins two sentences without <u>any</u> mark of punctuation or conjunction.

Example: Barney asked Thelma Lou to go on the hayride she had a severe allergy to new-moon hay.

A comma splice occurs when only a <u>comma</u> joins two sentences.

Example: Barney asked Thelma Lou to go on the hayride, she had a severe allergy to new-mown hay.

Either error may be corrected as follows:

> Barney asked Thelma Lou to go on the hayride, <u>even though</u> she had a severe allergy to new-mown hay.

> Barney asked Thelma Lou to go on the hayride; she had a severe allergy to new-mown hay.

> Barney asked Thelma Lou to go on the hayride. She had a severe allergy to new-mown hay.

> Barney asked Thelma Lou to go on the hayride, <u>but</u> she had a severe allergy to new-mown hay.

The first and last of the above corrections are probably most effective because they link the ideas logically and smoothly with <u>conjunctions</u>.

C. FAULTY SENTENCE STRUCTURE

The structure of a sentence is grammatically faulty if modifiers are placed incorrectly. A <u>modifier</u> is a word or phrase which adds to the meaning of another part of the sentence. Whenever possible, it should be placed <u>next to</u> the item it modifies. A <u>misplaced</u> <u>modifier</u> can result in an illogical meaning and confuse the reader.

Example: Climbing the ladder to Bonnie's room last night, Fred's head hit her father's pick-ax.

The way the sentence is constructed, it appears that Fred's head was climbing the ladder, since the opening phrases ("climbing the ladder to Bonnie's room last night") modifies "Fred's head." In fact, Fred himself (not his head) was climbing the ladder. So the sentence needs to be re-constructed as follows:

> Climbing the ladder to Bonnie's room last night, Fred hit his head on her father's pick-ax.

A <u>dangling</u> <u>modifier</u> results when a modifier cannot logically be attached to any part of the sentence.

Example: To satisfy her father, it was important that nobody call after 11 PM.

Revised: To satisfy her father, Myrtle saw that nobody called after 11 PM.

D. PARALLEL STRUCTURE

When a sentence contains two or more parts, usually joined with a conjunction, all the parts should be in the same grammatical form.

Example: The traveling salesman made several promises to his fiancee: never leave town without her permission, call her nightly when he was out of town, never call her collect, and keeping a record of all travel expenses.

The last item in the series of promises is not <u>parallel</u> with the first three (leave, call, call). The last item is in present-participle form, with an "-ing" ending (<u>keeping</u>). It would have to be changed to "keep" to make it parallel with the first three items.

Lack of parallelism can also appear in a sentence in which the verb is some form of <u>to be</u>. Since the verb <u>to be</u> functions like an equal sign in mathematics, a noun on one side of the verb must be in the same grammatical form as a noun on the other side of the verb.

Example: Speaking out of turn at the meeting would be to make a serious mistake.

Revised: To speak out of turn at the meeting would be to make a serious mistake.

E. SENTENCE BALANCE

<u>Balanced</u> sentences contain parts that are mirror-images of each other in form, or parts whose forms complement each other.

Example: <u>Either</u> you stop smoking <u>or</u> I move out of the apartment.

Example: Churchill ran for re-election after the war <u>not because</u> he was hungry for power <u>but because</u> he still felt duty-bound to the nation.

Sentence balance causes the reader to feel a certain psychological satisfaction. Once a structure is begun, the reader at least subconsciously expects it to be completed. The following sentence illustrates a lack of formal balance:

> Senator D'Amato expects to win re-election not only by wooing the labor vote, and he promises to strengthen his support for Israel.

Revised: Senator D'Amato expects to win re-election <u>not only by wooing</u> the labor vote <u>but by promising</u> to strengthen his support for Israel.

Chapter 8: Other Grammatical Errors

A. SUBJECT-VERB AGREEMENT

Verbs agree with their subjects when both are in the same number. That is, if a subject is singular, its verb must be singular in form. When the subject is plural, the verb must be plural in form.

Most errors involving subject-verb agreement occur in the present tense, third-person.

Example: He don't expect to win the bet.

In particular, watch for passages in which:

> (1) The verb and subject of the sentence are far apart. Often a prepositional phrase (or several) will intervene between the subject and verb.

> Remember: The object of a preposition cannot be the subject of the verb, even if it stands next to the verb, where the subject is often located.

Example: A girl with two boxes of fried chicken on her head is waiting for the guard to unlock the door.

"Girl" — not "boxes," "chicken," or "head" — is the subject of "is." The other nouns are all objects of prepositions.

> (2) The normal word order is inverted. Usually, the subject comes first in a sentence, followed by the verb. However, the word order can sometimes be turned around without changing meaning but making it harder to make sure the subject and verb agree.

Example: Three beat-up Volvos were rumbling past the reviewing stand.

Example: Rumbling past the reviewing stand were three beat-up Volvos.

No matter what the order of the words, the verb "were rumbling" must agree with "Volvos."

B. PRONOUN-ANTECEDENT AGREEMENT

A pronoun, like the antecedent it usually refers to, has number. It may be either singular or plural. Logically, if an antecedent is singular, then the pronoun should be singular. If the antecedent is plural, so too should the pronoun be plural.

One of the most common errors involving pronoun-antecedent agreement has to do with indefinite pronouns like:

anyone	no one	everyone
anybody	nobody	everybody
someone	none	
somebody	each	

These pronouns are singular, but when possessive pronouns are used with them, many writers incorrectly use plural forms.

Example: Everybody in the office asked for their own computer.

Revised: Everybody in the office asked for his (or her) own computer.

Another potential source of confusion is collective nouns, which name groups of people and thus can be considered singular or plural, depending on their use in a particular context.

Example: The team spent the entire morning arguing about their proposed pension benefits.

"Team," a collective noun, names a group of individuals. The team may be thought of as acting as a unit (hence, a singular noun) or as a number of individuals acting individually (hence, a plural noun). In the sentence above, the second interpretation applies. As a result, the plural "their" is the correct pronoun choice.

C. PRONOUN CASE

The form, or case, of a pronoun changes, according to how the pronoun is used in a sentence. The pronoun cases are called:

(1) subjective, (2) objective, (3) possessive, and (4) reflexive

(1) Subjective case pronouns are

> I, we, you, he, she, it, they, who

These pronouns are called subjective because they are usually used as subjects of verbs.

(2) Objective case pronouns are

> me, us, you, him, her, it, them, whom

They get their name from the fact they are used as objects in a sentence — direct or indirect objects of a verb, or objects of a preposition.

Example: <u>We</u> asked <u>her</u> to return without <u>him</u>.
               1   2   3

Blank # 1 is a subject slot (of the verb "asked"). So any pronoun in that slot must be in the subjective case. Both blanks # 2 and # 3 are object slots, so any pronouns in those slots must be objective case.

Remember: A direct object (if any) answers the question Whom? or What? after the verb. An indirect object (if any) answers the question To whom? or For whom? after the verb.

Example: Grampa gave her a kiss on the forehead.

"Kiss" is the direct object of "gave," and "her" is the indirect object.

Also, a pronoun after any form of <u>to be</u> will be in the subjective case. (Think of the verb as being like an equal sign in mathematics.)

Example: It is <u>he</u>, Sir Gawain, who will rescue us from the dreaded dragon.

(3) Possessive case pronouns, despite their name, will <u>not</u> contain apostrophes:

mine, ours, yours, his, hers, its, theirs

Example: I was willing to lend her my car, but Sheila wasn't willing to lend <u>hers</u> to anyone.

The pronoun "hers" takes the place of the phrase "her car."

(4) Reflexive case pronouns are

myself	ourselves
yourself	yourselves
himself	themselves
herself	
itself	

They are used to refer to a person or thing already mentioned in the sentence.

Example: Jennifer kept telling <u>herself</u> the job would get more challenging.

D. VERB FORMS

Verbs, of course, may change form, according to tense (past, present, and future). <u>Regular</u> verbs pose few problems for writers. A verb is <u>regular</u> if it forms its past tense and past participle by adding "-ed" to the verb.

Example: walk (present)
walked (past)
walked (past participle)

<u>Irregular</u> verbs, however, do not follow such a pattern.

Example: drink (present)
drank (past)
drunk (past participle)

The <u>past participle</u> is the verb form used with a <u>helping</u> (or auxiliary) verb (some form of <u>to be</u>, or <u>have, has</u>, or <u>had</u>).

Example: I <u>have</u> never <u>driven</u> to Miami by myself.

Example: Brenda <u>had lost</u> ten pounds when the doctor warned her about diet pills.

Example: The herd <u>was led</u> to the edge of the cliff.

An English handbook will contain a list of the most common irregular verb forms.

Some verbs, because of their similarities, can confuse writers. Their meanings, however, are different. Two examples are given below. See any English handbook for a full explanation of their differences in meaning, as well as a list of such confusing verbs.

lie vs. lay
rise vs. raise

Certain past participles are sometimes misspelled because the "-ed" ending is not clearly heard in pronunciation. Three common examples are

used to
supposed to
accustomed to

In a sentence that contains two or more verbs to express two or more separate actions, a writer must be sure that the tenses are logical for the <u>sequence</u> of the action.

Example: The fortune teller <u>had told</u> us to take another route home when Brett, the driver, <u>decided</u> to go the same way we <u>had come</u>.

All three actions are expressed in a past tense. But <u>two</u> of the actions ("had come" and "had told") occurred <u>before</u> the other action ("decided"). Consequently, those two actions are not expressed in the simple past, but in the <u>past perfect</u> tense, which uses the helping verb "had."

Using different tenses to express action in the past sets up a logical sequence of the actions for the reader.

E. ADJECTIVE AND ADVERB FORMS

An <u>adjective</u> performs one function: to modify nouns or pronouns.

An <u>adverb</u> will modify an adjective, a verb, or another adverb.

Many adjectives can be made into adverbs by adding "-ly."

Examples: sure surely
    fair   fairly
    extravagant extravagantly

A problem arises when a writer uses an adjective to modify a word which can be modified only by an adverb.

Example: Phil does <u>good</u> on pop quizzes.

Example: Cheryl was <u>real</u> sorry she got angry at her brother.

In both cases, an <u>adverb</u> is needed to modify the verb "does" and the adjective "sorry." The sentences should be revised as follows:

Phil does <u>well</u> on pop quizzes.

Cheryl was <u>really (very)</u> sorry she got angry at her brother.

Chapter 9: Punctuation

A. THE COMMA

Writers use commas in a wide variety of situations. Below are the most common, along with illustrations:

1. **Between items in a series:**

   The strikers expect to return to work, modify their demands, meet with company representatives, and work thirty days without a contract.

2. **Between coordinate adjectives and adverbs:**

   Isaac Stern's latest recording of the Sibelius Concerto has a silken, unhurried quality. (The comma could be replaced with *and*. Also, coordinate adjectives and adverbs are <u>reversible</u>.)

   The restorer touched up the painting more delicately, more carefully than the artist had. (Replacing the *and* between the adverbs with a comma is unusual but possible as a stylistic alternative.)

   My sister wants to transfer to a larger, more expensive university.

3. **Before a coordinate conjunction when it joins two independent clauses:**

   For weeks Barney pined over Thelma Lou, but she virtually ignored him.

4. **After a dependent clause when it precedes an independent clause:**

   Unless you apologize, I intend to follow my lawyer's advice and sue.

5. **After a transitional expression when it begins a sentence:**

   For example, seventy men responded to Ann Landers' survey.

6. **Before a transitional expression when it ends a sentence:**

   Our discussion of rap music will continue, however.

7. **Surrounding a transitional expression when it occurs in the middle of a sentence:**

   Revising the essay may, in addition, improve your grade.

8. **Setting off other words which interrupt the main idea:**

   Jerry Falwell, critics say, is not likely to stay out of national politics.

   Pasta, by the way, has fewer calories than some people think.

9. **After a long introductory phrase (more than three words):**

   Unable to satisfy his father, Ken left home in frustration.

10. **After a short introductory phrase if the sentence may be misread without a comma:**

    To begin with, half the students asked for extra help.

11. **Setting off words of contrast:**

    I wanted to pay for the sofa with Visa, not Master Card.

12. **Setting off dates:**

    Let's meet again on Wednesday, September 14, 1989, to review our progress.

13. **Setting off a noun of direct address:**

    When did you meet Duke Ellington, Mom?

    Do you like cats, Dr. Zorba?

    My friend, I'll gladly lend you the car.

14. **Setting off parts of an address or geographical location:**

    The mayor announced that Toulouse, France, would be Atlanta's sister city.

    No one in the sixth-grade class knew who lived at 10 Downing Street, London, England.

15. **Setting off a direct quotation from the identifying material in the sentence:**

    The bank guard screamed, "Come back with my dog!"

    "I suppose," she whispered, "everybody has a skeleton in the closet."

    "Please leave the table if you're done insulting my Veal Prince Orloff," the offended hostess announced.

16. **Setting off non-restrictive words, phrases, and clauses:**

    My oldest brother, Eddie, may quit his job.

    Emily, who enjoys mud wrestling, is one of the best mathematicians in the class.

My sister's fiance, wounded in Vietnam, counsels fellow veterans.

B. THE SEMICOLON

The semicolon has two main uses:

— To replace a period, but <u>only</u> when the two sentences are very closely related.

Example: Hitchcock's directing style peaked in *Psycho*; my own personal favorite, though, is *Notorious*.

— To separate items in a series when at least one comma must be used within any item in the series.

Example: The party nominated Derek Brown, who ran for the office once before; Marilyn DeVito, whose experience as a congressional aide may help her; and Gwen Phelps, the younger sister of last year's nominee.

C. THE COLON

The colon usually sets off a list or series from its introductory material.

Example: The interviewer said she was looking for three key traits in the candidates: integrity, candor, and ambition.

If the introductory material ends with some form of <u>to be</u>, however, a colon is not used.

Example: The interviewer said the three key traits she was looking for in candidates <u>were</u> integrity, candor, and ambition.

A colon may also separate a group of words from a clause when the group of words clarifies the clause.

Example: Professor Higgins made the obvious choice: settling down with Eliza.

D. THE APOSTROPHE

Apostrophes are used most often to show <u>possession</u>. A writer needs to distinguish between <u>singular</u> possession and <u>plural</u> possession.

Examples: the boy's parents = the parents of the boy (singular)

the boys' parents = the parents of the boys (plural, at least two boys)

the church's clergy (singular, one church)

the churches' clergy (plural, two or more churches)

For an <u>irregular</u> noun, which does not form its plural by adding "-s" or "-es," the singular or plural form of the noun is still used as a base.

Examples: The man's attraction to astrology

The men's attraction to astrology

The apostrophe is also used in informal writing to form <u>contractions</u> of words. The apostrophe replaces deleted letters.

couldn't = could not
isn't = is not

In addition, the apostrophe is used to form the plural of numbers and letters. The apostrophe helps avoid confusion.

Example: The word *popping* contains three p's.

Example: Out of boredom young Elvis scrawled dozens of 8's in his notebook.

PRACTICE

ENGLISH

TESTS

Practice English Test 1

Directions: In each of the passages which follow, certain portions are underlined and numbered. Most of these underlined sections contain errors and inappropriate expressions. You are asked to compare each with the three alternative passages in the answer column. If you consider the original version best, blacken the first choice. Otherwise, blacken the letter of the alternative you think best. If an item contains a question or statement to be completed, select the alternative which best answers the question or completes the statement.

PASSAGE ONE

One of the most unusual news programs on television is *The McLaughlin Group*, hosted by John McLaughlin. Each week four
        1
outspoken journalists gather with McLaughlin to have events
              2
discussed of the past week. The
2
program is taped in Washington on Friday it is shown by local sta-
            3
tions, usually over the weekend.

The show's participants are some of the best-known columnists and reporters in the country; Jack
              4
Germond, Fred Barnes, Morton
4
Kondracke, and Eleanor Clift. In addition, Pat Buchanan appears frequently. What distin-
        5
guishes the program from others that affect a "roundtable"-
       6
discussion format is its fast pace and highly vociferous

1A.	No change
B.	McLaughlin, however, each week
C.	McLaughlin; however, each week
D.	McLaughlin, but each week
2A.	No change
B.	with the intention to discuss
C.	to discuss events
D.	to get events discussed
3A.	No change
B.	Friday and it is shown
C.	Friday and is therefore shown
D.	Friday and shown
4A.	No change
B.	country: Jack Germond,
C.	country. Jack Germond,
D.	country, Jack Germond,
5A.	No change
B.	appears with a lot of frequency
C.	is on a great many occasions
D.	is on a great number of times
6A.	No change
B.	use
C.	put into effect
D.	put into application

exchanges between the five

panelists, which hardly ever
　　　　　　7

hesitate to interrupt each other.

Words can become so heated and

forceful, in fact, that a viewer

might think they are watching a
　　　　　　8

shouting match at times. Still,

McLaughlin is adept to keep the
　　　　　　　　9

discussions moving and ensuring

that a civilized atmosphere pre-

vails. Perhaps most of all,

McLaughlin has stamped the

program with his own self-

deprecating humor, It is a
　　　　　　　10

thing his most avid fans
　10

appreciate in the gentle mockery

panelists sometimes exchange

along with their comments.

McLaughlin is an editor for
　　　　　11
the *National Review* maga-
　　　　　11
azine. McLaughlin always
　　　　11
seems to be greatly enjoying

himself as he presides over

the weekly sessions.

PASSAGE TWO

Media coverage of American

politics have become nearly as
　　　　12

7A. No change
 B. panelists who
 C. panelists, who
 D. panelists whom

8A. No change
 B. he is
 C. he used to be
 D. they could have been

9A. No change
 B. adept for keeping
 C. adept by keeping
 D. adept at keeping

10A. No change
 B. humor; it is a thing
 C. humor, a thing, which
 D. humor, which

11A. No change
 B. McLaughlin, being an editor
　　 also for the *National*
　　 Review magazine,
 C. An editor for the *National*
　　 Review magazine,
　　 McLaughlin
 D. Plus being an editor
　　 for the *National Review*
　　 magazine, McLaughlin

12A. No change
 B. has become
 C. has became
 D. had become

controversial as the issues and

politicians <u>themselves, critics</u>
13
who attack the role of TV in

political campaigns often claim

that the medium over-simplifies

or distorts issues instead of

<u>clarifying it.</u> As a result,
14
politicians, campaign managers,

and a fairly new breed known as

"media consultants" learn

quickly that, <u>to survive, a</u>
15
<u>candidate must</u> reduce his message
15
to "thirty-second bites" for the

TV cameras. These thirty-second

bites are what TV newscasters can

easily fit into an evening news

program, <u>along with the other</u>
16
<u>events considered newsworthy</u>
16
<u>that day.</u>
16
In a so-called "age of

information," skeptics wonder

whether the public in a democracy

are truly being informed enough

about issues and candidates to

make intelligent choices at the

polls. Voters, who rely much more

on TV than any print medium as a

source of news and information,

13A. No change
  B. theirselves; critics
  C. themselfs; critics
  D. themselves. Critics

14A. No change
  B. having made it plain
  C. having clarified them
  D. clarifying them

15A. No change
  B. to survive, it is necessary
      that a candidate
  C. in order to survive, it is
      a must that a candidate
  D. survival necessitates that
      a candidate has to

16A. No change
  B. plus everything else
      happening on that day
  C. together with other stories
      happening in the news that
      should be on
  D. as well as other things
      that might have happened

then hearing little more than
                 17
buzz words, cliches, and slogans.

Even "debates" staged for the

cameras simply give candidates

one more forum for delivering

their familiar standard "bites."

Genuine clashes which involve

ideas and positions rarely occur.

Moreover, some insist that

TV, because of its visual nature
                 18
encourages voters to respond to

images rather than substance.

In the 1960s Marshall McLuhan's
                                19
pronouncement that "The medium
        19
is the message." Teddy Roosevelt,
                          20
for instance, tended to grin
              20
broadly or gesture emphatically
                 20
in public. Despite the fact John
  20   21
Kennedy's more appealing tele-

genic "image" drubbed that of
                       22
Richard Nixon in the 1960

Presidential debates, no major

presidential contender has

seriously considered a run for

the White House without hiring

an expert to advise them on
                  23
make-up, hair style, clothing,

speaking voice, and body move-

17A.   No change
  B.   and then hear little more
        then
  C.   then hear little more than
  D.   then hear little more then

18A.   No change
  B.   TV, because of its visual
        nature,
  C.   TV because of its visual
        nature
  D.   TV on account of it being
        visual

19A.   No change
  B.   McLuhan stated,
  C.   McLuhan stated;
  D.   McLuhan's statement,

20A.   No change
  B.   Teddy Roosevelt, as an
        example, used to grin
        broadly or gesture
        emphatically in public.
  C.   Teddy Roosevelt, for
        example, was a notorious
        grinner in public.
  D.   Omit underlined portion

21A.   No change
  B.   Until
  C.   Ever since
  D.   Before

22A.   No change
  B.   drubbed
  C.   attacked
  D.   was raised up over

23A.   No change
  B.   who would have the job of
        advising him
  C.   to advise him
  D.   whose job is that of
        advising him

116

ments for the cameras. <u>As the</u>
                              24
<u>use of television increases</u>
                24
<u>in American elections, even at</u>
                24
<u>the local level, its influence</u>
                24
<u>is not likely to wane.</u>
                24

PASSAGE THREE

Ralph <u>Ellison, being the</u>
                        25
<u>author of *Invisible Man*, one</u>
                        25
of the most important novels about

black life in America, grew up

in the 1920s in segregated Okla-

homa. His early years were mostly

typical <u>of other young black</u>
                    26
<u>males.</u> But having proved him-
    26
self an outstanding <u>student,</u>
                                27
<u>the state gave him</u> a schol-
            27
arship that enabled him to

attend Tuskegee <u>Institute.</u>
                        28
<u>At Tuskegee he became a student</u>
                        28
<u>of music.</u> <u>He then</u> set out for
        28   29
Harlem, at that time the mecca

for black artists in this

country. There Ellison met

Richard Wright and Langston

Hughes, two other prominent

writers of the <u>so-called</u> Harlem

24A. No change
  B. Television being used so
     much is likely to go on.
  C. Television's use in
     politics shows no sign of
     becoming less.
  D. Omit underlined portion

25A. No change
  B. Ellison, who wrote
     Invisible Man,
  C. Ellison, *Invisible Man*'s
     writer,
  D. Ellison, having written
     Invisible Man,

26A. No change
  B. of those which other
     young black males had
  C. of those experienced by
     young black males
  D. of that which young black
     males had

27A. No change
  B. student, he accomplished
     winning
  C. student, he had won
  D. student, he won

28A. No change
  B. Institute at which he
     studied music
  C. Institute, where he studied
     music
  D. Institute where he studied
     music

29A. No change
  B. After this, he
  C. After that, he
  D. Following that he

117

Renaissance. <u>Wright's *Native*</u>
                    30
<u>*Son* was published in 1940.</u>
                    30
Having tried his hand at

music, he now took up writing,

mostly short pieces with a

politically leftist slant.

Wright served as both mentor

and editor for the young Ellison

during the 1930s, a period when

many artists used their work to

explore social and political

issues <u>that came about in the Great</u>
                           31
<u>Depression</u>. Ellison, however,
   31
never committed himself to left-

wing causes as fully as many of

his contemporaries. Soon

Ellison was writing more fiction

<u>and less</u> political pieces. As the
   32
thirties came to an end, he had

begun to publish short stories that

anticipated some of the themes of

Invisible Man.

Following a stint in the

merchant marine during the war

years, he settled in Vermont,

where the novel started to

take shape. <u>Finally, in 1953,</u>
                      33
<u>the completed work was pub-</u>
                      33

30A. No change
  B. One novel by Wright, *Native
     Son*, was published in 1940.
  C. For example, Wright's
     Native Son was published in
     1940.
  D. Omit underlined portion

31A. No change
  B. which the Great Depression
     was the cause of
  C. which people talked about
     during the Great Depression
  D. raised by the Great
     Depression

32A. No change
  B. and not as much
  C. but less
  D. and fewer

33A. No change
  B. 1953 saw the book done and
     published at long last.
  C. It got its completion and
     publication in 1953.
  D. Omit underlined portion

lished. Immediately, critics
33
saw in its author a major

American novelist. Today Ellison's

reputation rests almost entirely

on *Invisible Man*, as yet his

only novel.

PASSAGE FOUR

To some, computers are the

bane of their existence; to

others, they mean miraculous
34
relief from drudgery. In par-

ticular, the personal computer,

or PC, has literally brought

home the question of whether

these machines do more to help,
35
or intimidate human beings.
35
Technology made it
36
relatively easy and inexpen-

sive to use a PC at home and

in the workplace, more people,

with no particular computer

expertise, are being given the

opportunity to use them, often

against their will. Some indi-

viduals feel at such a loss

getting used to all the new

names and the machines them-
37

34A. No change
  B. computers are other people's
  C. contrary to this, they mean
  D. then the computer can be turned to for

35A. No change
  B. help yet intimidating
  C. help or intimidating
  D. help or intimidate

36A. No change
  B. Technology makes it
  C. Now that technology has made it
  D. Technology is making it

37A. No change
  B. uncomprehending language
  C. jargon
  D. talk

119

selves <u>that</u> they may actually
       38

keep a safe distance from the

keyboard until they absolutely

have to approach it, and then

only in dread. <u>Your period of</u>
                39

<u>time</u> interacting with the PC
  39

may be short, ending in frustra-

tion and continued fear the

machine may never be mastered. [40]

38. A. No change
   B. so
   C. thus
   D. and

39. A. No change
   B. Your period
   C. Your time
   D. Their time

40. Which of the following makes the most effective first sentence of a paragraph that might <u>follow</u>?
   A. PC sales in 1987 shot up over the previous year's in most parts of the country.
   B. No brand of computer, unfortunately, is immune to the resistance some people show.
   C. Familiarity with the keyboard has a great deal to do with how fast you learn a word processing program.
   D. Students are finding more classroom applications for PC's as more educational software becomes available.

Practice English Test 2

Directions: In each of the passages which follow, certain portions are underlined and numbered. Most of these underlined sections contain errors and inappropriate expressions. You are asked to compare each with the four alternatives in the answer column. If you consider the original version best, blacken the first choice. Otherwise, blacken the letter of the alternative you think best. If an item contains a question or statement to be completed, select the alternative which best answers the question or completes the statement.

PASSAGE ONE

When it was first released in 1962, *The Manchurian Candidate* did not do brisk business at the box office, neither was it universally

1
acclaimed by the critics. But soon events of history, as well as internal corporate intrigue, would consign this political thriller to a twenty-three-year limbo. One explanation for the film's withdrawal in 1965 involves Frank Sinatra, who starred in the film and owns part of the rights. As a friend of the Kennedy family, his

opinion was that, at the very

2
least, it was in poor taste for such a movie to be playing so soon after the assassination of the President. At worst, it could be very dangerous, suggesting

3
unsubstantiated parallels with real life and even feeding ideas

1A. No change
   B. office neither was it
   C. office, nor was it
   D. office, also, it was not
   E. office, also it was neither

2A. No change
   B. family, it was felt
   C. family he felt
   D. family his opinion was
   E. family, he felt

3A. No change
   B. dangerous, inferring
   C. dangerous showing
   D. dangerous, implicating
   E. dangerous in inferring

to would-be assassins. *The*

Manchurian Candidate, <u>nonetheless</u>,
                                    4
is about a conspiracy to kill a

U.S. president which results from

brainwashing during the Korean

War. During the time it was

shelved, the movie <u>was not</u>
                        5
<u>scarcely shown</u>, mostly at film
        5
festivals. <u>In case</u> its cautious
                6
re-release in 1988 (limited to a

handful of cities at first) had

more to do with economics or a

belief the social and political

mood of the nation was right, only

the film's owners and distributor

can tell. In any case, the film

is <u>so</u> engaging and memorable a
    7
political thriller now as it was

in the early sixties.

PASSAGE TWO

What do Tammy Faye Bakker and

a Colorado ski slope have in common?

At one time, televangelists

were no joking matter. They

sometimes <u>striked</u> fear and awe
            8
into many politicians and ordinary

4A. No change
  B. that is
  C. after all
  D. for instance
  E. as a reminder

5A. No change
  B. was shown only rarely
  C. was not shown except
     scarcely
  D. was not scarcely shown
  E. was not scarcely being
     shown

6A. No change
  B. In the event
  C. Provided
  D. Deciding
  E. Whether

7A. No change
  B. such as
  C. as
  D. still
  E. Omit underlined portion

8A. No change
  B. struck
  C. have striked
  D. had striked
  E. are struck by

citizens. But since the fall of

the PTL ministry <u>due to</u> sexual and
                        9
financial irregularities, Jimmy

Swaggart's public confession of

"sinning" with prostitutes, and

Pat Robertson's abortive

presidential candidacy,

televangelists do not enjoy the

prominence and clout <u>which formerly</u>
                                10
<u>in the past they did</u>. Even Jerry
        10
Falwell, outspoken founder of the

Moral Majority, has largely

withdrawn from the very visible

role he played in national

politics and policy-making in the

early 1980s. Many observers

<u>pointing</u> to a self-destruct
    11
mechanism in both the

organizations and individuals

identified with the born-again

fundamentalist movement. The

success of their bold fund-

raising, often to promote

"conservative" public policy

positions and support like-minded

politicians, <u>leads</u> to what the
            12
ancient Greeks called *hubris* and

emboldened them to extremes of

9A. No change
  B. which was owing to
  C. that was caused by
  D. which was attributable
     to
  E. that was brought on it
     by

10A. No change
   B. they did in former
      times
   C. they once did
   D. that they formally did
   E. they used to formerly

11A. No change
   B. will have pointed
   C. had pointed
   D. point
   E. having pointed

12A. No change
   B. led
   C. is leading
   D. lead
   E. have led

behavior their followers could not

tolerate. <u>Once they are being shown</u>
                    13
as hypocrites, frauds, or con men,

these paragons of morality lost

the source of all their power and

influence: the trust of their

supporters. <u>While</u> the
                  14
fundamentalist movement in general

and televangelism in particular

can ever regain the political

status they once enjoyed may

depend more on the mood of the

country than the charisma of any

individual trying to restore lost

luster. Whatever fate may be in

store for <u>them, their</u> influence on
                 15
American politics and attitudes

has been an historic, if short-

lived, reality.

PASSAGE THREE

    For most of the seasons since

the team's move to Atlanta, Braves

blue <u>had been</u> overshadowed by
         16
Braves blues. Season after season

a succession of owners, general

managers, field managers, coaches,

pitching rosters, starting

rotations, and defensive

13A. No change
  B. Once exposed
  C. All at once revealed
  D. Once divulged
  E. To be exposed

14A. No change
  B. Unless
  C. However,
  D. As long as
  E. Whether

15A. No change
  B. it, their
  C. it, its
  D. them, its
  E. them, it's

16A. No change
  B. has been
  C. will be
  D. is being
  E. is

124

assignments <u>has</u> done nothing to
17
change the over-all record and

reputation of Atlanta's National

League baseball team. To be sure,

the team <u>has had it's</u> moments of
18
glory: specifically, Hank Aaron's

715th homerun, breaking Babe

Ruth's record; the career of Phil

<u>Niekro, the Braves'</u> famous
19
knuckleballer, which culminated in

the dedication of a statue at the

Stadium in his honor; winning the

Western Division pennant in 1982;

and of course the dependable

presence of outfielder Dale

Murphy, <u>the loss of which</u> on the
20
team would be absolutely

unthinkable.

   In general, though, the

Braves' performance over the years

has won a hard-core following of

eternal optimists whose specialty

must be rooting for underdogs.

Ted Turner, who owns the team,

also sees that Braves games are

carried by his "Super <u>Station"</u>
21
<u>thus</u> creating a far-flung viewing
21

17A. No change
   B. has not
   C. hasn't
   D. have not
   E. haven't

18A. No change
   B. had had their
   C. has had their
   D. has had its
   E. have had its

19A. No change
   B. Niekro, the Braves
   C. Niekro; the Braves'
   D. Niekro, the Braves's
   E. Niekro, with the
      reputation of the Braves'

20A. No change
   B. whose being lost
   C. the loss of who
   D. who's loss
   E. whose loss

21A. No change
   B. Station." Thus,
   C. Station," thus,
   D. Station," thus
   E. Station;" thus

audience on cable TV. A winning

streak usually means high ratings

for the televised games.

Financial difficulties seldom
                22
daunt the flamboyant tycoon. [23]
                22

22A. No change
  B. Ted Turner is not known to give in to financial challenges.
  C. Money problems rarely disturb Ted Turner.
  D. The flamboyant tycoon is seldom daunted by financial difficulties.
  E. Omit underlined portion

23.   A logical main idea for a following paragraph would be
  A. Ted Turner's business background.
  B. Dale Murphy's hitting record with the Braves.
  C. the sports programming of the "Super Station".
  D. improving the morale of both the team and fans.
  E. None of the above

PASSAGE FOUR

To: Whomever it may concern

From: A. Taylor

Subject: Job Reference

Date: April 1, 1965

This letter is written with
                24
regret over our loss of Deputy B.
                24
Fife's employment. Deputy Fife
        24
performed all assignments in a
                              25
manner pleasing to all concerned.
        25
He brought to the job a level-

headedness rarely found in young

people. In particular, his
            26
attendance record and attitude

24A. No change
  B. We regret losing Deputy B. Fife as an employee.
  C. This letter is written regrettably due to our loss of Deputy B. Fife.
  D. This letter is written out of regret over our loss of Deputy B. Fife's employment.
  E. We write this letter with regret that Deputy B. Fife is not in our employ any longer.

25A. No change
  B. with remarkable satisfaction to us all
  C. satisfactorily
  D. exceedingly satisfactory
  E. in a manner satisfactory to all concerned

26A. No change
  B. Just the same
  C. Therefore
  D. Notwithstanding
  E. On the contrary

were outstanding. Deputy Fife
                          27
possesses a trait envied by many in
                                27
his ability to self-discipline. I
                  27
perfectly understand his decision

to seek employment better suited

to his talents, this is something
              28
you should consider. As a first-
      28
rate employee, I hope you view
                          29
Deputy Fife favorably for the
          29
position he is applying for.

Please feel free to contact

me either by mail or by phone if

you would like to discuss Deputy

Fife's qualifications further.
                          30

27A. No change
    B. With his trait of self-
       discipline, Deputy Fife is
       envied by many.
    C. Deputy Fife possesses an
       ability to discipline
       himself, which is enviable.
    D. Deputy Fife's self-
       discipline is enviable.
    E. Deputy Fife has self-
       discipline, which is a
       trait envied by many.

28A. No change
    B. talents. I hope you
       consider his desire to
       better himself.
    C. talents, you should
       consider this.
    D. talents; you should
       consider this.
    E. talents, which is a thing
       you should consider.

29A. No change
    B. Deputy Fife's qualities
       should be viewed as right
    C. it is our desire that you
       view Deputy Fife favorably
    D. I trust you will look at
       Deputy Fife favorably
    E. Deputy Fife is most
       qualified

30A. No change
    B. farther
    C. furthermore
    D. additionally
    E. to a greater extent

PASSAGE FIVE

Practically every high school

senior who graduates with the

intention of going to college

knows they have to think seriously
        31
about a lot of things. For
        32
example, the kind of college

31A. No change
    B. he had ought
    C. she has
    D. they ought
    E. they need

32A. No change
    B. lots of things
    C. a whole lot of subjects
    D. loads of things
    E. many matters

127

atmosphere <u>ranking</u> high on the list.
33
<u>Given a choice, it is clear most college-</u>
34
<u>bound students</u> would probably
34
choose a residential campus, prefer-

ably a fair distance from home, where

they can be independent of Mom and

Dad. <u>However,</u> the added expense
35
and sometimes mediocre grades in

high school <u>perhaps prevents</u> them
36
from leaving home to attend college.

In such cases, then, a local commuter

institution, even a two-year

community college, becomes much

more feasible and attractive. Reluc-

tantly, those students with wanderlust

or a yearning for freedom apply for

admission to a nearby <u>college they hope</u>
37
to transfer to a more distant college

as soon as their academic record or

finances <u>allows.</u> Some feel frustrated
38
and resentful <u>due to having to settle for</u>
39
a college they perceive as decidedly

second-rate. <u>But,</u> in reality, they are
40
simply letting their thwarted

personal plans bias them toward

what this local commuter college

may actually have to offer.

33A. No change
B. ranks
C. had ranked
D. could have ranked
E. being

34A. No change
B. Making a choice, it is clear most college-bound students
C. When given a choice, it is evident that most college-bound students
D. Given a choice, most college-bound students
E. Given a choice most college-bound students

35A. No change
B. Dad, however,
C. Dad, but,
D. Dad but,
E. Dad; however

36A. No change
B. might have prohibited
C. may prevent
D. possibly prevents
E. perhaps prohibits

37A. No change
B. college while they hope
C. college; hoping
D. college hoping
E. college, having hoped

38A. No change
B. allows it
C. makes it possible
D. permits
E. allow

39A. No change
B. with having to settle on
C. having to be accepting of
D. at having to settle for
E. of being made to settle for

40A. No change
B. Otherwise
C. Although
D. Whereas
E. To conclude

Practice English Test 3

Directions: In each of the passages which follow, certain portions are underlined and numbered. Most of these underlined sections contain errors and inappropriate expressions. You are asked to compare each with the three alternative passages in the answer column. If you consider the original version best, blacken the first choice. Otherwise, blacken the letter of the alternative you think best. If an item contains a question or statement to be completed, select the alternative which best answers the question or completes the statement.

PASSAGE ONE

In the decades immediately after World War II, modern architecture meant a structure resembling a large glass box, usually cubical or rectangular in shape. The overall appearance of a "modern" building was angular and clean, with practically no decoration. This look, that dominated the design of public buildings until the 1980s, became known as the "international style." Such buildings were as much at home in Singapore as well as Peoria, Illinois. Even design features that might distinguish one architect from another was often difficult to find. One of the best-known recent examples of the

1A. No change
 B. being rectangular in shape
 C. rectangular
 D. like a rectangle in shape

2A. No change
 B. without practically no decoration
 C. with hardly no decoration
 D. with practically no decorated aspects

3A. No change
 B. look, which was
 C. look, which
 D. look

4A. No change
 B. along with
 C. with
 D. as

5A. No change
 B. seeming
 C. were
 D. seems

129

international style is the

World Trade Center in New

York, in all its monolithic
                    6
sleekness.

As the 1970s came to a

close, however, the
        7
international style started to

wane in popularity, both among

architects and the public.

People perceived the glass-box

design as cold and uninviting.

Consequently, architects began

experimenting with

alternatives; often borrowing
              8
from traditional styles that

had once been disdained by the

proponents of the international

style. One of the most controversial

of the early "post-modern" buildings

was the ITT Building in New

York, designed by Philip

Johnson, whose career had

always been mixed with the
                9
international style. Now he

was being ridiculed for a

building that some said looked

like an old-fashioned

grandfather's clock.

6A. No change
  B. its monolithic,
  C. its' monolithic
  D. it's monolithic

7A. No change
  B. in addition
  C. as a result
  D. therefore

8A. No change
  B. alternatives, often
  C. alternatives often
  D. alternatives. Often

9A. No change
  B. integrated
  C. identified
  D. Omit underlined portion

As more and more architects have helped develop a variety of styles to replace the glass box, buildings that recall more ornamental and curvacious designs of the past have become commonplace. Atlanta's IBM Tower, <u>in addition</u>, could not have been
                    10
built fifteen years ago.

Architects, following the public, have sensed a missing element in the glass-box design: a capacity to evoke positive emotions in those who view and use buildings. <u>The continued appeal of post-modern buildings will be the test of whether architects have succeeded in moving beyond the glass box.</u>
                    11

PASSAGE TWO

Perhaps the most famous description of Irving Berlin is also the most apt. <u>In the immortal terms of Jerome Kern,</u>
                    12
"Irving Berlin has no place in

10A. No change
   B. nevertheless
   C. consequently
   D. for instance

11A. No change
   B. Philip Johnson's best buildings do just that.
   C. The federal government has commissioned a study to determine why people respond emotionally to buildings.
   D. Omit underlined portion

12A. No change
   B. Like Jerome Kern has said,
   C. According to Jerome Kern,
   D. In the immortal language of Jerome Kern,

American music; he *is* American music." [13]

It seems unbelievable that the life of Irving Berlin had reached more than a
14
century. At the same time, it seems appropriate, as if he were a natural part of the landscape of American culture.

— As a son whose parents
15
were Jewish-Russian immigrants,
15
Berlin began his career in music singing for spare change on street corners. Later, as a singing waiter in New York's Chinatown, he became interested in writing his own songs, the first of them was
16
published when he was nineteen. Four years later, in 1911, came "Alexander's Ragtime Band," his first hit
17
for which he is still remembered.

Berlin was never formally trained in music. He was a true "natural," dictating it
18
to others for transcription.

He could play his tunes only

13. Which of the following would be an effective <u>final sentence</u> in the <u>first</u> paragraph?
   A. Kern was a real expert at spotting talent in others.
   B. Kern was, of course, referring to Berlin figuratively.
   C. In view of Kern's admiration, one wonders why the two composers never collaborated.
   D. None of the above

14A. No change
   B. spanned
   C. occupied
   D. had spanned

15A. No change
   B. Berlin had parents who were Jewish-Russian immigrants.
   C. With Jewish-Russian parents who were immigrants,
   D. The son of Jewish-Russian immigrants,

16A. No change
   B. songs; the first of which
   C. songs the first which
   D. songs, the first of which

17A. No change
   B. initial achievement
   C. first song which made it
   D. first song which succeeded

18A. No change
   B. "natural" that had it dictated
   C. "natural," dictating his music
   D. "natural;" his music dictated

on the black keys of the piano
and eventually bought an
instrument equipped with a
<u>lever it enabled</u> him to
      19
transpose melodies from one
key to another.

    Besides Berlin, only Cole
Porter, of America's greatest
popular song writers, wrote
both music and lyrics. But no
one approaches Berlin's output
and success as a composer of
songs for the theater and
movies. Songs from the scores
for *Top Hat, Holiday Inn,*
Easter Parade, and *Annie Get*
Your Gun endure and show no
signs of fading in popularity, <u>either</u>
                             20
<u>among performers or the public</u>.
     20

19A. No change
   B. lever that enabled
   C. lever, it enabled
   D. lever, that enabled

20A. either among performers
      or among the public
   B. between performers
      or the public
   C. for performers or by
      the public
   D. either among performers
      or by the public

PASSAGE THREE

    I have read many fictional stories,
especially science fiction and action
serials. Most readers, <u>such as I,</u>
                    21
expect a story to develop the main
character, as well as the plot. <u>It will</u>
                       22
<u>show you</u> how the protagonist thinks
  22
and feels as well as what he does.

21A. No change
   B. that are like myself
   C. for example, me
   D. like me

22A. No change
   B. They will show
   C. It will show
   D. They will show the
      reader

Many stories I have read describe

characters who are larger than life

and who do great deeds. These

characters are called heroes. I have

noticed three kinds of <u>heroes</u>
                                    23
<u>so I find them</u> memorable for
        23
the different ways they

achieve their goals. Three

different types of heroes <u>are</u>
                                  24
the virtuous warrior, the super-

genius, and the everyday hero.

  The virtuous warrior is a

soldier. He is constantly at

war, <u>however,</u> he views his
          25
killing as something that has

to be done. He is always

feared and respected by his

enemies. The virtuous warrior

is usually physically powerful

and has a <u>real keen sharp</u>
                        26
mind. He can make split-

second decisions and act on

impulse. But the virtuous

warrior is not just a killing

machine. He would never

involve friends or innocents

in his bloody battles, <u>nor</u>
                              27
<u>would he</u> ignore a plea for
   27

23A. No change
  B. heroes, yet I find them
  C. heroes, so I find them
  D. heroes whom I find

24A. No change
  B. were
  C. are:
  D. being

25A. No change
  B. though,
  C. but,
  D. for

26A. No change
  B. very keen, sharp
  C. very sharp
  D. real keen and sharp

27A. No change
  B. neither does he
  C. nor would he not
  D. also would he not

help. Mack Bolan, the hero of Don Pendleton's action series, *The Executioner*, is an example of a virtuous warrior. He vows to wipe out the Mafia, not out of revenge, but owing to he feels it has to be [28] done. He is known by his [28] enemies as "the Executioner" or "that damned Bolan," but comrades-at-arms and friends know him as "Sergeant Mercy."

Another type of hero is [29] the super-genius. A super- [29] genius is a far-seeing [29] individual who sets long-range goals and makes intricate plans to achieve these goals. Nothing ever surprises a far-seeing genius because every contingency is covered in his plans, which are made years in advance. [30] [31]

PASSAGE FOUR

Electronics technology has grown very rapidly over the last decade or so. It is growing due to the develop- [32]

28A. No change
  B. out of necessity
  C. because of it needing to be done
  D. on account of his feeling it has to be done

29A. No change
  B. Geeks will sure like the super-genius. He
  C. Who knows what a super-genius is? He
  D. Another type of hero, the super-genius,

30. Which of the following sentences could logically come next in the third paragraph?
  A. For example, Donal Graeme, the hero of Gordon Dickson's *Dorsai*, was bred to have a superior, agile intellect.
  B. In real life you don't have to be continuously at war.
  C. An example of how he manipulates people can be found in Gordon Dickson's *Dorsai*.
  D. In contrast, the everyday hero is a normal person thrown into a dangerous situation.

31. The next paragraph in the passage should logically be about
  A. the everyday hero.
  B. the author's preference for one type of hero.
  C. both the virtuous warrior and the super-genius, in summary.
  D. illustrations of these types of heroes from real life.

32A. No change
  B. It has grown due to
  C. This growth is largely due to
  D. This is largely due to

135

ment of integrated circuits.
33
Integrated circuits are large
33
complex circuits that are

reduced to microscopic size

and placed inside small

devices commonly referred to

as "chips." Chips can be

divided into two different

groups, analog chips, and
34
digital chips. There's
35
several main differences
35
between these groups.

One of these differences

is in internal structure and
36
design. Analog chips contain

discrete transistor networks,

along with other components

fabricated on them. These
37
components must be designed so

that they work within an

"operating region," since there may

be a wide range of duties for each

one. Therefore, these networks

must be dealt with very carefully,
38
on the other hand, digital
38
chips contain only basic

transistor networks that must

be designed to work in an "on"

33A. No change
B. circuits, integrated circuits are
C. circuits, or
D. circuits, being

34A. No change
B. groups: analog and
C. groups; analog and
D. groups, analog, and

35A. No change
B. There is several
C. There are a lot of
D. There are several

36A. No change
B. are
C. are a difference
D. differs

37A. No change
B. on itself
C. on themselves
D. on the chips

38A. No change
B. carefully. On the other hand,
C. carefully, on the other hand;
D. carefully, furthermore,

or "off" position. <u>Opposing</u>
                      39
<u>the analog chips</u>, they may be
            39
dealt with more loosely and

produced with more components

on one chip. There may be

hundreds or thousands of

components on a single digital

chip. [40]

39A. No change
   B. Opposite to the analog
      chips
   C. Unlike the analog chips
   D. Opposing the other type

40. Which of the following
    sentences would logically
    belong in a <u>concluding</u>
    paragraph for the
    passage?
   A. Digital chips are easier
      and cheaper to work
      with, although analog
      chips are probably more
      important to industry.
   B. Electronics has advanced
      rapidly since the
      development of
      integrated circuits and
      is expected to continue
      growing in the future.
   C. Although analog and
      digital chips are
      identical to the eye,
      they are much different
      in their internal
      structures and
      practical applications.
   D. All the above

Practice English Test 4

Directions: In each of the passages which follow, certain portions are underlined and numbered. Most of these underlined sections contain errors and inappropriate expressions. You are asked to compare each with the four alternative passages in the answer column. If you consider the original version best, blacken the first choice. Otherwise, blacken the letter of the alternative you think best. If an item contains a question or statement to be completed, select the alternative which best answers the question or completes the statement.

PASSAGE ONE

Dear Ms. Pratto:

I am writing to <u>put in an</u>
<u>1</u>
<u>application for</u> the entry-level
<u>1</u>
position advertised in the

Atlanta *Journal-Constitution*.

My work <u>experience, I know</u>
<u>2</u>
will convince <u>you of me being</u>
<u>3</u>
the best person for the job.

For the past two years, I <u>had</u>
<u>4</u>
<u>been working</u> as a grill cook and
<u>4</u>
counterman at the Waffle House

restaurant. <u>This</u> has provided
<u>5</u>
me with expertise in getting

along with all kinds of <u>people.</u>
<u>6</u>
<u>Including</u> co-workers and the
<u>6</u>
public. I fully expect this

1A. No change
  B. have my application considered for
  C. apply to
  D. make application to
  E. apply for

2A. No change
  B. details, I know,
  C. experience, I know,
  D. experience I know
  E. specifics, I know,

3A. No change
  B. you I am
  C. you of my being
  D. you, of my being
  E. you, I am

4A. No change
  B. work
  C. am working
  D. have been working
  E. will be working

5A. No change
  B. That
  C. This job
  D. It
  E. This working

6A. No change
  B. personalities. Including
  C. people including
  D. people; including
  E. people, including

position to be <u>rewarding but</u>
                       7
<u>challenging</u>.
        7
My academic credentials are

also impressive. In two months

I will <u>have bestowed</u> a B.S. degree
        8
in hotel-restaurant management

from Seersucker College in Sappe

City, South Dakota, <u>which</u>
                              9
<u>pleases my parents above all</u>.
        9
My grade-point average is about

2.9, a very <u>respectable</u> one.
                    10
More than my course content,

<u>just the same</u>, my college years
        11
in general have taught me how to

<u>think, planning</u> my time, and
        12
learn new skills and information.

As someone who changed majors four

times, <u>adjustment to new learning</u>
                          13
<u>situations comes easily</u>.   [14]
        13

7A. No change
  B. a reward but challenging
  C. a reward, but challenging
  D. rewarding, but a challenge
  E. rewarding but a challenge

8A. No change
  B. be endowed with
  C. receive
  D. acquire
  E. possess

9A. No change
  B. which especially delights my
      parents
  C. which satisfies my parents
      in particular
  D. which my parents are very
      happy about
  E. Omit underlined portion

10A. No change
  B. respectful
  C. respective
  D. reputable
  E. respected

11A. No change
  B. nonetheless
  C. therefore
  D. however
  E. nevertheless

12A. No change
  B. think, plan
  C. think; plan
  D. think, make plans for
  E. think, making plans for

13A. No change
  B. adjusting to new learning
      situations comes easy for me
  C. I can adjust to new
      learning situations easily
  D. adjustment to new learning
      situations come easily
  E. adjustment to new learning
      situations is easy for me

14. A paragraph which comes
      next in the passage could
      logically begin with the follow-
      ing sentence:

PASSAGE TWO

<u>Students that were</u> born
15
since 1960 or so probably have

little or no idea of the "counter-

culture" movement of the late 1960s

and early <u>seventies, it was</u> an era
16
of profound political, social, and

moral change in this country,

but people now in their twenties

generally take for granted most

of the changes that movement

made <u>possible. As if</u> open
17
premarital sex had always been

routine in American life.

One of the most telling, if

not always polished and

literate, sources of information

on the upheaval of the period

<u>was</u> a now-defunct publication
18
known as the *Great Speckled*

Bird. Between 1968 and 1974, it

documented the radical views of

a generation and <u>was proud of it</u>
19
<u>offering</u> an alternative to the
19
"establishment" press in the

Southeast. Much of the *Bird*'s

perspective, first grounded in

A. I will be glad to supply
   you with more detailed information about my work experience and academic background.
B. Before working at the
   Waffle House, I was an ap-
   prentice front-end manager at
   Big Star market.
C. Seersucker College attracts
   a great many non-traditional
   students like me.
D. My career goal during the
   first ten years of my life was
   to become a master chef.
E. Customer surveys at every
   restaurant I ever worked in
   usually rated me high.

15A. No change
  B. Students, who were
  C. Students, being
  D. Students,
  E. Students

16A. No change
  B. seventies. It was
  C. seventies, and it was
  D. seventies and it was
  E. seventies; thus, it was

17A. No change
  B. possible, provided that
  C. possible. The assumption
     that
  D. possible, as if
  E. possible. As though

18A. No change
  B. has been
  C. had been
  D. were
  E. used to be

19A. No change
  B. was proud of it's offering
  C. prided itself on offering
  D. prided itself to offer
  E. prided itself with offering

the Civil Rights <u>movement,</u>
            20
<u>eventually it</u> included a strong
     20
anti-Vietnam War position, as

well as a belief in personal

liberation <u>through</u> drugs and sex.
        21
    As the paper took stands on

more issues, controversy increas-

ingly racked the editorial staff itself.

One internal debate, <u>that is</u>, had to
            22
do with whether the *Bird* should

take a more extreme Marxist-

Leninist stance. Another grew

out of some staffers' growing

interest in feminism and

determination to fight sexism on

the paper's staff. <u>The claims</u>
              23
<u>of some are that</u> these often
     23
bitter arguments contributed to

the *Bird*'s demise. Part of the

education of every young adult

should include an understanding

of this important time in recent

American history. To a twenty-

year-old, 1968 may just as well

be 1768. [24} But <u>they're reading</u>
             25
old issues of the *Great Speckled*

Bird and other such "underground"

publications may be one of the best

20A. No change
    B. movement. Eventually it
    C. movement; eventually it
    D. movement; eventually
    E. movement, eventually

21A. No change
    B. by way of
    C. by the use of
    D. by utilizing
    E. in utilizing

22A. No change
    B. furthermore
    C. in any event
    D. for instance
    E. in point of fact

23A. No change
    B. Claims are sometimes made
    C. Some claim
    D. Frequently it is insisted
    E. It is many times argued

24. A new paragraph should start
    with the sentence in the
    passage which begins:
    A. One internal debate . . .
    B. Another grew out of . . .
    C. The claims of some are
       that . . .
    D. Part of the education . . .
    E. To a twenty-year-old . . .

25A. No change
    B. reading
    C. by reading
    D. in reading
    E. them reading

ways of bringing the period to life

again, _provided_ another
     26

generation may see its

shortcomings and appreciate the

ways it helped shape their own

values and behavior.

26A. No change
 B. thus,
 C. therefore,
 D. thereby
 E. so

PASSAGE THREE

In 1957 the Soviet launch

of _Sputnik_ startled and shocked

many Americans. The USSR <u>looked</u>
          27

<u>like it was</u> leading in a race
  27

with the US, not only in space,

but <u>in science and technology</u> in
       28

general. Immediately, American

leaders clamored for greater

support of the sciences, both

moral and financial. Without it

the Soviet Union would surely

outstrip America's ability to be

competitive in exploring and

using outer space for military

and other technical purposes.

A commitment to catch up to

the Soviet Union and even

surpass it culminated in

America's landing the first

27A. No change
 B. appeared like it was
 C. made you think it was
 D. appeared to be
 E. Omit underlined portion

28A. No change
 B. as a power in science and technology
 C. with science and technology
 D. promoting science and technology
 E. scientifically and technologically

human being on the moon in <u>1969</u>
                        29

<u>a goal set publicly by John Kennedy</u>
                 29

during his presidency. In recent

years, however, America's

commitment to science and tech-

nology seems to be in <u>an awful</u>
                       30

<u>nosedive</u>. One of the most
  30

disturbing facts <u>have been</u> that
              31

fewer young people are planning

careers in science and technology.

As a result, the nation's schools —

from elementary school through

graduate school — <u>is already</u>
                   32

experiencing a serious shortage

of mathematics and science

teachers. Those holding

advanced degrees, in particular,

are <u>scarce as hens' teeth</u>.
          33

<u>Because</u> industry is able to pay
  34

such highly trained professionals

better salaries than school systems

and universities. Their short

supply in the market makes major

companies willing to pay <u>well</u>
                   35

for their expertise. But if

trends continue, even well-off

companies like IBM and Kodak

<u>competing</u> more intensely for the
  36

29A. No change
   B. 1969. John Kennedy set it
     publicly as a goal
   C. 1969 which was set as a
     goal publicly by John Kennedy
   D. 1969, a goal set publicly
     by John Kennedy
   E. 1969; a goal set publicly
     by John Kennedy

30A. No change
   B. a downward direction
   C. a slide
   D. decline
   E. a state of decline

31A. No change
   B. are
   C. is
   D. seem to be
   E. will have been

32A. No change
   B. is sooner than expected
   C. is all ready
   D. are all ready
   E. are already

33A. No change
   B. scarce
   C. scarcer than hens' teeth
   D. more scarce than hens'
     teeth
   E. real scarce

34A. No change
   B. One reason is that
   C. This is caused by the fact
   D. One reason being that
   E. Owing to the fact

35A. No change
   B. good
   C. out-of-sight money
   D. great money
   E. a lot

36A. No change
   B. are competing
   C. compete
   D. will be competing
   E. have been competing

relatively small pool of

available engineers, physicists,

chemists, and technologists.

An obvious and short-term

solution to the problem is to

encourage young peoples interest
                     37

in math and science. Teachers

beside parents need to think of
 38

more ways to make these

demanding, often difficult,

disciplines appealing to children.

Solving math problems and perform-

ing experiments in a lab has to
                  39

attract young people because they

are as much fun as they are a way

of learning. [40]

37A. No change
  B. young peoples' interest
  C. young people's interest
  D. young people being interested
  E. young people having an interest

38A. No change
  B. and
  C. besides
  D. including
  E. plus

39A. No change
  B. must be
  C. have
  D. are necessarily
  E. is required

40. The next paragraph in the passage could logically be about
  A. a long-term solution to the problem.
  B. the short attention span of young children.
  C. Kodak's recruitment in colleges and universities.
  D. the abundance of scientists in the Soviet Union.
  E. young people's commitment to science after President Kennedy's speech about reaching the moon.

144

Practice English Test 5

Directions: In each of the pasages which follow, certain portions are underlined and numbered. Most of these underlined sections contain errors and inappropriate expressions. You are asked to compare each with the three alternatives in the answer column. If you consider the original version best, blacken the first choice. Otherwise, blacken the letter of the alternative you think best. If an item contains a question or statement to be completed, select the alternative which best answers the question or completes the statement.

PASSAGE ONE

I dreaded taking the class.

I had registered for Geography

110 because it was the only

course open at a convenient

time. Registering late

definitely has its drawbacks, I

kept repeating to <u>myself over</u>
                 1
<u>and over;</u> as I trudged from the
   1
parking lot to the first class.

Before <u>long; moreover,</u> I
         2
realized that this much-maligned

and misunderstood course would

benefit me in <u>lots of</u> ways. On
            3
the first day, the professor

gave a short test to get a sense

of what <u>us students</u> already knew
        4
about global geography. My test

results confirmed what I had

<u>suspected:</u> Kenya and Kalamazoo
   5
<u>might just as well had been</u> a
        6
few miles as a few thousand

1A. No change
  B. myself,
  C. me
  D. myself over and over

2A. No change
  B. long; though
  C. long, though,
  D. long moreover

3A. No change
  B. many
  C. loads of
  D. a lot of

4A. No change
  B. we, students,
  C. us, students,
  D. we students

5A. No change
  B. figured
  C. a hunch about
  D. thought on

6A. No change
  B. might not be
  C. might just as well have been
  D. might be

miles apart. My poor showing on

the test was comparable to <u>those</u>
                                    7
<u>of</u> everyone else in the class. A
 7
few students were not even able

to locate Africa on an unmarked

<u>map. But,</u> it was comforting to
         8
know that virtually the whole

class were <u>in the same boat</u>
                            9
<u>together</u>.
         9
 By the second week, we

discovered that the course

includes much more than place

recognition on a map. Geography

covers the study of population

make-up and the effects of

location, topography, and

climate on economics, social

customs, and culture in general.

For me and, I am sure, the

others as well, the course <u>was</u>
                                 10
an initiation into a new world,

actually the very world we all

inhabit, but do not really know. [11]

7A. No change
 B. that of
 C. tests by
 D. Omit underlined portion

8A. No change
 B. map. Yet
 C. map, yet,
 D. map, but,

9A. No change
 B. in a shared boat
 C. together in one boat
 D. in the same situation

10A. No change
  B. were
  C. have been
  D. are

11. Logically, the last
     paragraph in the passage
     could continue by
     discussing
  A. the resentment some
      students felt toward the
      professor.
  B. the uselessness of the
      course.
  C. the changed perspective of
      the students.
  D. none of the above.

PASSAGE TWO

From the public's point of

view, digital laser technology

in making recordings <u>seem</u> a

$\qquad$ 12

quantum leap beyond analog

methods. The first advantage a

listener discovers is <u>compactness;</u>

$\qquad$ 13

<u>which</u> explains why

13

the 5 1/4-inch plastic discs on

which the sound information is

stored are called compact discs,

or CD's. Currently, engineers

<u>are sharp enough to</u> record up

$\qquad$ 14

to seventy-five minutes of sound

on a disc. Another advantage is

durability. <u>You have to</u> inflict

$\qquad$ 15

a great deal of punishment on

one to make it unplayable.

But, of course, it is the

quality of the recordings <u>which</u>

$\qquad$ 16

<u>accounts</u> for the dramatic growth

16

of CD sales since they first

came on the market in the early

1980s. <u>Telarc, a company based</u>

$\qquad$ 17

<u>in Cleveland, was one of the</u>

$\qquad$ 17

<u>early leaders in marketing CD's.</u>

$\qquad$ 17

Although some of the early

digital recordings greatly

12A. No change
B. appear to be
C. look like
D. seems

13A. No change
B. compactness, which
C. compactness which
D. compactness, but it

14A. No change
B. have the ability to
C. can
D. have the knowledge to

15A. No change
B. You must
C. A user has to
D. You need to

16A. No change
B. which account
C. which make up
D. that account

17A. No change
B. Telarc, a company which is based in Cleveland, was one of the early leaders in marketing CD's.
C. One of the early leaders in marketing CD's was Telarc, located in Cleveland.
D. Omit underlined portion

exaggerated certain features,

those being high- and low-end
    18
percussion effects, recording

engineers have since refined

their techniques to create much

more natural and realistic

reproduction. Comparing an LP

analog recording of a Mozart

symphony with a digital

recording on CD, it is hard for
                          19
most people to return to
    19
listening to LP's on a routine

basis. The clean sound of

compact discs make the surface
                 20
pops and clicks on the typical

LP all the more noticeable.

Listeners, in a sense, become so
                              21
spoiled; they are unable (or
    21
unwilling) to tolerate the noise of a

stylus in contact with the vinyl LP.

Instead, they enjoy the pure,
    22
undistorted sound made when the

laser beam in the CD player reads

the musical data imprinted on the

disc. [23]

18A. No change
  B. like
  C. such as,
  D. like:

19A. No change
  B. it is difficult for most
      individuals
  C. it is difficult for most
      people
  D. most people find it hard

20A. No change
  B. brings out
  C. makes
  D. bring out

21A. No change
  B. so spoiled, that they are
  C. so spoiled, so they are
  D. so spoiled they are

22A. No change
  B. Besides
  C. Nevertheless
  D. Owing to this

23. A most effective and logical
     introductory paragraph for
     the passage could
  A. explain the evolution of
      laser technology in Japan.
  B. detail the early opinions
      of experts on CD sound
      quality.
  C. provide an overview of the
      dominance of analog
      recording through the
      1970s.
  D. None of the above

PASSAGE THREE

Isolation from the rest of the world was a long-standing American tradition. Until, that is, Japan's bombing of Pearl Harbor in 1941.

In the late 1930s, when pressures for the U.S. to aid Britain against Germany was intense, an organization known as America First actively opposed it. It was remembered what President Washington had said to the nation about avoiding "entangling alliances." Aviator and hero Charles Lindbergh was probably the best-known isolationist. He spoke forcefully in public about the dangers of fighting other nations' wars. The American public, by and large, agreed with the views of America First.

Those, who warned against the Nazi threat in Europe and the danger of not helping Britain were reviled as reckless interventionists. For example,

24A. No change
  B. tradition until, that is,
  C. tradition until, that is
  D. tradition; until that is

25A. No change
  B. had been
  C. has been
  D. were

26A. No change
  B. them
  C. such support
  D. this

27A. No change
  B. It was remembered that
  C. It was being remembered what
  D. Americans remembered what

28A. No change
  B. other nation's wars
  C. the wars of others'
  D. other nation's disputes

29A. No change
  B. Those who
  C. The individuals, who
  D. All, who

Claude Pepper, then a senator

from Florida, <u>was hung</u> in effigy
                    30
outside the Capitol after urging

more support for beleaguered

Britain.

    All this time, however, the

Roosevelt administration was

finding ways to bypass the

Neutrality Act passed by

Congress and assist the British

war effort. Few of them were

well publicized, but the

President himself, through his

public statements and his warm

relations with King George and

Prime Minister Churchill, <u>made</u>
                                31
<u>barely no</u> secret of where his
    31
and American sympathies <u>lay</u>. [33]
                          32

PASSAGE FOUR

To: All Department Personnel

From: J. Pierpont Bilodeau
          Department Manager

    <u>This memo will be short.</u>
             34
    <u>It looks like it is incumbent</u>
             35
<u>upon me to</u> remind you
    35
of two <u>real important things:</u>
         36
(1) All telephones and computer

terminals are to be secured at 5

30A. No change
   B. had been hung
   C. was hanged
   D. has been hung

31A. No change
   B. did not make no
   C. scarcely made no
   D. made no

32A. No change
   B. laid
   C. were laying
   D. lie

33.   The word *however* near the
      beginning of the last
      paragraph in the passage
      is appropriate because
   A. the paragraph continues the
      line of discussion begun in
      the preceding paragraph.
   B. the paragraph underscores
      the points made in the
      preceding paragraph.
   C. the paragraph echoes what
      was brought out in the
      first paragraph.
   D. the paragraph makes points
      that undercut the focus of
      the preceding paragraph.

34A. No change
   B. This memo will be brief.
   C. This memo will not be long.
   D. Omit underlined portion

35A. No change
   B. It looks like I need to
   C. It looks as if I have to
   D. I must

36A. No change
   B. very important matters:
   C. real important things;
   D. real critical things.

PM every day. (2) Official

business is not to be discussed

outside the department. Even

within the department, stuff

that is known to be confidential

is not to be <u>tossed about like</u>
                        37
<u>loose salad</u>.
     37
     The company, as well as

individual employees, is subject to

litigation if they <u>do it</u>.
                        38
     To top things off, persons

have been making unauthorized

calls on department phones after

hours. The monthly bills have

<u>become intolerant</u>. Guilty
          39
parties will be responsible for

all toll charges. [40]

37A. No change
  B. tossed about
  C. discussed loosely
  D. subject to be discussed

38A. No change
  B. keep at it
  C. do so
  D. keep it up

39A. No change
  B. gotten intolerant
  C. gotten beyond tolerance
  D. become intolerable

40. In which area(s) are the
     major weaknesses of
     the passage?
  A. Organization
  B. Diction
  C. Wordiness
  D. All the above

Practice English Test 6

Directions: In each of the pasages which follow, certain portions are underlined and numbered. Most of these underlined sections contain errors and inappropriate expressions. You are asked to compare each with the four alternatives in the answer column. If you consider the original version best, blacken the first choice. Otherwise, blacken the letter of the alternative you think best. If an item contains a question or statement to be completed, select the alternative which best answers the question or completes the statement.

PASSAGE ONE

A recent survey of physicians in thirteen Southern states <u>indicate that</u> stings by fire ants may be a growing problem. A large percentage of the victims are children. A small handful of individuals may even <u>experience dying,</u> mostly because they suffer several stings or <u>are</u> hypersensitive to the toxin. Typically, in such cases, the body experiences respiratory failure. Such allergic reaction to fire ant stings, allergists warn, <u>being</u> taken seriously by both victims and doctors. [5]

Fire ants apparently entered the southeastern U.S. early in this century from South <u>America, since</u> the 1940s they have migrated

1A. No change
   B. indicates,
   C. indicate,
   D. indicates that
   E. do indicate

2A. No change
   B. quit living
   C. die
   D. pass away
   E. give up the spirit

3A. No change
   B. are proving
   C. were
   D. will be
   E. will have been

4A. No change
   B. might could be
   C. has been
   D. should be
   E. ought be

5. Which of the following expressions would fit logically at the beginning of the second paragraph?
   A. Therefore,
   B. As a result,
   C. Nevertheless,
   D. On the other hand,
   E. None of the above

6A. No change
   B. America until
   C. America, until
   D. America since
   E. America. Since

152

steadily <u>northward; so that</u>

              7

their territory now includes

Tennessee and North Carolina. The

insects <u>seem unable</u> to tolerate

             8

winter temperatures much below

freezing.

    Doctors <u>needless to say,</u> usually

                9

recognize fire ant stings by a burning

sensation at first, followed by the

formation of pus at the site of the

sting in a day or <u>so. Fortunately,</u>

                    10

<u>however,</u> over-the counter

  10

antihistamines are effective

in treating most stings.

PASSAGE TWO

    As a language that has not been

routinely spoken for centuries, <u>it</u>

<u>is easy to refer to Latin as a "dead"</u>

              11

<u>language.</u> For years it has been

  11

studied primarily as a means to an end,

a <u>tool, for example,</u> law, medical, and

         12

pharmacy students learn at least some

Latin because so much of the jargon of

their professions <u>require</u> an

            13

understanding of Latin roots, prefixes,

and suffixes.

7A. No change

  B. northward so that

  C. in a northern direction

      so that

  D. northerly, provided

  E. northward. So that

8A. No change

  B. seem to not possess the ability

  C. appear incapable

  D. seem to lack the capability

  E. do not hardly seem able

9A. No change

  B. for example

  C. consequently

  D. therefore

  E. Omit underlined portion

10A. No change

  B. so. Fortunately moreover

  C. so. Fortunately, however

  D. so; fortunately, moreover

  E. so, fortunately, however

11A. No change

  B. people often refer to Latin as

      a "dead" language

  C. it is common for Latin to be

      called "dead"

  D. Latin, which is commonly

      referred to as "dead"

  E. Latin is often thought of as

      "dead"

12A. No change

  B. tool, for example;

  C. tool; for example,

  D. tool, especially

  E. tool, in particular,

13A. No change

  B. demand

  C. expects

  D. call for

  E. requires

In the last few years; however,
14
largely as a part of a national trend

toward reforming and improving

American education, foreign language

study, including Latin, is regaining

ground in the curriculum they had lost
15
over the past twenty years. One pro-

gram in Beloit, Wisconsin, illustrates
16
this. Starting in the fourth grade,
16
students are introduced to a Latin-

based curriculum in which Latin is

used not only as a subject of study

in itself but as a means of under-
17
standing other disciplines. Supporters
17
of the program, called Help Yourself,

claims it helps students develop into
18
independent analytical thinkers. An-

other unusual feature of Help Yourself
19
with it's insistence on the direct
19
involvement of parents and the

students themselves who serve as

mentors to those who follow them in

the program. If such programs succeed
20
and eventually proliferate across the

country, Latin's days as a "dead"

language may be numbered.

14A. No change
  B. years, however,
  C. years, however;
  D. years, but
  E. years but,

15A. No change
  B. they have lost
  C. they had been losing
  D. it had lost
  E. it will have lost

16A. No change
  B. gives an example of this trend
  C. illustrates this trend
  D. is an example of this
  E. is an illustration of this

17A. No change
  B. to help students understand
  C. it helps students understand
  D. as a means of getting into
  E. to get into

18A. No change
  B. claim
  C. argues
  D. maintains
  E. insists

19A. No change
  B. Yourself, is its
  C. Yourself, with its
  D. Yourself is it's
  E. Yourself is its

20A. No change
  B. Unless
  C. Until
  D. Before
  E. Since

154

PASSAGE THREE

"Desecration" of the American flag

has, from time to time, <u>arose</u> as an issue
                              21

in the nation's recent past. In particular,

during the Vietnam War, protesters

against U.S. policy burned the flag

publicly, displayed their own cynical

redesigns, or <u>weared</u> it on the seats of
                 22

their pants. [23]

Not until the summer of <u>1989, though,</u>
                          24

did the Supreme Court, in a 5-4 ruling,

declare that flag burning was protected as

free speech under the First Amendment

to the Constitution. To the surprise of

many, two justices in the majority had

been appointed by President <u>Reagan;</u>
                             25

<u>hardly</u> the first time a president was
 25

probably disappointed in an appointee to

the Court. <u>President Eisenhower once</u>
                  26

<u>admitted that nominating Earl Warren as</u>
                  26

<u>Chief Justice was one of the worst</u>
               26

<u>mistakes of his presidency.</u> Many Court
          26

observers explain the stands taken by

21A. No change
  B. rose
  C. put itself forward
  D. made appearances
  E. arisen

22A. No change
  B. wore
  C. had worn
  D. had wore
  E. have wore

23. Which of the following sentences would effectively conclude the first paragraph?
  A. For a time it was "cool" to do so.
  B. Vietnam veterans today get angry at the thought of it.
  C. Why shouldn't the police have arrested such people?
  D. Others wore stick-on flowers as peace symbols.
  E. None of the above

24A. No change
  B. 1989, moreover,
  C. 1989 moreover,
  D. 1989; however
  E. 1989; though

25A. No change
  B. Reagan, hardly not
  C. Reagan, hardly
  D. Reagan; it was not hardly
  E. Reagan. It was not hardly

26A. No change
  B. President Eisenhower once said nominating Earl Warren as Chief Justice was a great error.
  C. Naming Earl Warren as Chief Justice, President Eisenhower conceded, was one of his greatest mistakes.
  D. One of President Eisenhower's most serious blunders, he admitted, was appointing Earl Warren Chief Justice.
  E. Omit underlined portion

Justices Scalia and Kennedy as that of
                                27
conservative libertarians. As a result,

those that were outraged by the Court's
          28
decision feared the same two Reagan
         29
appointees would show a similar

libertarian bent when the Court

considered overturning the extremely

controversial Roe v. Wade decision

of 1973, legalizing abortion. [30]

PASSAGE FOUR

When many people think of

America's westward expansion, they

may envision a circle of covered

wagons; surrounded by screaming
         31
bands of blood-thirsty Indian

warriors. Actually, this Hollywood

version of America's development does

not square much with the reality, which

is dramatic in its own, perhaps
               32
understated, way.

The role of the mule, for example.
               33
Arguably, without it the U.S. might
                                34

27A. No change
   B. as being that of
   C. as being
   D. as those of
   E. as

28A. No change
   B. those, who were
   C. those being
   D. the ones who were
   E. those

29A. No change
   B. fearing
   C. being fearful
   D. was petrified
   E. were scared to death

30. A logical main idea for a
     following paragraph would be
   A. how Reagan Court appointees
       have taken libertarian posi-
       tions before.
   B. the legal background of the
       Roe v. Wade decision.
   C. illegal actions taken by oppo-
       nents of Roe v. Wade.
   D. the Senate's quick confirma-
       tion of Justices Scalia and
       Kennedy.
   E. public opinion of flag burning
       during the Vietnam War.

31A. No change
   B. wagons, that have been sur-
       rounded
   C. wagons surrounded
   D. wagons. Surrounded
   E. wagons, that are being sur-
       rounded

32A. No change
   B. its own,
   C. it's own
   D. its' own
   E. it's own,

33A. No change
   B. There is the role of the mule,
       for example.
   C. There's the role of mules, for
       instance.
   D. The mule's role, for example:
   E. The role of the mule, for
       example, was critical.

have been relegated to permanent
34
third-world status. However, mules,
35
of course, were indispensable to
35
transporting goods and

travelers on early canals in the

eastern third of the young nation.

Canals and other inland waterways

helped the economically struggling

nation beat out formidable natural
36
barriers like the Appalachian

mountain chain. Pilots on the Erie

Canal in New York State — or "Mr.

Clinton's Ditch" — knew how good
37
mules did in hauling boats alongside

their towpaths. Contrary to popular

views, the animals were valued for

their sure-footedness, intelligence,

and ability to recover from a hard
38
day's hauling. Treated almost like a

member of the family, owners often
39
assigned the job of caring for the mule
39
to the oldest son. [40]
39

34A. No change
B. will be
C. will have been
D. might could be
E. had been

35A. No change
B. Therefore mules of course
C. Therefore mules, of course
D. Mules of course
E. Mules, of course

36A. No change
B. whip
C. do in
D. overcome
E. beat

37A. No change
B. well
C. nice
D. spectacular
E. great

38A. No change
B. and were able to
C. and could
D. plus being able to
E. and they could

39A. No change
B. it was often the oldest son
who cared for the mule.
C. the mule was often cared for
by the owner's oldest son.
D. the job of caring for the mule
was often given to the oldest
son.
E. the care of the mule often
went to the owner's oldest son.

40. Which of the following details
could be logically included in
the first paragraph?
A. Typically, movie studios hired
whites to play American
Indians.
B. Indian attacks on white sett-
lers were usually filmed on
Hollywood back lots.
C. Six massacres of white sett-
lers inside circled wagons are
documented in contemporary
diaries.
D. All the above
E. None of the above

Practice English Test 7

Directions: In each of the pasages which follow, certain portions are underlined and numbered. Most of these underlined sections contain errors and inappropriate expressions. You are asked to compare each with the three alternatives in the answer column. If you consider the original version best, blacken the first choice. Otherwise, blacken the letter of the alternative you think best. If an item contains a question or statement to be completed, select the alternative which best answers the question or completes the statement.

PASSAGE ONE

One of the prospects facing college students about to graduate is attending graduate <u>school. Even</u> at
1
a time when so many students major in business and apparently want to start making handsome salaries as soon as possible.

To be sure, most universities have had to scale down their graduate programs (except those offering MBA's) since the mid-<u>1970s and</u>
2
the professional job market became glutted with graduates holding master's and doctoral degrees. Fields in the humanities and social <u>sciences, such as</u> English,
3
history, and sociology, were most severely affected. In the last few years, however, the demand for

1A. No change
 B. school. For
 C. school, for
 D. school, even

2A. No change
 B. 1970s whereas
 C. 1970s, when
 D. 1970s, whereas

3A. No change
 B. sciences such as
 C. sciences: such as
 D. sciences, such as,

such degree-holders had grown. No
          4   5
longer are men and women with
5
PhD's in Victorian literature being

forced to wait on tables or take

jobs in department stores,
                        6
consequently, more undergraduates
6
are seriously considering graduate

studies as an economically viable if
                                  7
not lucrative, option.

When a student does decide to

explore the possibilities of graduate

study, they may often begin by
8
browsing through catalogues and

perhaps writing to a few graduate

schools. Inquiring about the

likelihood of receiving some form of

financial aid is understandably one

of the student's top priorities. If a
        9
student is even remotely interested

in the possibility of a college teaching

career he or she will pay particular
10
attention to those universities that

offer stipends and tuition waivers for

taking on part-time teaching duties.

PASSAGE TWO

Our new lab facilities are well

equipped to a point, yet there is no

training in the proper use and care of

4A. No change
  B. has grown
  C. have swelled
  D. is multiplying

5A. No change
  B. Not any more are there
  C. No more is there
  D. No longer is there

6A. No change
  B. stores, as a result,
  C. stores. Consequently,
  D. stores, consequently;

7A. No change
  B. viable and
  C. viable though
  D. viable, if

8A. No change
  B. study, she
  C. study he
  D. study, some

9A. No change
  B. student
  C. students
  D. their

10A. No change
  B. career, he or she has paid
  C. career, they will pay
  D. career, he will pay

each and every instrument available.
                11
Most students, in addition don't know
            12
which equipment or parts in the

inventory are available. Many of these
                                    13
instruments are quite complex. Most

may be checked out, so the chances for

things to go crazy are much greater.
        14
The cost of repairing or replacing

instruments damaged through im-

proper use has to amount to quite a
            15
few dollars. Students without prior

experience are forced to master the use

of equipment by trial and error. The
                                16
reason is because most of the equip-
    16
ment lacks manuals. This should
                        17
disturb the college administration.

   Lab staff should conduct workshops

to familiarize students with the proper

care and use of equipment. A class size

of ten to fifteen would be ideal. Such

training would reduce the number of

equipment repairs, and allow for more
                    18
productive use of lab time.

   On the contrary, a master inventory
            19
list of parts and instruments should be

available at the start of the quarter.

Manuals should be available for

checking every piece of test equipment.

11A. No change
  B. the instruments
  C. every instrument, which is
       available
  D. each and every instrument

12A. No change
  B. students, on the other hand,
  C. students, in addition,
  D. students in addition

13A. No change
  B. Many of them
  C. A lot of them
  D. Much of these

14A. No change
  B. a mistake or malfunction are
  C. things to go haywire is
  D. a mistake or malfunction is

15A. No change
  B. have to amount
  C. have to come
  D. had to amount

16A. No change
  B. error
  C. error; the reason is
  D. error, the reason being

17A. No change
  B. That
  C. This problem
  D. These

18A. No change
  B. repairs and allowing
  C. repairs, which allow
  D. repairs and allow

19A. No change
  B. Moreover
  C. Likewise
  D. Whereas

These suggestions would be fairly
simple to implement. The administration would benefit from reducing
equipment repair costs. <u>We students</u>
20
would benefit by being better
prepared for our lab work. [21]

PASSAGE THREE

<u>Although</u> I'm not a woman-
22
hunting playboy, I have met my
share of women. Fort Walton Beach
is close to my home, so when I have
time, I can be found there. Usually
<u>there's women</u> everywhere on the
23
beach. All a man has to do is stand
<u>still, and</u> an abundance of females
24
will <u>enter your</u> line of vision. <u>It</u>
25
<u>is my determination</u>, playing on the
26
beach, that women can be classified
into three major <u>groups; beautiful,</u>
27
the friendly, and the beastly.

The beautiful are those who will
only let you watch <u>them, if you know</u>
28
<u>what I mean</u>. Most of them are stuck
28
up. They think they are better than
any <u>man alive maybe dead too.</u>
29
Sometimes, if you chase one long
enough and have a fool-proof plan,

20A. No change
 B. Us, the students
 C. Us students
 D. We, as students

21. The intended audience of this passage is likeliest to be
 A. the editor of the student newspaper.
 B. a student working in the lab.
 C. a supplier of lab equipment.
 D. None of the above

22A. No change
 B. Because
 C. Whereas,
 D. Provided

23A. No change
 B. women are
 C. there are women located
 D. there's women standing

24A. No change
 B. still, thus
 C. still, for
 D. still, and

25A. No change
 B. come into their
 C. come into your
 D. enter his

26A. No change
 B. I have determined
 C. My opinion is
 D. It is my opinion

27A. No change
 B. types: beautiful
 C. groups: the beautiful
 D. groups, the beautiful

28A. No change
 B. them, if you get the idea
 C. them if you get the meaning
 D. them

29A. No change
 B. man, alive or dead
 C. man that's living or dead
 D. man who is living or not

then you might land a <u>date. Which</u>
                              30
is not as easy as it sounds. Odds are

that your personality and hers won't

match. Usually you find these

women with men who have more

money, flashy cars, and expensive

clothes.

   The friendly <u>are the group of</u>
                        31
<u>women who</u> will walk up to you and
      31
say hello. They will help you

befriend them. <u>When searching for</u>
                        32
<u>words to make conversation,</u> so are
         32
they. These are the women I know

<u>real well</u>. I feel at home with them
    33
because I can relate to them. They

aren't only looking for the best in a

<u>man they</u> can also see the worst but
    34
make allowances.

   At the other end of the <u>spectrum</u>
                                 35
<u>there's</u> the beasts. This group
    35
includes unsightly women (who are

found in the other groups as well),

those who don't care about their

appearance and <u>having</u>
                     36
<u>attitudes that are completely awful</u>.
               36
These women excel at making fools of

themselves and being obnoxious.

30A. No change
  B. date; which
  C. date. Such success
  D. date. This

31A. No change
  B. women
  C. women are those that
  D. women, who

32A. No change
  B. While trying to make conver-
      sation,
  C. When you are searching for
      words to make conversation,
  D. When searching for words to
      make conversation

33A. No change
  B. best
  C. really good
  D. real good

34A. No change
  B. man, therefore they
  C. man. They
  D. man, they

35A. No change
  B. spectrum there were
  C. spectrum are
  D. spectrum there is

36A. No change
  B. have sour attitudes
  C. having completely awful
      attitudes
  D. have got rotten attitudes

They are careless about who their

friends are and what they do.
                          37
Although the beautiful, the

friendly, and the beastly are as

different as night and day, I could
                    38
find myself falling for a girl

from any group. In fact, I'm

convinced any man (especially a

desperate one) be finding a
                    39
companion or mate from any of my

three categories of women. [40]

37A. No change
  B. their actions
  C. what they are doing
  D. what their friends do

38A. No change
  B. different as night and day
  C. as different as night from day
  D. very different

39A. No change
  B. can find
  C. might could find
  D. find

40. The writer's overall attitude
     toward his subject could be
     described as
  A. cynical.
  B. arrogant.
  C. sexist.
  D. All the above

PREPARATION
for the
READING TEST

Reading

Preparing for the College Placement Exam in Reading

In this part of the book, you'll prepare for the CPE (College Placement Exam) in Reading. In this first section, you'll acquire some general knowledge about the test. In the next section, you'll take a diagnostic test to determine your strengths and weaknesses. In the middle sections (called chapters), you'll learn about: 1) the three major skills on the test; 2) strategies for improving your test score. The last section on the CPE in Reading contains five practice tests.

GENERAL INFORMATION ABOUT
THE COLLEGE PLACEMENT EXAM IN READING

The College Placement Exam in Reading consists of four passages covering academic reading in prose fiction, humanities, social science and science. Each passage contains several paragraphs. The test is designed to measure your knowledge of reading comprehension and vocabulary. There are generally ten multiple-choice questions per passage, and you are allowed 45 minutes to complete the test. A passing score on the test varies somewhat from college to college. Check with your particular institution for the passing score required.

The skills on the test can be divided into the following categories:

Skill	Number of Questions	Percentage of Test
1.) Vocabulary	8	20%
2.) Referring	16	40%
3.) Reasoning	16	40%
Total	40	100%

TEST-TAKING TIPS

Before going on to the other sections, look over these tips for taking the CPE in Reading. Try to review them from time to time since they will be helpful for taking the practice tests and for the actual CPE in Reading.

1) Be Prepared. Eat a well-balanced meal and get a good night's rest before the exam.

2) Arrive Early. Come ten to fifteen minutes early to get situated.

3) Think Positively. Think in terms of success. Negative thoughts create worry and unnecessary frustration.

4) Relax. Use your imagination to relieve anxiety. Picture your most favorite, peaceful place, and let yourself be there for a while. To relieve confusion, use a sense of humor. Think of everyone in the room dressed in clown suits with giant pencils in their hands. Or try the 3-12-6 method of relaxation. Inhale slowly and deeply for three seconds, hold your breath for twelve seconds, and then exhale slowly for six seconds. This technique increases your oxygen intake for clearer thinking. It also gets your mind off your stress.

5) <u>Read</u> <u>The</u> <u>Directions</u> <u>Carefully</u>. Be sure you understand the directions. If you don't, ask the monitor before the test begins.

6) <u>Be</u> <u>Aware</u> <u>Of</u> <u>The</u> <u>Time</u> <u>Limits</u>. Remember that the CPE Reading Test is forty-five minutes long. That means you should spend an average of about eleven minutes per passage.

7) <u>Develop</u> <u>An</u> <u>Approach</u> <u>For</u> <u>Answering</u> <u>The</u> <u>Questions</u>. First, skim the passage for the key words and main ideas. Second, read the passage carefully. Third, read the question a couple of times. Fourth, go back to the passage to confirm your answer. Don't depend on your memory alone.

8) <u>Don't</u> <u>Spend</u> <u>Too</u> <u>Much</u> <u>Time</u> <u>On</u> <u>Any</u> <u>One</u> <u>Question</u>. Return to difficult questions after you have completed the test. There may be extra time at the end.

9) <u>Answer</u> <u>Each</u> <u>Question</u> <u>On</u> <u>The</u> <u>Test</u>. It's better to make an educated guess than to leave a question unanswered. Leaving a question blank results in lost points. Therefore, eliminate one or two answers that look wrong, and make a guess. Guessing, however, is a last resort when all else has failed.

10) <u>Use</u> <u>Your</u> <u>Answer</u> <u>Sheet</u> <u>Properly</u>. Fill in each space neatly on your answer sheet. If you need to change an answer, erase it completely. Stray marks confuse the computer and may affect your score.

CPE Diagnostic Reading Test

INTRODUCTION

Before starting to review the upcoming chapters on reading strategies for the CPE, take this diagnostic test. Like the actual CPE reading test, it contains four passages with 40 questions. You will answer 10 questions on each passage.

The purpose of this diagnostic test is to pinpoint your strengths and weaknesses on the CPE Reading Test. You should then study the appropriate chapters in this section designed to help you pass the actual CPE Reading Test. After taking this diagnostic test, check your answers against the key and explanations at the end of this book. After this test, you will find an Evaluation Chart. Follow the steps for identifying the areas in which you will need to work. Of course, if you have time, the best preparation is to work through each of the chapters in this section. You should then take the five practice CPE Reading Tests at the end of this section to check your progress.

DIRECTIONS

Read each passage carefully. Then read each question and circle the best answer. Do not spend too much time on any one question. You can always return to it later if you have more time. You will have 45 minutes to complete the test.

CPE Diagnostic Test in Reading

PASSAGE ONE

LAURA

Laura drove the same road every day, saw the same houses, the same kids waiting for the bus. She was always just ahead of the bus, so the kids were all out waiting, staring past her down the road, looking for the bus that would take them too. The road told her where she was to go, forbade a shortcut across the field, told her when to stop, when to turn — much like her boss at work, her husband at home. She thought to herself: "Do what's expected and you'll be safe. Everything will be okay. Just like the kids on the bus. Never talk back. Don't think. Be good."

Could she cut free — just disappear for a while and find herself? No doing it her way at work, his way at home. Who was Laura? Did anyone know her? Rent a cabin in the off-season. It would be cheap now — her kids in school — no vacations. The lake would be calm, air brisk, sky blue — no haze from a too hot sun — just multicolored leaves to stare at, and sunshine frolicking on the water, and the tree branches reaching up to play — free to go beneath and find peace.

He said, "Stop at Sears after work, pick up the order, get some keys made, and get some new underwear, and we need milk."

She said, "Sure," so she is good. Laura remembered her childhood on the farm. She never asked questions, did her homework, fed the chickens, cleaned the water trough, did the dishes, changed the baby. Laura was a good girl, but who would remember her? People would say she just moved away.

1. The word <u>frolicking</u> in paragraph two most likely means

   A. hopping.
   B. playing.
   C. resting.
   D. walking.
   E. darkening.

2. Which answer best indicates the proper sequence of events in the passage?

   1. Laura stops at Sears.
   2. Laura daydreams about a cabin at the lake.
   3. Laura recalls her childhood.
   4. Laura drives past the school children.

      A. 2, 1, 4, 3
      B. 3, 2, 4, 1
      C. 4, 3, 2, 1
      D. 1, 2, 3, 4
      E. 4, 2, 3, 1

3. In which month of the year does the story most likely take place?

   A. August
   B. October
   C. December
   D. May
   E. February

4. According to the passage, the word <u>forbade</u> is used to mean

   A. prohibited
   B. permitted
   C. led
   D. welcomed
   E. signaled

5. Which of the following statements best describes the main point of the passage?

   A. Laura is angry and lonely but enjoys nature.
   B. Laura longs for her childhood where she could be good again.

C. She admires the school children for their carefree lives.
D. Laura feels trapped in a routine existence and would like to escape.
E. She is elated about her up coming vacation and cannot wait to move away from her neighborhood.

6. As a child, Laura lived

   A. in the suburbs.
   B. near a school.
   C. in the country.
   D. in the city.
   E. on a farm.

7. What conclusion can you draw about her relationship with her husband?

   A. They are happily married.
   B. They have their differences but accept their relationship.
   C. Laura is tired of doing her husband's bidding but fails to communicate that to him because of her need to "be good."
   D. Laura's husband loves her because she is cooperative.
   E. Laura never questions any aspect of their relationship.

8. Laura is probably a

   A. working mother.
   B. secretary.
   C. working wife.
   D. teacher.
   E. housewife.

9. Where is Laura going?

   A. To run some errands.
   B. To sneak away for a short vacation.
   C. To pick up her children from school.
   D. To get some keys made.
   E. To her place of employment.

10. In the passage, Laura's car is

    A. behind the bus.
    B. beside the bus.
    C. across the street from the bus.
    D. in front of the bus.
    E. far away from the bus.

PASSAGE TWO

Drama is one of the oldest art forms, and its exact origins remain a mystery. Yet it is primarily through the Greeks that we understand much of our dramatic heritage. During the 600's B.C., festivals honoring Dionysus, god of wine and fertility, took place. Choruses of performers dressed as satyrs (half man and half goat) danced and sang songs celebrating their ancestors and spring's renewal of the earth. These events usually culminated in the sacrificial killing and eating of a goat, representing Dionysus, so that the power of nature would once again surge through all living things. When in 534 B.C. Thespis introduced to this ritual an actor and speeches, real drama began to develop in ancient Greece.

Tragedy and comedy both evolved from these rites of Dionysus. Myths provided subject matter, and a chorus danced or sang to music. Tragedy was solemn, serious, and ended in heroic defeat. On the other hand, comedy aimed to amuse the audience and usually ended happily.

Performances of Greek drama occurred in a stadium-like outdoor theater with seats sloping down to and curved about halfway around a circular stage called an orchestra. In the back of the stage was the skene or stage house which later became a backdrop for the action. Gods descended from the roof by a crane; thus, impossible situations could be solved through deus ex machina. Scenery was not elaborate. Simple objects and painted screens were used to suggest setting. Masks and vivid costumes also played important roles in Greek drama. Because of the size of the theater, actors wore huge masks with exaggerated features so that the spectators could see the characters from a great distance.

11. According to the passage, Dionysus was

   A. half goat and half man.
   B. an early actor.
   C. a god of fruitfulness.
   D. a Greek actor.
   E. a chorus of singers.

12. In paragraph one, culminated means

   A. ended.
   B. erupted.
   C. required.
   D. started.
   E. continued.

13. In paragraph two, which pattern of organization does the author use?

   A. Definition
   B. Comparison
   C. Description
   D. Comparison/contrast
   E. Argumentation

14. The tone of the passage is

   A. critical.
   B. informative.
   C. skeptical.
   D. humorous.
   E. dramatic.

15. The phrase deus ex machina in paragraph three probably refers to

   A. the roof of the stage house.
   B. an impossible situation.
   C. introducing a famous person into the action.
   D. a dramatic exit from the action.
   E. intervention by a supernatural force.

16. Try to recall the times you viewed or visited various public places. Which of the following would most closely resemble an ancient Greek theater?

   A. a classroom
   B. a shopping mall
   C. a supermarket
   D. a church
   E. an auditorium

172

17. According to the passage, the reason actors wore masks was to

A. hide their true identity.
B. make excitement on the stage.
C. make facial expressions visible to the audience.
D. emphasize their god-like qualities.
E. stand out from the scenery.

18. According to this passage, the true origin of drama is

A. Greece.
B. a mystery.
C. the rites of Dionysus.
D. Thespis' introduction of an actor.
E. tragedy and comedy.

19. According to the passage, which of the following statements is not true?

A. Tragedy was solemn and serious whereas comedy was amusing.
B. Consuming goat meat was a part of the spring festival of Dionysus.
C. Actors performed in front of the stage house.
D. The audience watching Greek theater surrounded the stage on all sides.
E. During the early fifth century B.C., Thespis added a speaking actor to the spring celebration.

20. This passage is primarily about

A. the development and presentation of Greek drama.
B. the types of Greek drama.
C. the early Dionysian festivals of spring that became Greek drama.
D. the role of the stage, scenery, and masks in Greek drama.
E. the beginning of Greek drama.

PASSAGE THREE

After the Civil War, the United States underwent many rapid changes. With peace restored, the nation turned its energy toward growth, industrialization, and the accumulation of wealth. Cities expanded as people left rural areas seeking a better life, but most were destined to a life in crowded slums. European immigrants provided cheap, plentiful labor for factories. The business boom created a wealthy upper class and a growing middle class, but common laborers, who formed the lower class, toiled long hours for starvation wages. Their lot was <u>penury</u>. It became evident that economic progress excluded a large segment of the population while a small but influential group of businessmen accumulated huge fortunes. Consequently, several movements to reform the country's economic, political, and social systems emerged.

The Populist Party was one movement that criticized oil, steel, and railroad monopolies. Composed primarily of farmers and laborers, this party appealed to rural ideals and blamed bankers and industrialists for weakening agriculture through unfair costs for services.

The goals of the Progressive Movement were similar but more comprehensive than those of the Populists. The Progressives believed that the quality of life throughout society should be improved. A government policy of <u>laissez-faire</u> was unacceptable. Congress needed to enact legislation that would protect workers and prevent an imbalance in the distribution of wealth. During the presidencies of Teddy Roosevelt and William Howard Taft, new laws controlling monopolies, protecting consumers, and limiting child labor were passed.

The Progressive Movement intensified during the presidency of Woodrow Wilson. To insure the common good of all citizens, Congress passed the 16th Amendment which permitted the levying of an income tax, so that needed services could be provided. The Federal Trade Commission (FTC) was instituted to deal with customer complaints about unethical business conduct while the Clayton Antitrust Act all but eliminated monopolies. With the passage of the 17th Amendment, senators were now elected directly by the people rather than elected through the influence of special interest groups within the state legislatures. The 19th Amendment gained the right to vote for women.

Thus, through a combination of social concern and government leadership, reform of the country's economic, political, and social systems occurred. At the same time, the United states blossomed into a major industrial power with a limitless future.

21. The term <u>laissez-faire</u> in paragraph three means

    A. sympathy.
    B. monopoly.
    C. democracy.
    D. noninterference.
    E. exploitation.

22. In the passage, the author suggests that before the Civil War the United States was

    A. agricultural with moderate income.
    B. urban and industrialized.
    C. wealthy and stable.
    D. changing rapidly.
    E. a major world power.

23. The author explains the topic through

    A. critical evaluation.
    B. argumentation.
    C. historical analysis.
    D. emotional appeals.
    E. historical examples.

24. What is the author's attitude toward the upper class in the passage?

   A. sympathetic and supportive
   B. accepting yet detached
   C. critical and distrustful
   D. indifferent and unconcerned
   E. sarcastic and bitter

25. Which of the following statements best summarizes what the passage is saying?

   A. The Progressive Movement established a balance in the distribution of wealth in America while the Populist Movement was not as successful in achieving that aim.
   B. The post-Civil War industrial boom created a strong economy in the United States but with a large class of poorly paid workers.
   C. The poor became poorer and the rich got richer in the years following the Civil War.
   D. The presidency of Woodrow Wilson accomplished more for the public welfare than any previous administration.
   E. After the Civil War, rapid industrialization created economic imbalances and gave rise to reforms designed to correct the situation.

26. In the first paragraph, the best definition of penury is

   A. despair.
   B. poverty.
   C. sickness.
   D. starvation.
   E. loneliness.

27. From the information in this passage, we can determine that the time period discussed is

   A. 1700-1775.
   B. 1776-1830.
   C. 1830-1865.
   D. 1921-1948.
   E. unclear.

28. The Clayton Antitrust Act helped to discourage

   A. child labor.
   B. economic progress.
   C. consumer exploitation.
   D. immigration.
   E. monopolies.

29. According to the passage, immigrants furnished the labor for industrial expansion. Based on the chart below, about how many immigrants came from Northern and Western Europe?

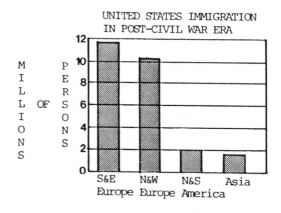

   A. 10.5 million
   B. 5 million
   C. 11 million
   D. 11.5 million
   E. 12 million

30. For populists, which group was the most excluded from the American economy?

   A. immigrants
   B. industrialists
   C. bankers
   D. farmers
   E. consumers

PASSAGE FOUR

People with allergies exhibit an abnormal sensitivity to substances called allergens which are usually harmless to the ordinary person. Hippocrates, the father of medicine, first documented hives, a skin rash resulting from the ingestion of certain foods. About 10% of the population suffer from severe allergic disorders while 40% to 60% experience minor allergies from substances ranging from hair and insect venom to certain foods and fungi.

Determining the causes of allergies is a complex yet valuable part of patient diagnosis. A detailed case history of the patient aids investigation since a person's occupation, environment, food, and general habits may aggravate allergies. For example, a husband's irritability was traced to his wife's makeup. Far more common than conjugal allergy, however, is exposure to tobacco smoke. The condition of asthmatic children living with parents who smoke worsened in 65% of the cases. Another common diagnostic tool for finding allergies is the patch test. This procedure involves the scratching of minute amounts of various materials into the skin and then reading the reaction. An immediate swelling at the scratch point indicates a positive test and may suggest an allergy.

Although a complete cure for allergies is rarely possible, researchers have devised various methods of treatment. Often-times, two categories of medications are recommended: daily or routine medications and medications for the attacks. Daily or routine medications such as antihistamines assist persons with occasional episodes of asthma or hay fever. Temporary side effects like jitteriness, headache, or stomach ache are common, but they disappear after a few days. Medications for attacks are usually only for acute situations in which breathing becomes difficult. Frequent use of these medications should be avoided because of trembling and headaches. In addition to medications, allergy patients can receive injections of allergic substances on a regular basis for up to three years or longer. These allergy shots contain extracts of pollen, dust, or mold spores. The patient gradually develops increased resistance to those substances and decreased allergic symptoms.

Ultimately, the best treatment for allergies entails the control of one's environment, and that means avoiding or reducing allergens in the home and workplace. Suspect foods in the diet should be eliminated, and insidious molds and dusts should be minimized in living areas.

31. Your family recently brought a kitten home from a pet store, and, as the little kitten romps around the house, your sister sneezes frequently. According to the passage, what would be the best procedure to follow?

    A. Return the kitten to the pet store.
    B. Give your sister anti-histamines to stop the sneezing.
    C. Keep the kitten in the basement or garage.
    D. Require her to get allergy injections for three years or longer.
    E. Make an appointment for her to visit an allergist.

32. With which of the following statements would the author of this passage most likely agree?

    A. Allergy shots are the most effective treatment for allergy symptoms.
    B. Allergies become more prevalent in the fall than at any other time of the year.

C. Tobacco smoke tends to aggravate some types of allergies.
D. Severe allergic disorders far outnumber minor allergies.
E. Allergies are a psychosomatic illness.

33. The point of view expressed in the passage is probably that of

A. a nurse.
B. a journalist.
C. a patient.
D. a teacher.
E. a nonsmoker.

34. In the last paragraph, the word insidious means

A. useless.
B. gray.
C. microscopic.
D. dangerous.
E. unusual.

35. Conjugal allergy in the second paragraph refers to

A. cosmetics.
B. marriage.
C. house.
D. bedroom.
E. wife.

36. According to the passage, why is the patch test part of an allergy diagnosis?

A. to prevent a severe allergic reaction
B. to insert medication under the skin
C. to combine several procedures into one step
D. to isolate the patient's specific allergies

37. In paragraph three, the author explains the topic by means of

A. classifying and defining.
B. comparing.
C. reasons and examples.
D. contrasting.
E. illustrating.

38. What method(s) listed is (are) the most important for allergy treatment?

1. medications
2. injections
3. environmental control

A. 2
B. 3
C. 1
D. 1, 2, 3
E. 1, 2

39. All of the following are side effects of allergy medications except

A. trembling.
B. headache.
C. stomach ache.
D. wheezing.
E. jitteriness.

40. From the passage, one can conclude that

A. the primary causes of allergies are mold and pollen.
B. the workplace is more likely to cause allergies than the home.
C. allergies can be lessened through careful diagnosis and treatment.
D. Hippocrates is the father of allergy science.
E. a patient's case history is more valuable for diagnosis than a patch test.

DIAGNOSTIC READING TEST
EVALUATION CHART

On the chart below, circle the number of questions that you answered incorrectly and evaluate the results. Then turn to the appropriate skill area (listed by page number), review the discussion and strategies and complete the exercises for improving that skill. Finally, complete the practice tests to further prepare yourself for the College Placement Exam in Reading.

SKILLS	
VOCABULARY 1, 4, 12, 15, 21, 26, 34, 35	REFERRING (Facts and Details) 6, 9, 10, 11, 18, 27, 28, 29, 30, 32, 38
REFERRING (Sequence, Cause and Effect) 2, 17, 36	REASONING (Stated or Implied Main Idea) 5, 20, 25
REASONING (Inferences, Conclusions) 3, 7, 8, 16, 22, 31, 33, 40	REASONING (Organizational Patterns, Tone, Irrelevant Questions) 13, 14, 19, 23, 24, 37, 39

CHAPTER 10
Vocabulary Strategies

Understanding words is an essential skill you will need for passing the College Placement Exam (CPE) in Reading. Each of the four passages on this test will contain two questions about the meanings of words. That equates to 8 out of 40 questions or 20% of the test. In addition, the CPE will require you to decipher the meanings of other unfamiliar words, so that you can comprehend the ideas expressed in each passage. Therefore, the knowledge of words is really a fundamental skill necessary for the successful completion of the CPE. Ultimately, a rich vocabulary will help you answer all of the questions on this test.

On the CPE, vocabulary questions will generally be phrased with the following stems:

1. The best definition for _____ is
2. _____ most probably means
3. As used in the passage _____ means
4. _____ is closest in meaning to

Some experts estimate that the English language has over 1,000,000 words. An educated person may be familiar with 50,000 of those words or less than 5% of the total. Fortunately though, as we attend school, work, and gain more experiences, learning new words continues right to the end of our lives.

The best vocabulary strategies that will prepare you for the CPE are: 1. Understanding meanings by context. 2. Understanding meanings by word parts. Of course, you may sometimes know what the words mean, but their definitions may vary depending on how they are used in the passage. So it's always helpful to use these two strategies.

There are other vocabulary strategies such as using a dictionary. However, since you cannot look up words during the test, we will focus on explaining context analysis and word parts.

MEANING BY CONTEXT

When you encounter a puzzling word on the CPE, you can often determine its meaning by reading the words or sentences that come before or after it. This particular strategy is called context or contextual analysis. Readers use this method frequently because it's easy and quick.

Let's take the word run, for example. In our language, run has many meanings. How is it used in the following sentence?

Last night on the news, there was a report of a run on the stock market. Investors bought shares of companies as soon as they became available.

If you figured out that run means buying stock quickly, you were correct. The meaning of run was explained in the sentence following the word. Definition cues are the most common strategies readers use to find the meanings of words in context.

Another useful context strategy is defining a word by searching for its opposite meaning. Let's look at the word gregarious in this sentence.

Gina is very shy, but her boyfriend, Rick, is gregarious.

If you guessed that gregarious means outgoing or sociable, you were right. The cue for the definition, but, signals that the statement following it suggests the opposite of what preceded it. We call this context method a contrast cue.

Although you'll learn other context strategies as you read, you should find the definition and contrast cues most helpful. Just remember, some of the key words associated with context strategies:

KEY WORDS

Definition Cues	Contrast Cues
or, defined as, because, that is, for example, such as	but, however, yet, while instead of, nevertheless

MEANING BY WORD PARTS

Our English-speaking ancestors borrowed many words from other languages. Over the last 2,000 years, words from Latin, Greek, German, French, and Spanish have enriched English. Particularly important for college reading, are words or parts of words taken from Latin and Greek. In fact, well over 50% of our vocabulary comes from these classical languages.

Of course, you don't need to take a course in Latin or Greek. There are simpler strategies you can develop for expanding your vocabulary. Many meanings of words can be acquired through a thorough knowledge of word parts. These parts consist of prefixes, roots, and suffixes. Becoming familiar with these basic word parts unlocks the meanings of countless words in our language.

Let's examine a word that contains a prefix, root, and a suffix. Can you figure out the meaning from its word parts?

The speaker's voice was inaudible.

If you said it means not able to be heard, you're correct. Here's how the Latin word parts work. The prefix "in" means not, the root "aud" deals with hearing, and the suffix "ible" refers to an ability. Let's look at one more example.

The child's appetite for ice cream was nearly insatiable.

If you guessed it means not able to be satisfied, you're right. Insatiable has the same prefix (in) and a similar suffix (able) as inaudible. "Satia" is the Latin root for satisfy.

As you can see, one advantage of learning word parts is that once you know them, you can apply your knowledge to new words. You start figuring out meanings of words with similar prefixes, roots and suffixes.

Here is a list of some common prefixes, suffixes, and roots. You can also consult longer lists available in reading or English textbooks. Review them, and they will help you define meaning from word parts.

LIST OF WORD PARTS

PREFIXES

Prefix	Meaning	Example
a	not	amoral
ex	outside	exterior
mono	one	monologue
pre	before	pre-Civil war
super	above, over	supernatural

ROOTS

Root	Meaning	Example
annum	year	annual
cred	believe	credit
port	carry	export
scrib	write	prescription
var	change	varied

SUFFIXES

Root	Meaning	Example
ate	make	animate
hood	state of	childhood
ism	doctrine of	communism
or, er	person who	investigator
tude	state of	multitude

VOCABULARY TIPS FOR THE CPE

Before doing the practice CPE exercises at the end of this chapter, try to study and apply the following vocabulary tips for the CPE Reading Test.

1. Read frequently. Because you will be tested on words from the humanities, social sciences, and the sciences, try to read magazines and books that deal with these subjects. A high school or college textbook in English, art, biology, or history would be a good place to start. Scholarly articles in *National Geographic*, *Newsweek*, *Time*, or *Psychology Today* are also useful. As you read, try to determine the meanings of new words by context or word parts. Use the flashcard technique discussed below, so you can develop a collection of new words and word parts.

In addition, libraries and bookstores carry many books which build vocabulary. Here are some good ones:

The Must Words by Craig and Peter Norback
Word Forms by Gordon
30 Days to A More Powerful Vocabulary by Funk and Lewis
SAT High Frequency Word List in *Barron's SAT* by Brownstein and Weiner

2. <u>Make flashcards</u>. Flashcards are an easy and effective way to learn new words. Buy packs of 3x5 index cards and start collecting words from your reading or listening experiences. You can carry these cards conveniently and review them during your spare time.

The success of this strategy comes from <u>writing down</u> the material to aid your memory. Follow these steps.

FRONT OF CARD

1. On the front of the card, print the word in large letters.
2. Beneath it, write the pronunciation.
3. Then add the sentence in which you found the word.
4. Finally, if you can, think of a mnemonic device (memory aid) to help you recall the meaning. Make a mental or visual association. For example, the word <u>pen-ury</u> sounds like penny and, since it means extreme poverty, you have given yourself a clue to the definition. For <u>hydrophobia</u>, you could draw a man running away from a shower. (It means fear of water.) Don't worry about your lack of artistic ability. You're the only one who will see your drawing anyway. The purpose of the visual is to help you remember and the more humorous or outrageous it is, the better you will usually succeed.

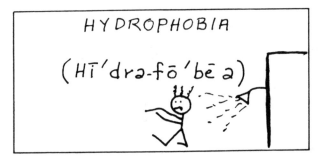

BACK OF CARD

1. <u>Write</u> the definition or definitions.
2. <u>Write</u> your own sentence using the word.

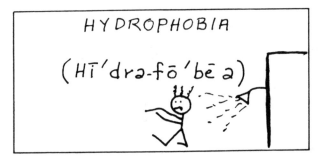

3. <u>Review choices carefully</u>. Before choosing an answer on the CPE, check all of your choices. Don't mark the first answer you see, even though you may feel the pressure of time. Look at all the answers, so you can arrive at the best choice.

4. <u>Do the Practice Vocabulary Exercises</u>. Be sure you practice your context and word parts strategies. Work through the exercises at the end of this chapter. The Practice Reading Tests at the end of this section will also help you answer vocabulary questions on the CPE.

PRACTICE EXERCISES ON VOCABULARY STRATEGIES

Directions: Read the following passages. Then try to define the meanings of the underlined words. Use either context or word parts strategies. Write your definitions in the spaces provided. Answers for these exercises are in the answer key at the end of this book.

EXERCISE 1

In a pure <u>monopoly</u>, only one individual or group controls an industry or manufactures a product. In the early 1900's, such a situation existed. Single corporations dominated the oil and steel industries. As a result, consumers paid <u>fixed</u> prices for products. Instead of allowing this situation to continue, the government passed laws limiting monopolies, which fostered the development of several producers of the same goods. Unlike monopolies, these oligopolies promoted more competition for oil or steel products, and, thus, the costs for these products decreased.

Today, however, <u>variable</u> <u>costs</u> associated with production and foreign competition have encouraged frequent <u>mergers</u>, or the combining of corporations into one large business. Economists are watching this development anxiously. For some, at least, these mergers <u>portend</u> a return to the monopolies of the early 1900's.

1. <u>monopoly</u>(paragraph 1)_____
2. <u>fixed</u> <u>prices</u> (paragraph 1) _____
3. <u>oligopolies</u> (paragraph 1) _____
4. <u>variable</u> <u>costs</u> (paragraph 2) _____
5. <u>mergers</u> (paragraph 2) _____
6. <u>portend</u> (paragraph 2)_____

EXERCISE 2

In our city of the future (indeed, in some European cities today) waste disposal will at last be coupled with <u>reclamation</u>. Nature's Rule that all essential materials must cycle within the system will become a way of life, for no other reason than necessity. There is simply no <u>recourse</u> but to change to a system where the circular movement of materials essential for our needs will be patterned after that of nature.

In our city of the future, it is likely that domestic and industrial solid waste will be collected and transported to <u>reclamation</u> centers and separated into combustibles and into metals and glass for recycling. The combustibles may be burned to power the system - or perhaps they may be <u>degraded</u> to produce methane (also used for power) and compost for city gardens and parks. It is quite possible that the value of recovered materials will offset the costs of collection and processing.

Sewage disposal systems will probably be linked directly to natural ecosystems at least for tertiary phases of water treatment. Studies have demonstrated the <u>feasibility</u> of using forests and agricultural lands as recycling systems, where nutrients are incorporated by the <u>Producer Players</u> before they can <u>intrude</u> into waterways, and where water can be returned to recharge city aquifers. In the future, the forest disposal systems will be cropped periodically to remove "excess" nutrients and prevent the overloading of cycles.

The primary concern in recycling materials in the future is the enormous energy that will be required to drive these cycles. The closing of the last mines of precious metals and industrial minerals will signal the end of our free ride. Just as great expenditures of energy were required by nature to separate, concentrate, and store mineral reserves eons, ago, so, too, will we require great amounts of energy to repeatedly complete each phase of the cycle. But when all costs (including those of energy and environment) are considered, recycling still uses less energy than is used exploiting virgin materials; recycling also causes less air and water pollution and generates less solid waste. Recycling is one of the basic ecological Rules of the Game by which we must abide.

An abundant supply of energy will be critical if we are to prevent cycles from running amuck. And this presents a paradox because anticipated great increases in the use of coal and shale oil, the most likely stopgap energy sources, will result in great intrusions and disruptions of the sulfur, nitrogen, and carbon cycles - cycles that already are overloaded.

From *Understanding the Game of the Environment* by David R. Houston. Washington, D.C.: United States Department of Agriculture Forest Service, 1979, p. 845.

1. reclamation (paragraphs 1 and 2) _____
2. recourse (paragraph 1) _____
3. degraded (paragraph 2) _____
4. feasibility (paragraph 3) _____
5. Producer Players (paragraph 3) _____
6. intrude (paragraph 3) _____
7. free ride (paragraph 4) _____
8. exploiting (paragraph 4) _____
9. virgin (paragraph 4) _____
10. amuck (paragraph 5) _____
11. paradox (paragraph 5) _____

CHAPTER 11
Referring Strategies

To score well on the College Placement Exam in Reading, you will need to develop your referring skills. <u>Referring</u> means understanding what is directly stated in the passage. Researchers in reading sometimes call this skill <u>literal comprehension</u>, the recognizing of the important details that contribute to the meaning of the passage. Besides understanding the details of a selection, referring also involves the ability to note relationships between those details. In other words, you should be able to see logical connections between facts. For example, a story will begin and end in a certain <u>sequence of events</u>. A passage about AIDS might trace the <u>causes</u> <u>and</u> <u>effects</u> of that disease.

On each of the four reading passages, you can probably expect five questions which require referring skills. That is a total of 16 questions or 40% of the CPE reading items. Consequently, referring is a crucial competency for this exam. Learning referring strategies will help you make a higher score.

Try to become familiar with these question stems that require referring skills on the CPE. Spot the typical wording of the questions, and you will know you will be looking for facts or details in the passage.

1. According to the passage, the author states that
2. Which of the following is <u>not</u> supported in the passage?
3. Who, what, when, where, or why questions
4. The correct sequence of events in the passage is
5. Which of the following statements is true?
6. The blood passes through the lungs <u>because</u>
7. The passage states that one of the <u>primary</u> <u>reasons</u>

Now let's take a closer look at the two aspects of referring that are important for the CPE in reading. They are: 1) Facts and Details, and 2) Relationships.

FACTS AND DETAILS

Facts and details explain or clarify the meaning of a passage. If you can locate this information quickly and correctly, you will have a better chance of passing the CPE. The author may use <u>events</u> in a story, <u>reasons</u> in a historical analysis, or <u>examples</u> in a discussion of polluted rivers. No matter what label we give them, they all are, in one way or another, facts and details that aid in understanding the topic.

What referring strategies, then, will be useful for identifying facts and details in a passage? Several strategies can be developed. One involves <u>skimming and scanning</u>. An example may help here. Have you ever taken a trip on an airplane? Or perhaps you watched a movie in which people flew on an airplane. As the plane gets ready to land, you and the other passengers start surveying the scenery which is becoming more visible. Questions or observations start forming such as: What's that tall building over there?, Why do the highways look like a plate of spaghetti?, The ocean is bluer than I thought it would be., Those aren't ants. They're cars!

In this example, you were using both skimming and scanning. You <u>skimmed</u> for important landmarks or interesting objects in the scenery. Then you <u>scanned</u> by raising questions, making observations, and seeking answers. Actually, we employ these strategies daily, whether we are looking for a place to eat or finding someone's number in the phone book.

Skimming and scanning on a CPE reading passage are very similar. When you <u>skim</u> the passage, look for key words and get a sense of the topic (what the passage is about). First, you need to look for the main ideas which are sometimes in the first or last sentence of each paragraph. Then, <u>read</u> the passage carefully. Finally, look at the questions. Note the key words in the answer choices that are also in the passage. <u>Scan</u> or locate the answer to your question and blacken the appropriate circle on your answer sheet.

Another referring strategy centers around the <u>5 W's</u>. When you listen to the news on television, or read the newspaper, you'll find out about a crime, peace treaty or community event. You'll learn <u>who</u> was involved, <u>what</u> happened, <u>when</u> and <u>where</u> it occurred and <u>why</u> it happened. These are the <u>5 W's</u>. Sometimes a newscaster will explain <u>how</u> events occurred also. These <u>5 W's</u> and <u>how</u> are tip-offs for questions about facts and details in a passage. Seeing them in a question will tell you what kind of thinking you should use to get the answer.

Now let's summarize what we've learned about referring. Here are the strategies to use for locating facts and details in a CPE reading passage.

1. <u>Skim</u> the passage. Notice <u>key</u> <u>words</u> and the <u>general</u> <u>topic</u>.
2. <u>Read</u> the passage carefully.
3. <u>Scan</u> the question and the answer choices. Look for the <u>5 W's</u> or <u>how</u>, the clues to fact and detail answers.
4. Try to match key words in your answer choice with those in the passage.
5. <u>Choose</u> the <u>best</u> answer, <u>but</u> always verify your response by going back to the passage.

RELATIONSHIPS

Recognizing relationships between facts and details is another referring skill needed for the CPE. Basically, you should be particularly sensitive to sequences and cause-effect relationships.

For the CPE in reading, <u>sequence</u> <u>relationships</u> will usually require you to make connections between events. For example, you may encounter a passage of short fiction (like a short story). Let us say this passage is about a first date. There would be a <u>sequence</u> <u>of</u> <u>events</u> in chronological (time) order starting with the first meeting, continuing through the dinner and dance, and ending with a good night kiss. Or you may read a historical passage about the Civil War. Again, there would be a series of events in chronological order.

Questions dealing with sequences will be worded as: In which order did the events occur, or what is the correct sequence of events in the passage? You would know, then, to review the events from the earliest one to the most recent one in the passage. There are also key words that will help you figure out the sequence of events. Here are some common ones:

before	first
after	second
then	third
when	finally
next	most important

Detecting <u>cause-effect</u> <u>relationships</u> is also important for the CPE. The author may analyze the reasons (<u>causes</u>) for an event or observation, the results (<u>effects</u>) of those events, or both together. Let's illustrate what causes and effects are and how they may be related.

> Every dawn the sun rises and floods the earth with light for a new day. Because of this sunlight, plants make food. Animals eat the plants, and, human beings are able to consume animal meat. This food chain results from the beneficial rays of our sun.

Cause-effect relationships occur in this passage. The cause or reason for life of all kinds is light from the sun. The effects (results or consequences) are plant, animal, and human life. We could also say that the cause or source for animal life is plants and a significant cause or reason for human life is meat derived from animals. As you can see, cause-effect relationships focus on <u>why</u> something happens and <u>what</u> the results might be, and they are often interrelated.

Using our previous example, CPE questions about causes or effects will be phrased as: <u>Why</u> do plants depend on the sun? The <u>reason</u> for daylight is, Animals eat plants <u>because</u>. The questions tend to focus on causes more often than effects. Again, there are key words in CPE passages and questions that hint at cause-effect relationships. Some common ones are:

<u>causes</u>	<u>effects</u>
because	result
why	consequence
reason	outcome
basis	therefore

Let's review the strategies that will be useful for referring questions on the CPE in Reading.

SEQUENCES

1. Be alert to the sequence of events in a passage, particularly in short fiction and history.
2. Learn the key words used in passages and questions about sequence.
3. Practice listing events chronologically from newspaper articles, history books or short stories.

CAUSE-EFFECT RELATIONSHIPS

1. Notice cause-effect relationships in passages, particularly in science and short fiction.
2. Learn the key words used in passages and questions dealing with cause and effect.

3. Practice listing causes and effects from science or news articles in *Time* or *Newsweek*. Try to see how they are related.

PRACTICE EXERCISES ON REFERRING

Directions: In these passages, you will be tested on both word meanings and referring. In this way, you'll continue sharpening your vocabulary strategies as well as practicing referring strategies. Skim and then read the following passages. In the spaces provided, write your definitions, using context or word parts. Then, in one sentence or less, answer the fact and detail questions and the relationship questions. Answers to these questions are in the key at the end of this book.

EXERCISE 1

Canice headed for the streets again. That morning, she had combed her graying hair back into a neat <u>bun</u>. Her maroon Sunday overcoat gave her a respectable appearance. As she walked past the Community Gospel Church, children ran and played near cars parked up against the Wood Street apartments. "You or your car aren't safe far from home," she thought.

Veering away from the church now, Canice passed the Fifth Street Elementary. The phrase "strung out" was <u>scribbled</u> in big white letters on the side of the school building. Suddenly, she saw the hungry eyes of her grandchildren, Alonzo and Tasha in her cramped flat. "Real food, please! No more beans and grits," they seemed to say.

A large, abandoned three story building loomed ahead of her. Canice's <u>wary</u> eyes shifted in every direction. No one would notice her now. As she quickly entered, Canice met Jason. He slipped the "<u>20-cent bags</u>" into the lining of her overcoat. Inside each bag were chunks of cocaine worth $20 each on the street. She would make $100 selling them after she paid off Jason. At the R&O Supermarket, Canice could already see the smiling lady at the checkout counter. "Mrs. Lewis, we appreciate your business. You always pay cash for your groceries," she would say.

1. <u>bun</u> (paragraph one) _____
2. <u>scribbled</u> (paragraph two) _____
3. <u>wary</u> (paragraph three) _____
4. "<u>20-cent bags</u>" (paragraph three)_____
5. Who is Canice? _____
6. Where is Canice going?_____
7. What is the main reason Canice deals in illegal activities? _____
8. When (time and day) does the story occur? _____
9. The checkout lady at the supermarket is happy because_____
10. How many places does Canice notice in her neighborhood? _____
11. What happens just before Canice meets Jason? _____
12. According to the passage, the primary consequence of poverty for Alonzo and Tasha is_____

EXERCISE 2

Diarrhea is by far the most frequent health problem of travelers to developing countries. Of the estimated 300 million international travelers who will cross the world's frontiers this year, at least 16 million persons from industrialized countries, including more than 8 million U.S. residents, will travel to developing countries. Approximately one-third of these travelers to developing countries will get diarrhea. The economic impact of travelers' diarrhea (TD) is substantial, because fear of sickness is one of the major deterrents to tourism. International tourists worldwide spend over $100 billion annually, and the economies of many nations depend on this travel. For educational, recreational, political, and financial reasons, this international exchange should be fostered.

The incidence of TD varies markedly by destination and may depend in part on the number of dietary indiscretions made by the traveler and on the style of travel. TD is caused by a variety of infectious agents, and the spectrum of clinical illness varies considerably. However, this illness in travelers is usually not severe; high fever, vomiting, or bloody stools occur in only a minority of cases.

Dietary prudence and hygienic measures are safe and simple preventive techniques, but they do not eliminate entirely the risk of diarrhea. Prophylactic measures such as antidiarrheal drugs and oral antimicrobial agents have been used. TD is treated with a variety of regimens including oral electrolyte solutions, antidiarrheal compounds, and antimicrobial drugs, prescribed either singly or in combination.

There continues to be a debate concerning whether the risk of antimicrobial agents is worth the benefit; whether early therapy of ill travelers is preferable to daily prophylaxis of all travelers; whether all currently employed treatment strategies are useful; and whether given groups of travelers, such as vacationers, students, or business travelers, should be selectively advised to follow special regimens.

— *National Institutes of Health Consensus Development Conference Statement, 5:8, U.S. Department of Health and Human Services, Bethesda, Maryland, 1985.*

1. deterrents (paragraph one) _____
2. incidence (paragraph two) _____
3. indiscretions (paragraph two)_____
4. prudence (paragraph three) _____
5. prophylactic (paragraph three) _____
6. antimicrobial (paragraphs three and four)_____
7. regimens (paragraphs three and four)_____
8. The main reason tourists avoid travel to other countries is because ____
   _____
   _____
9. How many people from industrialized nations travel to developing countries each year? _____
10. According to the passage, travelers' diarrhea is normally a serious illness. True or False _____

11. Which group is most prone to travelers' diarrhea?
    A. students
    B. United States citizens
    C. visitors from industrialized countries
    D. business people

12. What major effect does travelers' diarrhea have on countries that rely on tourism? _____

13. Name three causes of travelers' diarrhea. _____

14. Based on the passage, are preventive measures better for the treatment of travelers' diarrhea than drug remedies? Explain. _____

    _____

    _____

CHAPTER 12
Reasoning Strategies

The College Placement Exam in reading also requires the use of your reasoning skills. Unlike referring, <u>reasoning</u> deals with information that is not directly stated in the passage. Another name for reasoning is <u>inferential comprehension</u> or <u>critical comprehension</u>. This level of reading comprehension involves recognizing and relating the implied information that contributes to the meaning of a passage. For example, in a story passage, an author might describe a strange character breaking the window of an empty restaurant in the middle of the night and then entering through that window. Though the author might never directly mention the word "stealing" or "breaking and entering," the information presented would suggest or imply these actions. You draw an <u>inference</u> from the stated details.

An author may also want to convey a certain attitude or effect in a passage. We call this effect a <u>tone</u>. The author might never directly state his (her) attitude towards the subject, but, as readers, we can detect the tone by the use of words. The tone of the following sentence is suspenseful, though it is never explicitly stated. The author creates uncertainty about the nurse's safety.

> Old man Tucker flew down the hallway in his new wheelchair, and, directly in his path, was the head nurse.

On the CPE in reading, you will probably find three to four questions in each passage that will require reasoning strategies. That is a total of 16 questions or 40% of the test. Consequently, reasoning is an essential skill for passing the CPE in reading.

Now let's review question stems that relate to reasoning skills. Become familiar with the wording of these questions. When you see them, you know you'll need to use reasoning. Notice the key words (<u>underlined</u>) that relate to reasoning.

1. From this passage, we can <u>infer</u>
2. Which of the following statements is the best <u>conclusion?</u>
3. The <u>tone</u> of the passage is
4. The author <u>implies</u> or <u>suggests</u> that
5. The <u>point of view</u> expressed in the passage is
6. All of the following statements are mentioned in the passage <u>except</u>
7. The <u>main point</u> of the passage is
8. Which <u>organizational pattern</u> is used in this passage?

In the next two sections, we'll discuss reasoning skills and strategies for the CPE in reading. They are: 1) Making Inferences and 2) Structural Analysis.

MAKING INFERENCES

As you learned earlier, making inferences involves the ability to read between the lines. You draw a conclusion or make a judgment based on what is stated or suggested by the author.

Helpful strategies for inferring information from a passage include the following:

1. <u>Understand the stated facts and ideas</u>. Go over the main points, details, and key words carefully. Remember, any conclusions you draw must be based on information directly stated in the passage.

2. <u>Read the question and each response carefully</u>. Try to narrow your choices to responses that contain stated information from the passage. Eliminate choices that do not contain facts or ideas mentioned in the passage.

3. <u>Reason out your best choice</u>. Focus on the most logical answer. Always confirm your answer by going back to the passage and reviewing the evidence for your choice.

One kind of inferential reasoning you will need to use on the CPE in reading is <u>inferring the main idea</u> of a passage or paragraph. The <u>main idea</u> communicates what the passage or paragraph is basically about. Sometimes it is a direct statement that summarizes the topic under discussion. Here is an example:

> <u>There are many fixed expenses for students attending college.</u> Rent or mortgage payments involve the most expense. Next is the cost of tuition, books and fees. Car payments and car insurance also affect finances. Finally, food, medical bills, and entertainment must be considered when planning for a college education.

The underlined sentence is the main idea of the paragraph. Notice how it expresses the central thought — the many fixed expenses of college students. It also appears in the beginning of the paragraph. You can often pinpoint main ideas in the first sentence or sometimes in the last sentence of a paragraph. Being able to locate main ideas in a passage is obviously important for understanding the major points an author is communicating. In addition, without a sense of the main ideas in a passage, you would have an even harder time making inferences since your understanding of implied information is derived from your understanding of the stated information.

Inferring the main idea should not be difficult if you remember that you are still looking for the basic topic in a passage. The only difference is that instead of being directly stated, the main idea is implied or unstated. You just need to apply the three steps for inferring. Read the following paragraph and see if you can infer the main idea.

> The blood carries oxygen from the lungs to each cell in the body. In addition, the blood carries carbon dioxide away from the cells to the lungs where it is expelled as a waste product. Nutrients like protein and glucose depend on the blood for their dispersal throughout the body. Metabolic by-products in the form of urea and creatine are also transported by the blood to the kidneys and spleen.

If you decided that the author was describing the functions of the blood, you were right. The details and facts provided the clue, but nowhere in this passage is this idea directly stated. You made an inference about the <u>main idea.</u>

Besides inferring the main idea, you will also need to <u>make</u> <u>inferences</u> or <u>draw</u> <u>a</u> <u>conclusion</u> from the passages on the CPE Reading Test. You form an opinion based on what the author states or suggests in the passage. What conclusion can you draw about Minnie and Rex in this scene?

Minnie got out of bed at dawn while Rex snored loudly until 10:00 A.M. He rose slowly, yawning and stretching for a good hour. Minnie had already cooked breakfast, painted the front fence, and plowed half the field. "Time to get up and finish the plowing!" she yelled. Rex hollered back that the weather was still a bit chilly to work outdoors.

You can draw many conclusions about Minnie and Rex from this passage. Among them are:

1) Minnie seems overworked.
2) Rex appears lazy.
3) Minnie is an early riser.
4) Rex sleeps late.
5) Minnie and Rex do not get along very well. They yell back and forth at each other.

You can probably draw other conclusions as well, but the author never directly states that Minnie works hard or that Rex is lazy. The language and details suggest the conclusions. You make inferences about these characters based on their descriptions.

Another important type of inferring is <u>predicting</u> <u>outcomes</u>. Sometimes this skill is called applying ideas. Basically, what this means is that you as a reader must take information from a passage and apply it to a new situation not mentioned in the passage. Read this passage and then answer the question.

As the demand for a product increases, the price of the product often decreases. As the demand for a product decreases, the price of that product generally increases.

You watch a television special on the new Frisbee craze. Americans everywhere are flying Frisbees in parking lots, on suburban lawns, backlots and barnyards. Based on this passage, would the price of Frisbees be high or low?

If you chose low, you're right. A demand for a product usually decreases the price. You applied what you read about product demands to a new situation not specifically discussed in the passage. You predicted an outcome.

STRUCTURAL ANALYSIS

Along with making inferences, reasoning questions on the CPE in reading require an understanding of how the author presents and organizes information in a passage. In other words, you will be asked questions that involve a <u>structural</u> <u>analysis</u> of a passage.

One of the skills for analyzing structure on the CPE in reading is identifying organizational patterns. <u>Organizational</u> <u>patterns</u> refer to the various ways an author develops an idea in a paragraph or passage. These methods or patterns aid in explaining a topic. To answer questions correctly about organizational patterns, you should learn the meanings of the following organizational patterns and then practice recognizing them on the practice reading tests and in your general reading:

1) Narrative — telling a story, a series of related events leading to a climax — Examples: "The First Time I Fell in Love," "The Time I Barbecued the Back Deck"

2) Description — creating a word picture through the use of one or more of the five senses — Examples: "My Mother's Face at Christmas," "Sunrise on the Beach"

3) Illustration — use of examples to develop or clarify the main idea — Examples: "Examples of Mexican Food Eaten in the United States," "Examples of Women Athletes"

4) Process Analysis — explaining how to do or make something; giving directions — Examples: "The Stages of Photosynthesis," "Steps for Building a Better Memory"

5) Classification, Listing — dividing a topic into types or categories — Examples: "Types of Personalities," "Breeds of Dogs"

6) Comparison — explaining similarities between two ideas — Examples: "Similarities Between the United States and Canada," "How My Brother and I Are Alike"

7) Contrast — explaining differences between two ideas — Examples: "Differences Between Plants and Animals," "Buying a Used Car versus Buying a New Car"

8) Analysis — taking an idea apart and discussing each part separately — Example: "Basic Elements of Ocean Water," "Analysis of my Brother's Dirty Wash"

9) Argumentation — discussion of a controversial issue: author usually presents both sides of the issue but favors one side over the other — Examples: "Why Handguns Should be Banned," "AIDS is a Lifestyle, Not a Disease"

10) Definition — explaining the meaning of a term or concept — Examples: "What Love Is," "The Meaning of Environmental Preservation"

11) Theorizing or Hypothesizing — making an assumption on the basis of reasoning or evidence — Examples: "Theories About the Origins of the Earth," "Hypotheses About the Composition of Water"

12) Opinion — explanation of an author's feelings or views on a topic — Examples: "My Hopes For The Future," "Why I Believe in a College Education"

13) Cause and Effect — discusses reasons or results — Examples: "Causes of Heart Disease," "Effects of the Civil Rights Movement"

14) <u>Persuasion</u> — an urging to action on a controversial issue — Example: "A Formula For Educational Change," "Remedies For Urban Congestion"

Another aspect of understanding structure in a passage is determining tone. <u>Tone</u> is the attitude of an author toward the information presented. It is sometimes referred to as the feeling a writer puts into a passage. The author's view of the subject matter can vary from optimism to neutrality to pessimism and can cover several shades in between. Here are some common tones found in reading material:

serious	critical	amusing
humorous	factual	supportive
angry	sympathetic	objective
condemning	sarcastic	subjective
admiring	respectful	neutral

Using the above mentioned tone words, see if you can identify the correct tone for the following statements:

1. I thought that there would be this beautiful time after adolescence, but I went straight from acne to gray hair.

2. Some business workers exhibit aggressive Type A personalities. Others lean more toward the easier going Type B characteristics.

3. You lazy bum! Why don't you get a job!

4. He gently dried Lola's tears, held her close, and told her he'd fix her bicycle.

Answers:

1. humorous, amusing
2. serious, factual, objective
3. angry, condemning, critical
4. sympathetic, respectful

You should also be sensitive to the points of view expressed in a passage. <u>Point of view</u> deals with who is presenting the information in a passage. Is it an astronomer in a passage about meteors? Is it one of the characters in a story passage? Remember, an author may write a passage, but the point of view expressed may be entirely different. Authors frequently become personae (other persons) in a passage, so you cannot assume that a writer's point of view is the same as one of the characters he (she) creates. Let's look at the following passages. Try to determine the point of view in each.

PASSAGE ONE

I liked Professor Hubbell very much. She always made English easy to understand. I never felt lost in her class. In fact, I think I learned more in her course than in any other class I ever took.

PASSAGE TWO

Petroleum has a greater variety of uses than perhaps any other substance in the world. The reason petroleum has so many uses lies in its complicated molecular structure. Crude oil is chiefly a mixture of many different hydrocarbons, which are molecules made up of the elements hydrogen and carbon. Some of these hydrocarbons are gaseous, and some are solid. Most of the hydrocarbons, however, form a liquid.

In Passage 1, the point of view expressed is probably that of a student. The word "Professor" and "class" are clues. In Passage 2, the author writes the passage from the point of view of a scientist — perhaps a chemist or geologist. The clues are "molecular" and "hydrocarbons." The subject is technical and scientific.

A final strategy for analyzing structure on the CPE in reading is recognizing irrelevant statements in a selection. Irrelevant statements are examples, facts, or ideas not mentioned in a passage. You will be asked to identify those irrelevant statements. Questions may be worded as: Which of the following facts (or statements) is not mentioned in the passage? The author mentions all of the following statements except... After reading the following example, try to answer the questions about an irrelevant statement.

The culture of Mexico has influenced American food in many ways. For example, dishes like chili, tacos, and burritos are Mexican in origin. Oranges, lemons, and limes came to us through the Spanish missionaries who settled in California. Finally, America's love affair with beef owes much to early Mexican cowboys. Their ranching in the great Southwest fostered an interest in raising cattle for hungry consumers in the East.

The author mentions all of the following examples except

      A. lemons and limes
      B. cattle raising
      C tacos and burritos
      D. enchiladas
      E. chili

If you answered enchiladas, you are correct. This example is not discussed in the passage. The CPE Practice Tests in reading contain more practice with this kind of analytical skill.

Now let's summarize what we've learned about reasoning strategies on the CPE in reading.

MAKING INFERENCES

1. Remember that you should understand the stated information (main ideas and details) before you begin drawing conclusions or making inferences.
2. Use these steps for inferring:
   a.) Read the passage.
   b.) Gather your evidence (stated information).
   c.) Make your inference and confirm your choice by reviewing the evidence in the passage.
3. Practice inferring main ideas, drawing conclusions and predicting outcomes from newspaper and magazine articles, textbooks, and even television programs.

STRUCTURAL ANALYSIS

1. Learn the basic organizational patterns mentioned in this chapter.
2. Be sure you understand the meanings of the tone words listed in this chapter.
3. Notice the point of view expressed in what you read.
4. Practice identifying organizational patterns, tone, and point of view in stories, newspaper articles and magazines, and in textbooks.

PRACTICE EXERCISES ON REASONING, REFERRING AND VOCABULARY

Directions: Read the following passages carefully. Then answer the questions on reasoning, referring and vocabulary. In this way, you'll continue developing strategies for the College Placement Exam in reading. Answers to these questions are in the key at the end of this book.

EXERCISE 1

The collapse of the Roman Empire in 479 A.D. ushered in a period of uncertainty. The Roman genus for social organization no longer unified the diverse cultures of a vast empire. Rival political factions fought each other for control of lands. The economy declined because established trade routes were no longer safe or had disappeared entirely. Much of the art and literature of the classical world perished in the ruins of ancient cities.

Despite these upheavals, however, pockets of Roman heritage survived. A reweaving of European culture in the new Christian era gradually occurred. With the coming of Christianity, the new Germanic traditions began mingling with the older Greco - Roman culture. The resulting, hybrid, feudalism, developed into an elaborate system that mirrored both Roman and German social organization.

Feudalism arose out of necessity. In a lawless, chaotic age, fragmented groups needed to band together for mutual survival. Feudalism inherited its hierarchical structure from the Romans. Each human being was a link in a chain of relationships. At the bottom were the serfs, followed by the lords and bishops and kings. Near the top was the Pope since he was sometimes a worldly and spiritual leader. At the highest point was God, ruling over all. German social organization stressed the loyalty of warriors to a powerful chieftain. This system evolved into an alliance of a king with his noblemen and knights. Consequently, feudalism provided a foundation on which a new society could be built.

REASONING

1. What is the main idea in the first paragraph? In the third paragraph?

2. Based on the first paragraph, what can we infer about the quality of life in the Roman Empire before its fall?

3. If feudalism existed in the United States today, which of the following posi-

tions would be most comparable to a king? a) manager of a city, b) governor of a state, c) president of the country

4. Which organizational pattern does the author use in the first paragraph? In the third paragraph?

5. The tone of this passage can best be described as_____.

6. Who is most likely presenting the information in this passage? (point of view)

REFERRING

7. According to the passage, why did feudalism emerge after the fall of the Roman Empire?

8. Based on the passage, what was the most important contribution of the Roman Empire to feudalism?

9. Name the lowest and highest members of feudalistic society.

VOCABULARY

Meanings of words:

10. genius (paragraph 1) _____

11. factions (paragraph 1) _____

12. hybrid (paragraph 2) _____

13. hierarchical (paragraph 3) _____

EXERCISE 2

In our own culture, creating poetry is a solitary act perfected through trial combinations of words and sounds. If we write something we don't like, we can always scratch it out and begin anew. The act of composing a finished product before a critical audience is beyond our realm of experience.

Before the existence of written language, poets from many countries created their narratives and songs during fast-paced performance. Their poems were not worked out and memorized in advance. Instead, they were <u>shaped</u> during performance according to audience response. What is it about oral tradition that makes this <u>feat</u> possible?

In 1933, oral tradition was very much alive in parts of rural Yugoslavia where Milman Parry and Albert Lord recorded Serbo-Croatian epic singers, <u>guslari</u>, as a living <u>analog</u> to their theory of the oral origin of the *Iliad* and the *Odyssey* ...

During their field research, Parry and Lord found that the rapid oral creation of metrical lines is done by using familiar expressions and patterned speech evolved over centuries of performance by guslari who could neither read nor write. The tales are built around <u>recurrent</u> themes absorbed by the singers in much the same way infants acquire language. Themes and formulas are useful, but not <u>fixed</u>. Each recreation by a singer is, in fact, an original creation.

Studies of heroic epics have been the focus of considerable research, but some scholars believe that this work has overlooked the prevalence of poetry in many aspects of oral tradition. With the help of a National Endowment for the Humanities Research Grant, four specialists formed an <u>interdisciplinary</u> team to investigate the theory that the oral process in guslari tales is not a singular phenomenon, but rather a mode of thinking and communicating that pervades the entire culture.

— *Newsletter for the National Endowment for the Humanities. VII:5, Washington, D.C., 1977.*

REASONING

1. What is the main idea in the second paragraph? In the fourth paragraph?

2. What does the existence of an oral tradition suggest about the use of language in rural Yugoslavia?

3. The tone of paragraph four can best be described as _____
   _____.

4. Which organizational pattern does the author use in the fourth paragraph? In the fifth paragraph?

REFERRING

5. In the first and second paragraphs, the author indicates that one difference between poetry written in isolation and poetry spoken before an audience is _____
   _____
   _____

6. What techniques do the guslari favor for the oral transmission of their tales?

7. Why have scholars and specialists been interested in the guslari tales?

VOCABULARY

Meaning of words:

8. shaped (paragraph 2) _____

9. feat (paragraph 2) _____

10. guslari (paragraph 3) _____

11. analog (paragraph 3) _____

12. recurrent (paragraph 4) _____

13. fixed (paragraph 4) _____

14. interdisciplinary (paragraph 5) _____

PRACTICE READING TESTS

Practice CPE Reading Test One

PASSAGE ONE

SCHOOL

Sitting up in bed, Tom began to think. "I don't want to go to school, but what excuse will work? I don't have a fever, but yes, I feel a headache coming on. There it is, all over my forehead. A guy like me, nearly six feet tall shouldn't have to worry about parents trying to stop me from not going to school."

"The other kids think it must be nice to have a father who is a doctor. They say, 'Wow! Dude! With the money he makes, you can have anything!' What they don't know is the pressure. Dad tells me never to miss a day of school and to get all A's like he did."

"Yes, the top of my head is really starting to hurt a lot. A few minutes more and the pain won't go away for hours. My dad's very moral too. He taught me not to lie. He can lay on more guilt for just one little lie than any son can bear. My head better really hurt."

"Yes, Dad, I'm awake."
"No, I don't feel like breakfast today. I've got a headache. A bad one."

"Son, I majored in headaches in medical school. You can trust me. What is it?"

"It's a killer headache, Dad. It feels like ten algebra books are stacked on top of my head."

"It sounds serious, Son. You'd better stay home from school. You must be coming down with that flu that's going around, and you'll be contagious for 48 hours or so. Better cancel that date with Cindy tomorrow night. You won't be her friend if you make her sick."

It feels like it will probably be gone by tonight."

"Oh, it's a predictable headache. Yes, it's going to be gone by the time your first period class starts. You'd better get going, Son. It's a long walk to school if you miss the bus."

1. What was the author's intent in the passage?

   A. to describe
   B. to amuse
   C. to explain
   D. to compare
   E. to argue

2. What is the meaning of the word predictable in the last paragraph?

   A. possible
   B. ordinary
   C. severe
   D. convenient
   E. small

3. What is the correct sequence of events in the story?

   1. Dad asks his son if he wants breakfast.
   2. Son decides he is not going to school.
   3. Father tells son to hurry.
   4. Son makes a date with Cindy.

   A. 3, 4, 1, 2
   B. 2, 1, 3, 4
   C. 3, 1, 2, 4
   D. 4, 3, 1, 2
   E. 4, 2, 1, 3

4. The main reason the son tries to avoid school is because

   A. he has to get A's all the time.
   B. he is old enough to decide what to do.
   C. he has the flu.

D. he pretends to have a headache.
E. he is sick.

5. What is the meaning of the phrase <u>lay on</u> in paragraph 3?

   A. impose
   B. refuse
   C. shout
   D. preach
   E. count

6. In the conversation, the father's attitude is

   A. unsuspecting.
   B. proud.
   C. annoyed.
   D. sympathetic.
   E. skeptical.

7. Where does the story most likely take place?

   A. in the city
   B. in a large hospital
   C. in a suburban home
   D. in the boy's bedroom
   E. in the father's office

8. The story is told from the point of view of

   A. the author.
   B. the son.
   C. the father.
   D. the doctor.
   E. the teacher.

9. The best statement of the main idea of this passage is

   A. school should be missed only for serious reasons.
   B. fathers demand a lot from their children.
   C. no one should ever get a headache.
   D. fathers who are doctors are better at diagnosing illnesses than regular parents.
   E. telling a lie is wrong, but liars are never punished.

10. Which of the following is <u>not true</u> according to the passage?

   A. The son is six feet tall.
   B. The father is older than the son.
   C. The son has a headache.
   D. The father believes in honesty and achievement.
   E. The father and son are the only characters.

PASSAGE TWO

The conflict between children and parents is a universal theme found frequently in literature. This conflict is universal because it is not confined to one country's literature. Archaeological evidence reveals that family friction existed from the beginning of written literature. The resolution of the parent-child conflict can be tragic at times, although some authors have treated the topic humorously, or even satirically.

Authors who portray the parent-child conflict seem to sympathize more often with the child rather than with the parent. In *Romeo and Juliet,* Shakespeare focuses on the plight of two young lovers who are forbidden marriage because of a feud between their families. Juliet's cranky father values social status much more than Juliet's love for Romeo. The reasons why their families forbid their marriage are seen as petty and selfish. Finally, in *The Wild Swans,* the Danish author, Hans Christian Anderson, tells the story of a wicked queen stepmother who banishes a young princess from the castle and turns her brothers into swans. However, the innocent princess cures her brothers of the swan curse and eventually becomes the queen of the land instead.

Sometimes a parent-child conflict in literature depicts the parent favorably and the child unfavorably. The Old Testament story of King David and his son, Absalom, centers around a father-son conflict that ends in tragedy. Absalom, David's son, tries to murder his father and take the king's wives for his own. David is humble and <u>benevolent</u> throughout this ordeal and commands that Absalom not be slain in battle. Despite the King's efforts, another brother kills Absalom in battle anyway.

Occasionally, the authors poke fun at both parents and children. Their differences give rise to humorous situations. In *The Fantastics,* a Broadway musical, two fathers try to trick their <u>gullible</u> son and daughter into marrying each other. The fathers stage a rape, so the son can rescue the daughter from her abductor. However, the plan backfires, the children discover that the rape is a trick, and no marriage takes place. The author sympathizes with neither the parents nor the children. All four appear petty and foolish in the end.

11. What is the best definition of of <u>benevolent</u> in the third paragraph?

    A. quiet
    B. truthful
    C. vindictive
    D. indifferent
    E. kind

12. The attitude of the author toward the subject is

    A. critical.
    B. objective.
    C. argumentative.
    D. subjective.
    E. supportive.

13. According to the passage, authors seem to sympathize most frequently with

    A. parents.
    B. children.
    C. families.
    D. young lovers.
    E. princes and princesses.

14. Which of the following works portrays the parent-child conflict humorously?

    A. *David and Absalom*
    B. *Romeo and Juliet*
    C. *The Wild Swans*
    D. *The Fantastics*
    E. Shakespeare

15. Based on the information in the passage, one can infer that

    A. parent-child conflicts first appeared in literature 200 years ago.

B. Romeo and Juliet finally got married.
C. *The Wild Swans* ends happily.
D. David tries to kill Absalom but is unsuccessful.
E. rape is a frequent cause of family conflict.

16. According to the passage, parent-child conflicts in literature resolve themselves

   A. in various ways.
   B. in tragic patterns.
   C. through humor or satire.
   D. with sad endings.
   E. neither sadly nor happily.

17. The word <u>gullible</u> in the fourth paragraph means

   A. gull-like.
   B. young.
   C. silly.
   D. lucky.
   E. naive.

18. Which of the following statements would be the best conclusion for the passage?

   A. Shakespeare presents the parent-child conflict most realistically.
   B. Parents always triumph over their children in family conflicts.
   C. *The Fantastics* is more entertaining than other literary works because it is a musical.
   D. Absalom is King David's only son.
   E. Parent-child conflicts in literature have existed for a long time.

19. Parent-child conflicts could be reduced if

   A. daughters would not run away with their boyfriends.
   B. sons would not be so jealous of their fathers.
   C. parents would allow their children more freedom.
   D. parents and children would try to understand each other.
   E. parents and children would not communicate with each other.

20. This passage is primarily about

   A. parent-child relationships.
   B. sympathetic treatment of children in literature.
   C. parent-child conflicts in literature.
   D. recent research on parent-child conflicts.
   E. examples of literature from the past 2000 years.

PASSAGE THREE

Gestalt psychologists believe that human beings and animals solve problems by perceiving relationships between different parts of a stimulus. The resulting insight or <u>cognitive structure</u> becomes evidence that learning has occurred. The individual then stores this new pattern of organization in the memory for possible application to future situations.

Unlike behaviorists, Gestalt psychologists hold that mental processes are not a matter of making random associations between stimuli. Learning involves an organized perception of reality generated by connecting experiences together.

In further opposition to the behaviorists, the Gestaltists do not arrange experiments with predetermined conclusions. Instead, they create problematic situations which would be resolved through human or animal insight. In their view, organisms interact ingeniously with the environment rather than reacting passively in a series of conditioned responses.

Wolfgang Kohler (1887-1967), an early Gestalt psychologist, worked with chimpanzees on the island of Tenerife. Suspending a banana from the ceiling of their cage, he watched how the chimps tried to reach their food. At some point, the chimpanzees seemed to suddenly perceive a relationship between some boxes in the cage. By stacking and climbing them, the animals were able to reach and eat the banana. With poles of varying lengths, the results were also the same. The chimpanzees eventually "<u>figured out</u>" how to join the pole sections together so they could knock down the banana. Subsequently, they applied their knowledge of pole use to new situations.

Wheeler and Perkins found that even fish display primitive forms of insight. In their experiments, goldfish would only receive food if they responded to different light intensities. Although these researchers varied the light intensities, the fish learned how to choose the brightest, medium, or dimmest light to get their food.

Objections to Gestalt psychology arise out of its tendency to view all learning as insight. For example, some tasks like memorizing a telephone or Social Security number are repetitive or mechanical. However, Gestaltists contend that even memorization includes finding a pattern of meaning in those numbers. While insight does not necessarily mean comprehending all aspects of a situation, it does involve the identifying of relationships in those numbers. Sensing a pattern in a task is enough for insightful learning to occur.

21. According to the passage, objections to Gestalt psychology focus on its

    A. tendency to emphasize memorizing.
    B. repetitive tasks in learning.
    C. tendency to overlook the role of insight.
    D. emphasis on insight and patterns of learning.
    E. narrow interpretation of learning

22. In which ways do the Gestaltists and behaviorists differ?

    I. Nature of experiments
    II. Use of animal or human subjects
    III. Role of insight

    A. I
    B. I and II
    C. I, II and III
    D. II and III
    E. I and III

206

23. Besides chimpanzees, this passage states that Gestalt psychologists have also done research with

A. monkeys.
B. humans.
C. animals.
D. goldfish.
E. behaviorists.

24. The best meaning for figured out as used in the passage is

A. reasoned.
B. discussed.
C. confused.
D. admitted.
E. overcame.

25. In the first paragraph, the phrase cognitive structure most nearly means

A. question.
B. formula.
C. clue.
D. understanding.
E. shape.

26. With which of the following statements would the author most likely agree?

A. For Gestalt psychologists, learning involves the ability to perceive relationships between experiences.
B. Learning occurs in different patterns by making random associations.
C. Wheeler and Perkins were not as successful as Kohler in their research.
D. Gestaltists and behaviorists agree on the nature of the learning process.
E. Lower organisms do not display learning as readily as higher organisms do.

27. For the fourth paragraph, the best statement of the main idea is

A. animals are capable of finding food even if it is hard to reach.
B. Kohler's experiment with chimpanzees shows that insightful learning can occur.
C. for chimpanzees, poles work better than boxes for learning tasks.
D. Kohler was an early Gestalt psychologist who experimented with chimpanzees.
E. chimpanzees can be motivated to use tools if they are hungry.

28. In paragraphs 1 and 2, the topic is explained through

A. narration.
B. comparison.
C. analogy.
D. contrast.

29. In which of the following situations would Gestalt psychology most likely be used?

A. Eating a hot dog
B. Studying for a mid-term examination
C. Sleeping in a warm bed on a cold night
D. Dressing for work every morning
E. Watching chimpanzees eat a banana at the zoo

30. For Gestalt psychologists, one of the primary reasons for storing information in the memory is to

A. avoid mistakes in the future.
B. expand one's understanding.
C. decrease anxiety.
D. adapt the information to other situations.

PASSAGE FOUR

Containing 72% of the earth's supply of fresh water, 90% of the world's ice, with winds blowing as fast as 185 miles per hour, and with temperatures <u>plunging</u> to 100 degrees below zero, Antarctica's landscape is breathtaking, its climate life-taking. For centuries, Antarctica was almost unknown. In 1838, the U.S. Navy commissioned Lieutenant Charles Wilkes to explore the South Pole near the center of Antarctica. He saw enough of Antarctica to prove it was a continent. In 1911, a British team and a Norwegian team had a race to the South Pole. Five Norwegians reached the Pole first and returned unharmed. The British party perished in the bitter cold.

Antarctica remains full of mysteries and contradictions. Scientists have uncovered plant, tree, and animal fossils of species originally found only in warm climates. Today there are only lichens, mosses, three flowering plants, one herb, and two grasses that grow where the ice recedes in the December summer. What triggered the <u>metamorphosis</u>? No one knows.

Antarctica has the coldest (–126.9 degrees Fahrenheit) temperature ever recorded. It contains enough ice to cover the United States with a layer two miles thick. In some places, the ice is 14,000 feet deep, covering mountains and valleys that are below sea level. In the mountains near the sea, scientists have found the purest air in the world, studied the sun circling 24 hours a day overhead, and drilled into glaciers, bringing up samples that froze before the last ice age over 1.5 million years ago.

In this, the coldest place on earth, is Mt. Erebus, an active volcano with a steaming, 1,000 degree centigrade, bubbling lake of lava in the middle. How about a sauna in an ice cave and a dinner cooked in a volcanic hot spring? A U.S. company will take you to the South Pole for $35,000 apiece. Once you get there, your life will be in constant, imminent peril, and pretty much in the hands of your guide. There are no hotels, and the 1,000 or so scientists who live there now really don't want you, will not share their quarters with you, sell you souvenirs, let you land on their ice strip, nor be liable for you. They will, however, try to rescue you in an emergency.

31. In the second paragraph, the word <u>metamorphosis</u> can best be defined as

    A. change.
    B. vegetation.
    C. fossils.
    D. mystery.
    E. situation.

32. Where is Mt. Erebus located?

    A. the earth
    B. Antarctica
    C. near the sea
    D. at the South Pole
    E. in a volcano

33. According to the passage, why did the British and the Norwegians have a contest?

    A. to explore an unknown continent.
    B. to prove that the South Pole exists.
    C. to measure their ability to resist cold.
    D. to determine which group would reach the South Pole first.
    E. to decide which team could survive in a dangerous environment.

34. In paragraph 3, the word <u>samples</u> probably refers to

    A. plants.
    B. plants and animals.
    C. air.
    D. water.
    E. ice.

35. Paragraph three is primarily

    A. analogy.
    B. criticism.
    C. description.
    D. process analysis.
    E. historical background.

36. The best statement of the main idea of the passage is

    A. a visit to the South Pole is risky and expensive.
    B. few plants and animals survive in the bitter cold of Antarctica.
    C. Antarctica is a continent filled with beauty and peril.
    D. Antarctica was one of the last continents to be explored.
    E. sub-zero cold, snow, and ice are always present in Antarctica.

37. The author states that the reason warm-weather species no longer exist in Antarctica

    A. seems to be a mystery.
    B. results from the short summers.
    C. is now being researched.
    D. is only partly understood.
    E. has to do with the glaciers.

38. Based on the information in the first paragraph, if Antarctica's climate would gradually become as warm as Florida's, what would most likely happen to the rest of the earth?

    A. Many places would be colder than they are now.
    B. Some places would be colder and others warmer than they are now.
    C. Antarctica would have a more tropical climate with palm trees and sunshine.
    D. Many parts of the world would experience earthquakes and volcanic eruptions.
    E. Coastal areas of the world would become flooded.

39. Of the three items below, which would be the most important for a college student's knowledge of Antarctica?

    1. A cost of $35,000 for a tour
    2. Presence of glaciers and volcanoes
    3. Coldest climate on earth

    A. 1
    B. 2
    C. 2 and 3
    D. 1 and 2
    E. 3

40. Plunging in paragraph one means

    A. shifting.
    B. dipping.
    C. rising.
    D. flying.
    E. remaining.

Practice CPE Reading Test Two

PASSAGE ONE

A NIGHT TO REMEMBER

The long June day ended all too quickly for the Jones family. Claude, Hazel, and their children, Mattie and Ernest, had gone for a picnic in Ashley Park. The cool night breezes felt good, <u>dispersing</u> the heat of a Georgia afternoon. Claude glanced up across the trees toward the town's skyline. Beyond the electric lights, stars began twinkling in the darkening sky. "Such a peaceful place, " he thought, "and no rat race to run." He pulled a bloom of wild honeysuckle and gave it to Hazel. She smiled. "Let's remember this good time," he said.

The Jones family packed the blankets, folding chairs, and cooler into the old Chevy station wagon. As they left the park, Claude looked in the rearview mirror for one last glimpse of what he told Hazel was paradise. Paying little attention to the car following them, he noticed the children napping against their seats.

The car followed the Jones family even more closely now. In his mirror, Claude saw the driver flash his headlights on and off. Hazel thought it might be the police, but Claude thought the car should be clearly marked, and why wouldn't a police officer use a flashing light? "We can't go home," he whispered to Hazel. She took out a pen and wrote a full description of the dirty blue Mustang and got the license plate number. Claude decided to drive to the Pinetree Mall instead. Then he made a sharp U-turn around the road divider. The driver behind him did the same. Claude felt a <u>sinking feeling</u> in his gut.

Claude recalled that the police station was less than two miles from the mall. "That's where we'll go," he concluded. Pulling up to the station, Claude hobbled out the door in his sneakers, yelling at Hazel to lock it and lean on the horn. The strange driver behind them suddenly backed away from the curb and drove off in a cloud of dust. Just then, Claude entered the police station.

1. Claude is

    A. Hazel's father.
    B. a member of the Jones family.
    C. Hazel's husband.
    D. Mattie's uncle.
    E. Ernest's brother.

2. In paragraph three, the best meaning for <u>sinking feeling</u> is

    A. dread.
    B. excitement.
    C. confusion.
    D. sadness.
    E. indifference.

3. Which of the following statements best expresses the main point of the passage?

    A. Georgia summers are unpredictable.
    B. The Jones family knows how to fight crime.
    C. Evil is sometimes present in the happiest of situations.
    D. Picnics are safer in the daytime than at night.
    E. Claude Jones is brave and scared.

4. In paragraph one, <u>dispersing</u> most likely means

    A. mixing.
    B. bringing.
    C. raising.
    D. adding.
    E. scattering.

5. In which order do the events in the story take place?

    I. The Jones family leaves Ashley Park.
   II. Claude finds the police station.
 III. A strange car follows the Jones family to the mall.

    A. I, II, III
    B. I, III, II
    C. III, II, I
    D. III, I, II
    E. II, I, III

6. Claude's feelings about Ashley Park suggest that

    A. he does not appreciate nature.
    B. he enjoys the night air.
    C. he prefers to be with Hazel rather than with Mattie and Ernest.
    D. he considers it an escape from life's worries.
    E. he would rather live in the country.

7. After the picnic, the Jones family had planned to

    A. shop at the mall.
    B. return to their house.
    C. leave the city.
    D. visit the police station.
    E. drive around town.

8. How often does the Jones family go on a picnic to Ashley park?

    A. The story does not say.
    B. They go once in a while.
    C. They go once a month.
    D. They go every Fourth of July.
    E. This was their first time.

9. The mood of the last paragraph can best be described as

    A. hopeless.
    B. sentimental.
    C. humorous.
    D. tragic.
    E. suspenseful.

10. Which method of organization does the author use in the third paragraph?

    A. exposition
    B. description
    C. comparison
    D. narration
    E. analysis

PASSAGE TWO

For Black America, the Harlem Renaissance triggered a burst of artistic energy. Between 1920 and 1940, New York City's Harlem district was a hub for aspiring writers, painters, sculptors and musicians. They shared in common a need to find and express their true Black identity in an impersonal environment where it could be easily lost. For several generations, Northern and Southern Blacks had lost touch with their history since slavery often fostered the breakup of family groups, and few could trace their ancestors. Consequently, for many, artistic expression was one way of asserting Black identity. In addition, art created a sense of unity between the present and the forgotten past.

Aaron Douglas, a Black painter from Kansas, was one artist who expressed the African heritage Black Americans share. Beginning as an illustrator for white magazines such as *Vanity Fair*, he soon developed his own unique style. He favored the more abstract designs of African art and often painted two-dimensional figures. Douglas frequently portrays them dancing or making music which are two key motifs in African art. One of his most famous paintings is a group of four murals now housed at the New York Public Library. Completed in 1934, these large wall panels show the history of Black Americans from their African origins to contemporary urban society. Black silhouetted figures stand out against green or violet backgrounds. A feeling of movement flows out from the painting to the viewer. Primitive African tribesmen carry spears and tired sharecroppers work the soil. In the last mural, a musician proudly plays a saxophone, affirming the centrality of music in Black culture.

Richard Barthe, a sculptor of the Harlem Renaissance, also stressed African roots in his statues. *African Dancers* (1933) depicts the freedom and joy of primitive dancing. The young girl's expression is almost mystical. Another work, *Feral Benga* (1935), shows a male dancer raising a curved machete in his right hand. Barthe achieves a graceful balance in the figure by lowering the left hand near the legs. Thus, he repeats the motion of the sword in a downward movement.

11. According to the passage, Black American artists turned to their African past for inspiration because

    A. no one had explored their African heritage.
    B. they wanted to forget their present condition.
    C. the art of Africa was older and richer than American art.
    D. they needed to assert their Black identity.
    E. they liked using music and dancing in their works.

12. What is the author's attitude toward Black American art?

    A. He is negative and critical.
    B. He is objective and neutral.
    C. He is sympathetic and complimentary.
    D. He is argumentative and opinionated.
    E. He is boastful and self-centered.

13. In paragraph two, the word silhouetted most likely means

    A. outlined.
    B. bulky.
    C. fragile.
    D. restless.
    E. tiny.

14. According to the passage, what major work was created in 1934?

    A. *African Dancer*
    B. The Douglas murals
    C. Harlem Renaissance
    D. *Vanity Fair*
    E. *Feral Benga*

15. Based on the passage, which of the statements below would the author support?

    1. Art provides a continuity between the past and the present.
    2. Slavery was one reason Blacks lost their artistic heritage.
    3. Richard Barthe created impressive paintings and sculptures.
    4. Aaron Douglas and Richard Barthe were artists of the Harlem Renaissance.

    A. 1, 2, 3, 4
    B. 2 and 4
    C. 1, 2, and 4
    D. 1 and 4
    E. 1 and 2

16. According to the passage, Aaron Douglas included sharecroppers in his paintings because

    A. they were part of Black history.
    B. they were interesting subjects to paint.
    C. he enjoyed variety in his work.
    D. his father was a sharecropper.
    E. they were easy to draw on murals.

17. In paragraph two, motifs means

    A. gods.
    B. colors.
    C. sports.
    D. subjects.
    E. fantasies.

18. This passage focuses primarily on

    A. African art from 1920-1940.
    B. the effects of slavery on Black Americans.
    C. the influence of the Harlem Renaissance on Black American artists.
    D. Aaron Douglas, a Black-American painter.
    E. the Harlem Renaissance and its relationship to African history.

19. In paragraph one, we can infer that Black artists needed to express their identity because New York City was

    A. huge.
    B. friendly.
    C. exciting.
    D. miserable.
    E. unfriendly.

20. The passage states that the Harlem Renaissance started in

    A. the 1930's.
    B. the 1920's.
    C. the 1940's.
    D. 1922.
    E. 1934.

PASSAGE THREE

The earliest hunters and gatherers belonged to the Lower Paleolithic Period. Lasting 1,850,000 years, these human-like creatures scavenged for the remains of animals and did not become skilled hunters or users of fire until the end of that period. They lived in the open or in caves.

In the Middle Paleolithic Period, Neanderthal Man dominated the hunting and gathering societies and used symbols, speech, clothing, and tools. During the Upper Paleolithic Period, advanced hunting and gathering societies emerged. These societies used the spear thrower, the bow and arrow, many diverse tools, and began to live in earth houses and tents. They drew pictures, sculpted, performed fertility rites, and practiced magic. In the one thousand year period of the Mesolithic Era, hunting and gathering societies reached their apex. They began to fish, gather wild grain, domesticate wild sheep and dogs, and manufacture advanced tools and weapons.

In contrast to the hunting and gathering societies, the horticultural societies came into being rather recently, around 7,000 B.C. The Horticultural Period is called the era of effective food production. This society was characterized by more permanent dwellings, cultivation of the soil, more possessions, use of pottery, weaving, metals, and contained larger populations than the hunting and gathering societies. Advanced horticultural societies derived from these basic characteristics and persisted longer in China. Horticulture developed independently in prehistoric America, and the Mayan civilization was one of the most advanced societies of this type.

Around 3,000 B.C., another kind of society began to form. This society, which is called the Agrarian, made a tremendously important contribution to human progress. That contribution was the plow. It freed society to use animal energy, and it helped to sustain the fertility of the soil. Writing was mastered by only a few. Formal legal systems were created, and grains were the main medium of monetary exchange.

A merchant class soon emerged, creating products which stirred the desires and needs of the population. Literate and illiterate classes became very distinct. The smelting of iron proved to be the most important technological advance of the Agrarian societies. Advanced Agrarian civilizations discovered the catapult, gunpowder, the screw, the wheelbarrow, and windmills. The size of these societies ranged from tiny towns to great countries. Division of labor became more pronounced.

21. The word apex in the second paragraph is used to mean

    A. land.
    B. death.
    C. highest point.
    D. goal.
    E. lowest point.

22. As used in the first paragraph, scavenged most likely means

    A. avoided.
    B. ran.
    C. hopped.
    D. looked.
    E. fought.

23. In this passage, what is the main method of organization?

    A. personal opinion
    B. contrasting ideas
    C. historical analysis
    D. cause and effect
    E. critical evaluation

24. The author states that horticultural societies were

    A. larger and persisted longer than previous societies.
    B. more dependent on gathering and hunting than previous societies.

C. less dependent on farming than agricultural societies.
D. more war-like and independent than other societies.
E. more successful in China than in other places.

25. The ancient Egyptian civilization was an example of an advanced Agrarian society. Based on this fact, one can conclude that

   A. most Egyptians were merchants.
   B. there were few laborers and much wealth.
   C. all classes were well-educated.
   D. Egyptian culture was complex and sophisticated.
   E. Egyptian civilization was successful and lasted for 300 years.

26. Which of the following tools was most valued by inhabitants of the Paleolithic Periods?

   I. spear
   II. bow and arrow
   III. fishing pole

   A. I
   B. I and II
   C. I and III
   D. II and III
   E. I, II, and III

27. The primary purpose of paragraph three is to

   A. tell about the Mayan civilization.
   B. show how horticultural societies changed.
   C. describe food production in the horticultural society.
   D. give examples of advanced horticultural societies.
   E. discuss the Horticultural Period.

28. It can be inferred from the passage that one of the necessary requirements for an advanced civilization is

   A. adequate housing.
   B. diverse tools.
   C. enough food.

D. strong weapons.
E. smelting of iron.

29. According to the passage, which of the following is not a product of Agrarian societies?

   A. windmills
   B. plow
   C. screw
   D. weaving
   E. writing

30. In the last sentence of paragraph four, the phrase "monetary exchange" suggests that grains were used for

   A. money.
   B. food.
   C. animal feed.
   D. status.
   E. sacrifice.

PASSAGE FOUR

Matter consists of four states: solid, liquid, gas, and plasma. However, plasma exists only at very high temperatures. It is matter composed of very highly charged atomic particles. In plasma, ions and electrons move around in wave-like motions unlike gases where the motion of particles is random. Magnetic forces also affect plasma, and because it exhibits properties different from solids, liquids or gases, scientists consider plasma to be a fourth state of matter.

The surface of the sun is in a plasma state. Gases in the atmosphere surrounding the sun, known as the corona, reach a temperature of 3,000,000 degrees F. which causes them to expand. These gas atoms collide, lose their electrons, and become electrically charged particles called ions. As these ions constantly leave the atmosphere of the sun, they become solar wind. The strong magnetic forces around the earth prevent particles from the solar wind from hitting our planet.

On the earth, plasma occurs naturally in lightning bolts. Heating or passing an electrical current through gases can create plasma. Applying this principle, technicians heat neon gas to make a luminous plasma used for florescent lighting in our many shopping districts. Heating argon gas with electricity will create plasma useful in arc welding. When the plasma is sprayed on the metals to be welded, filler material is applied. With the extremely high temperatures present, it is possible to merge metals that would be difficult to weld by any other method.

In the future, scientists will use a plasma heated millions of degrees to develop a controlled thermonuclear reaction for energy production. The problem is that so far no one has found a container that would not melt from such heat. At those temperatures,

plasma also tends to escape from its container. If the walls of this container were cooled to avoid melting, the plasma would become too cold to produce fusion. This blending of plasma particles to generate energy is an important goal for the researchers of tomorrow.

31. The main topic of paragraph three is

    A. practical uses for plasma.
    B. electricity and plasma.
    C. plasma at high temperatures.
    D. the presence of plasma in lightning.

32. Plasma around the sun changes to solar wind because

    A. the plasma clashes with the earth's magnetic forces.
    B. the corona absorbs the plasma.
    C. the plasma turns into superheated ions.
    D. the sun explodes periodically.
    E. the plasma's ions and electrons combine.

33. What is the principal problem connected with using plasma in a thermonuclear reaction?

    A. The reaction is uncontrollable.
    B. The plasma becomes very hot.
    C. The plasma becomes too cold.
    D. The container is too small.
    E. The container melts.

34. In paragraph one, random is used to mean

    A. purposeful.
    B. calm.
    C. constant.
    D. haphazard.
    E. slow.

35. If plasma could be used for energy production, what would be its broadest application?

    A. Fueling automobiles.
    B. Generating electricity.
    C. Heating and cooling homes.
    D. Creating water power.
    E. Supplying food.

36. In the second paragraph, the author explains the subject through

   A. analysis.
   B. argument.
   C. classification.
   D. sequence of events.
   E. description.

37. Why is plasma considered a unique type of matter?

   A. Plasma is similar yet different from solids.
   B. Only plasma is composed of electrons and ions.
   C. Plasma is present only at certain temperatures and responds to magnetism.
   D. Plasma is more common than other elements.

38. In the fourth paragraph, the best definition for <u>fusion</u> is

   A. gas.
   B. heat.
   C. electricity.
   D. compounds.
   E. bonding.

39. The tone of this passage can best be described as

   A. biased.
   B. subjective.
   C. humorous.
   D. dramatic.
   E. objective.

40. The reader can infer that the author of this passage is probably a(n)

   A. lawyer.
   B. scientist.
   C. physician.
   D. business manager.
   E. engineer.

Practice CPE Reading Test Three

PASSAGE ONE

HOME AGAIN

Josh sat in 100 mile long bumper to bumper traffic on Interstate 75. The cars inched slowly south out of Chattanooga, Tennessee. He had just finished installing cabinets in two new drugstores. "122 years after the Civil War, we're still fighting the Battle of Atlanta," he thought.

Josh had plenty of time to think now. He remembered how snow paralyzed the city months ago. Atlanta had become one big amusement park. If you dared to drive, you could choose between bumper cars, skate and shake, or the backslide advance. He could still see the helpless old man in his big Buick sliding backward down a country road. Smart people stayed at home.

David would be finishing sixth grade soon. This boy had <u>sprung up</u> like a Georgia pine. Josh imagined that one day David would lift him over his head with one hand. Fantasy videos, StarTrek, and science were his main interests, with school far down on the list. The court settlement allowed David to visit his father every other weekend. With regular shots, the boy's allergies were no longer a problem, so they'd be able to fish at Cross Creek on Saturday. Josh looked forward to tilling the garden in a few weeks. Removing rocks was a constant chore. Surely the rock pile was big enough now to build the Great Wall of China.

The traffic began moving again. When Josh got back, he'd pack the tent, sleeping bags, and cooking gear in the truck. Then he'd be picking up David. They'd be together for the whole weekend in a <u>secluded</u> mountain woodland with no one around for miles. He could already smell the freshly caught trout sizzling over an open fire.

1. In paragraph three, the phrase <u>sprung up</u> means

   A. grown.
   B. shook.
   C. fallen.
   D. jumped.

2. Why is Josh leaving Chattanooga?

   A. to install new cabinets in some drugstores.
   B. to take his son fishing.
   C. to pack his truck.
   D. to visit Atlanta.

3. From the passage, we can conclude that Josh is

   A. married.
   B. separated.
   C. dating.
   D. divorced.

4. The word <u>secluded</u> in paragraph four most likely means

   A. beautiful.
   B. distant.
   C. high.
   D. quiet.

5. The correct sequence of events in the passage is

   I. Josh thinks about picking up David.
   II. Josh remembers a recent snowfall
   III. The traffic moves toward Atlanta.
   IV. Josh sits in stalled traffic on Interstate 75.

   A. I, II, III, IV
   B. II, IV, III, I
   C. IV, II, III, I
   D. IV, II, I, III

218

6. The best statement of the main idea of this passage is that

   A. Traffic jams occur frequently on Interstate highways.
   B. Snow creates problems on Atlanta's roads.
   C. Josh and David enjoy fishing at Cross Creek.
   D. A traffic delay allows time to reflect on one's life.

7. At what time of year does the story occur?

   A. early winter
   B. spring
   C. summer
   D. winter

8. When Josh uses the expression "fighting the Battle of Atlanta," we can infer that the traffic is

   A. pleasant and peaceful.
   B. funny and unusual.
   C. risky and heavy.
   D. smooth and steady.

9. According to the passage, during snowy weather, Josh would probably

   A. walk to work.
   B. remain at home.
   C. drive carefully.
   D. travel on back roads only.

10. What is the tone of the last paragraph?

    A. expectant
    B. fearful
    C. humorous
    D. neutral

PASSAGE TWO

The musical is a distinctly American art form, a blend of drama, music, singing, and dancing. Written for the stage, this popular form of entertainment includes a simple story line with touches of comedy. Its primary purpose is to amuse an audience and to offer unique song and dance numbers. A musical usually consists of two acts. The first act has richer musical material. The second act contains frequent <u>reprises</u> which repeat portions of the most memorable tunes and dances from the first act.

The style of a musical is simpler than an opera. Whereas opera is almost entirely sung, the musical mixes dialogue and song. While operatic characters convey an air of heroism and nobility, the actors in a musical are ordinary and down-to-earth. An opera is typically the result of one composer, with specialized musical training, working alone. In a musical, a team of artists — songwriters, playwrights, designers, technicians — <u>collaborate</u> on a production.

The two basic kinds of musicals are musical comedy and musical drama. Singing and dancing make musical comedy. The story line is often weak and flimsy, and producers build the show around star performers, catchy songs, and spectacular dances. *Gentlemen Prefer Blondes* (1949) highlighted Carol Channing and the hit song "Diamonds Are A Girl's Best Friend." Musical drama combines songs and dances with a stronger plot, deeper characterizations, and more serious themes. The songs develop the story and reveal characters. A good example of musical drama is *Showboat* (1927) which takes place along the Mississippi River in the 1800's. Another example is *Man of La Mancha* (1965) based on Cervantes' world-famous novel. This musical drama successfully captures the complexities of the main character, a frustrated but lovable idealist. The songs,

dialogue, dancing, and story all contribute to a highly unified production.

11. Paragraph two is primarily about

    A. opera and musicals.
    B. musical drama.
    C. musical comedy.
    D. the American musical.

12. In the second paragraph, what is the best definition of <u>collaborate</u>?

    A. struggle
    B. work together
    C. break up
    D. avoid

13. The earliest musical drama mentioned in the passage is

    A. *Gentlemen Prefer Blondes.*
    B. *Showboat.*
    C. *Man of La Mancha.*
    D. Cervantes.

14. The author views the musical as

    A. less complex than opera.
    B. more complex than opera.
    C. more recent than opera.
    D. longer than opera.

15. The author develops the ideas in the first paragraph by

    A. presenting an opinion.
    B. developing a sequence.
    C. defining a term.
    D. giving examples.

16. As used in the passage, the best meaning for <u>reprises</u> is

    A. songs.
    B. dances.
    C. operas.
    D. repetitions.

17. Based on the passage, which of the following statements would be correct?

    I. Musicals serve to entertain the audience.
   II. Carol Channing is the greatest star of musical comedy.
  III. Musical drama is more unified than musical comedy.

    A. I, II, III
    B. I, II
    C. I, III
    D. II, III

18. According to the passage, opera and the musical differ because

    A. the musical is more popular than opera.
    B. opera has more characters than the musical.
    C. the musical presents songs in a complex style.
    D. opera contains more singing than the musical.

19. According to the author, musical comedy relies heavily on well-known stars because

    A. stars make less money for the show.
    B. its story line is not very substantial.
    C. stars draw a bigger audience.
    D. it is a tradition in show business.

20. Based on the passage, how many acts does a musical generally contain?

    A. one act
    B. two acts
    C. three acts
    D. four acts

PASSAGE THREE

For a time after the Civil War, newly freed slaves voted, held offices, and served in the legislatures of the Southern states. Black Americans made quick political gains. In some states with large Negro populations, Black control of local and state government seemed <u>imminent</u>. White fears of a takeover by a Black majority provoked the Southern states to withdraw voting rights from Blacks. A pattern of separate and unequal schools, housing and employment further eroded political progress for Blacks. Even in Northern states, Blacks could only live in overcrowded slums and could not find jobs except as servants or unskilled workers.

Black politics in the United states evolved in response to these problems of oppression in a racially divided society. Therefore, an <u>activist orientation</u> was crucial since the resolution of current complaints determined success. Concerns about segregated units in the Armed Forces or wage balances in the workplace could not be put off indefinitely.

As a result of these historical issues, most Black political movements stress the solving of racial imbalances in a timely fashion. However their approaches vary. Constitutionalism bases its arguments for equality on the promises of the United States Constitution, particularly the Fourteenth and Fifteenth Amendments. The Constitutionalists focus on legal action and political pressure to achieve the goal of racial integration. On the other hand, Nationalism emphasizes complete separation from white society. Only then can Blacks achieve full equality. Some Nationalists advocate a return to Africa where an independent nation can be established. Others want land within the United States. In either case, political and economic liberation from white society is essential. The Black Muslims illustrate the Nationalist viewpoint. They have established their own living areas, businesses and farms within the United States.

Another important Black political movement is Socialism. For Socialists, Black Americans suffer not because of their race but because of rigid class distinctions in American society. These distinctions reward the rich and privileged classes and neglect the poor who are mostly Black. The Socialists believe in cooperating with white groups since some whites also suffer from class discrimination. Thus, changing the political system involves an alliance of liberal, labor, and civil rights forces.

21. As used in paragraph one, <u>imminent</u> most likely means

    A. near.
    B. impossible.
    C. desirable.
    D. far away.

22. What is the best meaning for <u>activist orientation</u> (paragraph two) ?

    A. dependence on the past
    B. stress on long-range goals
    C. strategies of cooperation
    D. emphasis on immediate solutions

23. According the passage, which of the following explain(s) the unequal treatment of Blacks in the United States?

    I. Segregated housing and schools
    II. Importing of slaves from Africa
    III. Rigid class distinctions

    A. I, II
    B. III, II
    C. I, III
    D. I, II, III

24. According to the passage, which of the following is <u>not</u> an example of a Black political movement?

A. Black Muslims
B. Constitutionalism
C. Nationalism
D. Democratic Party

25. Based on the chart below, which of the following conclusions can best be drawn about Blacks in political office?

Number of Black-Americans in Political Office

1960-1990

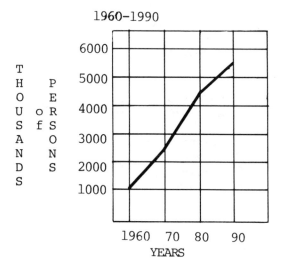

A. Numbers of Black-Americans in political office remained the same from 1980-1990.
B. Numbers of Black-Americans in political office increased dramatically from 1960-1990.
C. Black-Americans gained more political offices in 1960 than in 1990.
D. Black-Americans have achieved total political equality since 1960.

26. One can infer from the passage that prejudice against Blacks in the North was

A. greater than their oppression in the South.
B. similar to their oppression in the South.

C. less than their oppression in the South.
D. limited to certain states.

27. How are the Constitutionalists and the nationalists alike?

A. Both believe in racial integration.
B. Neither group promotes separation from white society.
C. Both groups rely on the United States Constitution.
D. Both groups support racial equality.

28. This passage can best be described as

A. critical
B. pessimistic
C. informative
D. biased

29. The passage states that political gains for Black-Americans in the South occurred

A. before the Civil War.
B. during the Civil War.
C. after the Civil War.
D. in the early 1900's.

30. The author states that Socialists tend to focus on

A. Black-White differences.
B. class distinctions.
C. the problems of poor Blacks.
D. violent overthrow of the government.

PASSAGE FOUR

To study the stars is an adventure in time travel. To contemplate the origins of the universe is an exciting discovery. How did the universe begin? Where did the stars and planets come from? One cannot know how or where, but only that the universe does exist. Obviously <u>it</u> is here — the countless stars, other galaxies that look like stars to the naked eye, the sun, earth, and other planets, the moon, and us. The theories command attention.

The first theory suggests that the universe began 10 or 20 billion years ago and continues expanding forever until it will disappear over the cosmic horizon. In the second theory, the universe <u>oscillates</u> between death and rebirth, having no beginning and no end, with no information carried over from previous ages. This theory may seem frightening except that the estimated time frame is between 10 and 100 billion years from birth to death to rebirth—more than enough for humanity to rule the earth. In this theory, exploding gases propel galaxies, driving them farther and farther, gradually stopping, reversing direction, and drawing the universe in on itself until another inevitable expansion.

The one certainty all theories have in common is that the universe is getting larger — at least for now — and has been expanding for billions of years. <u>Quasars</u>, peculiar and brilliant galaxies, are the farthest objects away from us that we know about. As these quasars recede from us, they emit light in longer radio waves which scientists call red shifts. Astronomers can tell that quasars and other galaxies are moving away from us and from each other. At least they were 10 or 12 billion years ago. That's how long it takes the light from those moving bodies to reach the earth.

What we see today happened before the earth was formed a mere 4.5 billion years ago. What has happened to those quasars since then? Have they gone over the cosmic horizon into nowhere? Have they disappeared? Has their direction reversed and are they now headed toward us? We can only know where they were and the direction they were moving 10 to 12 billion years ago. Where they are today is only speculation.

31. In paragraph one, the underlined word <u>it</u> refers to

    A. discovery.
    B. adventure.
    C. stars.
    D. universe.

32. In paragraph three, the author presents the topic by means of

    A. comparison.
    B. description.
    C. narration.
    D. opinion.

33. In paragraph two, the word <u>oscillates</u> means

    A. stands.
    B. shines.
    C. explodes.
    D. moves.

34. According to the passage, how do astronomers use "red shifts?"

    A. to explain the age of the universe
    B. to develop theories about creation
    C. to distinguish different types of shifts
    D. to determine movements of quasars

35. Which of the following statements best expresses the main idea of paragraph four?

    A. Questions about the routes taken by quasars have still not been answered.

B. Quasars are disappearing over the cosmic horizon.
C. Quasars were formed before the earth began 4.5 billion years ago.
D. Now that the direction of quasars has reversed, they will be moving toward the center of the universe.

36. Pretend you are an astronomer living 100 billion years in the future. Your job is to observe quasars in the universe. Based on the second theory in this passage, what would the universe be doing?

   A. contracting
   B. stabilizing
   C. expanding
   D. dying

37. The word quasars in paragraph three refers to

   A. stars.
   B. the universe.
   C. patterns of light.
   D. a type of galaxy.

38. According to the passage, the earth is part of

   A. a quasar.
   B. the Milky Way.
   C. a galaxy.
   D. the universe.

39. Galaxies move across the universe because

   A. they follow regular paths of movement.
   B. they consist of expanding quasars.
   C. they contain gases which propel them.
   D. they expand as they grow older.

40. According to the first theory, when did the universe begin?

   A. 100 billion years ago
   B. 50 billion years ago
   C. 20 billion years ago
   D. 5 billion years ago

Practice CPE Reading Test Four

PASSAGE ONE

If clay is one of the most versatile of the craft materials, glass is perhaps the most fascinating. Few people, when presented with a beautiful glass form, can resist holding it up to the light, watching how light changes its appearance from different angles.

While there are thousands of formulas for glass, its principal ingredient is usually silica, or sand. The addition of other materials can affect color, melting point, strength, and so on. When heated, glass becomes <u>molten</u>, and in that state it can be shaped by several different methods. Unlike clay, glass never changes chemically as it moves from a soft, workable state to a hard, rigid one. As glass cools it hardens, but it can then be reheated and rendered molten again for further working.

Glass as a material holds many risks, both during the creative process and afterward. The shaping of a glass object demands split-second timing — quick decisions and quick handwork — while the glass remains hot. What's more, a finished glass piece is the most fragile of all craft wares. One quick blow can shatter it irreparably. There is something almost heroic about an artist who would spend days, weeks, even months making an object that is so <u>vulnerable</u>.

Glassmaking is nearly as old a craft as ceramics, but it was not until the Roman era, shortly before the birth of Christ, that the first great period of glassmaking as an art began. The Roman era saw the invention of the blowpipe — an instrument that has changed very little in two thousand years. To blow glass, the artist dips up a portion of <u>molten</u> glass at the end of the pipe and then blows through the pipe to produce a bubble. The bubble can be shaped or cut by various methods while it is still hot. Besides blowing, other ways of forming glass include molding, pressing, and rolling.

. . . About a thousand years later, another great era of glassmaking took place in Italy. This time it centered on the city of Venice. By the year 1291 there were so many glass factories in Venice, with so many furnaces burning day and night, that the entire city seemed in danger of going up in flames. As a result, the Senate demanded that all the glass factories be removed to the island of Murano, where many remain to this day.

From Living With Art by William McCarter and Rita Gilbert. New York: Alfred A. Knopf, Inc., 1985, p. 295.

1. When did glassmaking first become an art form?

   A. in 1291
   B. in the Roman era
   C. after the birth of Christ
   D. during the Middle Ages

2. The word <u>molten</u> in paragraphs two and four most likely means

   A. melted.
   B. brittle.
   C. volatile.
   D. rough.

3. What effect did the numerous glass factories have on the government of Venice?

   A. The government said the factories caused fires.
   B. The government wanted furnaces burning in the day only.

C. The government indicated that the factories should remain where they were.
D. The government requested that factories be built only on the island of Murano.

4. The closest meaning for the word vulnerable (paragraph three) is

A. worthless.
B. enduring.
C. fragile.
D. costly.

5. The main focus of paragraph two is on

A. the peculiarities of glass and clay.
B. the composition and properties of glass.
C. the ingredients found in glass.
D. the shape and color of glass.

6. What is the traditional method of working with glass?

A. rolling
B. molding
C. blowing
D. cutting

7. According to the passage, glass is easier to work with than clay because

A. clay cracks and falls apart at higher temperatures.
B. glass accepts color more easily than clay does.
C. clay is more versatile than glass.
D. glass keeps its same properties whether it is heated or cooled.

8. A glassworker can shape glass only when it is

A. rigid.
B. warm.
C. thick.
D. liquefied.

9. The passage states that glass is composed primarily of

A. silica.
B. angles.
C. bubbles.
D. clay particles.

10. Based on the passage, which of the following statements are valid conclusions about the art of glassmaking?

I. Inferior glass objects result from poor timing and slow work.
II. Glassmaking's greatest achievements occurred in Venice.
III. Glassmaking involves creativity, patience, and timing.

A. I
B. I, II
C. I, III
D. I, II, III

227

PASSAGE TWO

As a result of widespread ocean dumping and other pollution problems, marine scientists are studying the populations of various marine organisms in an attempt to determine the effects of pollution. Marine biologists, ecologists and fishing industry investigators are compiling data on aging of marine organisms, including such factors as the relationship between the size and age of the organism, its longevity, its rate of growth and growth differences among species. These factors hold clues to many questions of importance.

Of particular interest because of its great economic value is the surf clam that inhabits the U.S. Atlantic Coast. There exists a method of determining the age of the surf clam by examining photographic blowups of a section of the clam that contains annual rings or growth bands, like a tree. Though useful, this technique has shortcomings, among them difficulty in finding the often faint initial ring and difficulty in getting an accurate count in older clams, whose rings become crowded and run together.

Professor Ernest G. Hammond and a group of students at Morgan State University, Baltimore, Maryland, in cooperation with Goddard Space Flight Center, have been conducting research for several years on a way to apply space developed digital image processing techniques to age determination in clams.

Digital image processing is the use of computers to convert sensor data into informative images. The idea of applying it to clam-aging investigations came from Kevin Peters, a Morgan State graduate student. The Morgan State/Goddard technique involved development of a computer program to create digitized images of clam sections with annual rings. The computerized image can then be enhanced — manipulated to emphasize certain features — in order to improve and amplify the information that can be extracted from the image.

A lengthy series of tests established that the technique offers a number of advantages in aging studies not only of clams but of other shellfish and marine organisms that have growth bands. Among these advantages, with respect to clam studies, are greater contrast between each annual ring, making it easier to get an accurate count, clearer delineation of the initial ring and the ability to create adequate separation of the crowded ring areas of older clams by enhancing and enlarging the image. The technique also showed promise for being able to reveal information regarding the rate of the organism's growth during seasonal and environmental changes that the organism undergoes.

From *Spinoff 1988* by James J. Haggerty. Washington, D.C.: National Aeronautics and Space Administration, 1988, p. 101.

11. As used in paragraph four, the word extracted means

    A. taken.
    B. reversed.
    C. stolen.
    D. erased.

12. Based on the passage, the surf clam lives primarily

    A. near Baltimore, Maryland.
    B. along the Atlantic Coast.
    C. in lakes and rivers.
    D. in deep oceans.

13. All of the following are advantages of digitized images except

    A. distinct initial rings.
    B. clearer delineation of rings in older clams.
    C. developmental changes based on the seasons and environment
    D. economic potential of clam species.

14. The main idea of the passage is that

    A. scientists have discovered a new technique called digital image processing which limits a closer examination of surf clams.
    B. new computer imaging techniques have proven useful in studying how environmental changes affect the growth patterns of clams.
    C. pollution of the environment affects many marine organisms including surf clams.
    D. many scientific investigators study growth rings of clams to monitor changes in the population of these marine organisms.

15. The best definition for compiling (paragraph one) is

    A. scattering.
    B. losing.
    C. gathering.
    D. disregarding.

16. The purpose of this passage is

    A. to narrate.
    B. to argue.
    C. to list.
    D. to inform.

17. According to the passage, what is the main reason that computerized images of surf clams are superior to photographic images?

    A. the degree of enhancement
    B. the size of the image
    C. the cost of image processing
    D. the amount of data generated

18. The growth rings in older clams cannot be photographed accurately. In which paragraph does this fact support the main idea?

    A. Paragraph 1
    B. Paragraph 2
    C. Paragraph 3
    D. Paragraph 4

19. Marine organisms are of particular importance to scientists because

    A. they grow at constant rates.
    B. they are distributed widely.
    C. they are sensitive to pollution.
    D. they vary in size and shape.

20. Of the following traits, which become less distinct in older clams?

    A. initial rings
    B. shell size
    C. annual rings
    D. shell color

PASSAGE THREE

. . . I just watched Sonny's face. His face was troubled, he was working hard, but he wasn't with it. And I had the feeling that, in a way, everyone on the bandstand was waiting for him, both waiting for him and pushing him along. But as I began to watch Creole, I realized that it was Creole who held them all back. He had them on a short rein. Up there, keeping the beat with his whole body, wailing on the fiddle, with his eyes half closed, he was listening to everything, but he was listening to Sonny. He was having a dialogue with Sonny. He wanted Sonny to leave the shoreline and strike out for the deep water. He was Sonny's witness that deep water and drowning were not the same thing — he had been there, and he knew. And he wanted Sonny to know. He was waiting for Sonny to do the things on the keys which would let Creole know that Sonny was in the water.

And, while Creole listened, Sonny moved, deep within, exactly like someone in torment. I have never before thought of how awful the relationship must be between the musician and his instrument. He was to fill it, this instrument, with the breath of life, his own. He has to make it do what he wants it to do. And a piano is just a piano. It's made out of so much wood and wires and little hammers and big ones, and ivory. While there's only so much you can do with it, the only way to find this out is to try; to try and make it do everything.

And Sonny hadn't been near a piano for over a year. And he wasn't on much better terms with his life, not the life that stretched before him now. He and the piano stammered, started one way, got scared, stopped; started another way, panicked, marked time, started again; then seemed to have found a direction, panicked again, got stuck. And the face I saw on Sonny I'd never seen before. Everything had been burned out of it, and, at the same time, things usually hidden were being burned in, by the fire and fury of the battle which was occurring in him up there.

Yet, watching Creole's face as they neared the end of the first set, I had the feeling that something had happened, something I hadn't heard. Then they finished, there was scattered applause, and then, without an instant's warning, Creole started into something else, it was almost sardonic, it was Am I Blue. And, as though he commanded, Sonny began to play. Something began to happen. And Creole let out the reins. The dry, low, black man said something awful on the drums, Creole answered, and the drums talked back. Then the horn insisted, sweet and high, slightly detached perhaps, and Creole listened, commenting now and then, dry, and driving, beautiful and calm and old. Then they all came together again, and Sonny was part of the family again. I could tell this from his face. . . .

From "Sonny's Blues" by James Baldwin in The Norton Introduction to Fiction Jerome Beaty, ed. New York: W. W. Norton and Company, pp. 298-299.

21. The phrase strike out for the deep water (paragraph one) suggests that Sonny should

A. drown rather than stay in shallow water.
B. swim in a deep lake or river.
C. play a challenging piece of music.
D. imitate Creole's style of music.

22. Which of the following statements best summarizes paragraph four?

A. The musicians play Am I Blue.
B. Creole plays an emotional song.
C. The audience hears a blending of horns and piano.
D. Sonny is accepted as a talented musician.

23. The major reason that the musicians in the bandstand appear reserved (paragraph one) is because

    A. Sonny seems anxious.
    B. Creole dominates the group.
    C. they fear the audience.
    D. no one wants to lead them.

24. Based on the context, the best definition for detached (paragraph four) is

    A. unfastened.
    B. disgusting.
    C. agitated.
    D. distant.

25. Who is telling the story?

    A. the narrator
    B. Sonny
    C. one of the musicians
    D. Creole

26. As revealed in the passage, Sonny can best be described as

    A. enthusiastic and blissful.
    B. intense and struggling.
    C. shy and apathetic.
    D. calm and peaceful.

27. In which order do the events in the passage take place?

    I. Sonny has difficulty playing the piano.
    II. Creole makes music with his fiddle.
    III. Sonny's piano playing impresses Creole.

    A. I, II, III
    B. III, II, I
    C. II, I, III
    D. II, III, I

28. Why does the author discuss the piano (paragraph two)?

    A. to point out the complex nature of musical creativity
    B. to describe the many parts of a piano
    C. to understand Creole's thoughts and feelings
    D. to aid in understanding Sonny's musical training

29. In paragraph three, the author expresses a tone of

    A. frustration.
    B. optimism.
    C. elation.
    D. amusement.

30. As used in paragraph three, stammered most likely means

    A. blended.
    B. improved.
    C. hesitated.
    D. collided.

PASSAGE FOUR

So remarkable was the kingdom of Ghana during the age of Africa's great empires that writers throughout the medieval world praised it as a model for other rulers. Medieval Ghana also holds a central place in the historical consciousness of the modern state of Ghana. Since this former British colony attained independence in 1957, its political leaders have hailed the medieval period as a glorious heritage. The name of the modern republic of Ghana — which in fact lies far from the site of the old kingdom — was selected to signify the <u>rebirth</u> of an age of gold in black Africa.

The nucleus of the territory that became the kingdom of Ghana was inhabited by Soninke people who called their ruler <u>ghana</u>, or war chief. By the late eighth century Muslim traders and other foreigners applied the word to the region where the Soninke lived, the black kingdom south of the Sahara. The Soninke themselves called their land "Aoukar" or "Awkar," by which they meant the region north of the Senegal and Niger rivers. Only the southern part of Aoukar received enough rainfall to be agriculturally productive, and it was in this area that the civilization of Ghana developed. Skillful farming and an efficient system of irrigation led to the production of abundant crops, which eventually supported a population of as many as 200,000 people.

The Soninke name for their king — war chief — aptly describes his major preoccupation in the tenth century. In 992 Ghana captured the Berber town of Awdaghast, strategically situated on the trans-Saharan trade route. Thereafter Ghana controlled the southern portion of a major caravan route. Before 1000 the rulers of Ghana had extended their influence almost to the Atlantic coast and had captured a number of small kingdoms in the south and east. By the beginning of the eleventh century, the king exercised <u>sway</u> over a vast territory approximately the size of Texas. No other African power could successfully challenge him.

From <u>A History of World Societies</u> by John P. McKay, Bennett D. Hill, and John Buckler. Boston: Houghton Mifflin Company, 1988, p. 461.

31. In paragraph three, the word <u>sway</u> most likely means

    A. confusion.
    B. movement.
    C. authority.
    D. silence.

32. According to paragraph three, the main concern of the Soninke king was

    A. control of more territory.
    B. selecting a strategic position on the Atlantic coast.
    C. maintaining present borders.
    D. defending Ghana against Berber invaders.

33. As used in the passage, the best definition for <u>rebirth</u> (paragraph one) is

    A. reversal.
    B. end.
    C. voice.
    D. revival.

34. Why did the northern region of Aoukar remain undeveloped?

    A. Muslim traders controlled the region.
    B. The area received plentiful rain.
    C. The land was dry and unproductive.
    D. Most of the population was concentrated in the southern region.

35. The passage implies that modern Ghana is

    A. less powerful than ancient Ghana.
    B. more powerful than ancient Ghana.
    C. equally as powerful as ancient Ghana.

D. There is not enough information to determine which was more powerful.

36. Which of the following was not a characteristic of the kingdom of Ghana?

    A. prosperity
    B. famine
    C. agriculture
    D. monarchy

37. The major focus of the passage is on

    A. the heritage of modern Ghana.
    B. the king's importance in ancient Ghana.
    C. Ghana's role in ancient trade routes.
    D. African kingdoms in the medieval period.

38. Which of the following influences affected the expansion of ancient Ghana?

    I. Conquests
    II. Population Growth
    III. Agriculture

    A. I
    B. I, II, III
    C. I, III
    D. II, III

39. The passage progresses from a discussion of

    A. modern Ghana to the major victories of its ancient kings.
    B. farming to its applications today.
    C. the Soninke people to independence in 1957.
    D. the battles for territory to the establishment of a peaceful society.

40. According to the passage, which of the following statements is an opinion rather than a fact?

    A. In the tenth century, several rulers of ancient Ghana conquered lands to the south, east, and in the trans-Sahara region.
    B. Ghana gained independence from Great Britain in 1957.
    C. The organization of ancient Ghana was a remarkable example for other rulers.
    D. Irrigation helped to produce abundant crops in ancient Ghana.

Practice CPE Reading Test Five

PASSAGE ONE

Ecology is the study of organisms and their environment as a biological unit, or system. Actually this is a somewhat older definition of ecology. A newer definition is that ecology is the study of the structure and function of nature. One problem with the older definition is that it makes a distinction between organisms and their environment, instead of seeing them as part of a unified living system.

In discussing the structure of an ecological system, or ecosystem, it is useful to consider four basic elements: 1) the nonliving components of the system, 2) producer organisms, 3) consumer organisms, and 4) decomposer organisms.

The nonliving components are the various elements of the physical environment which are necessary for the growth of the living creatures in the system. These include such things as heat and light from the sun, the gases oxygen and carbon dioxide, water, as well as such elements as nitrogen, phosphorus, potassium, calcium, sulfur and magnesium.

The producer organisms are always green plants. They are organisms which convert sunlight and various chemicals into the substances which they need to live and grow.

Consumer organisms can be divided into two groups. The first kind are animals that feed on plant life. These are called primary consumers or herbivores. The second kind are animals which feed on herbivores and sometimes on one another. These are called carnivores. There may be several levels of carnivores depending on the complexity of the ecosystem.

Decomposer organisms are bacteria and fungi which break down complex compounds from dead members of the ecosystem and release simpler substances into the environment so that they can be used again.

In an ecosystem these different groups are organized into a system of feeding relations called a food chain. In a food chain, the consumers are dependent on the producers for their food, the carnivores are dependent on the herbivores, and the higher carnivores are dependent on the lower carnivores . . .

Perhaps a simple example will make this clearer. Let's consider the ecology of a grassland. . . . In a typical grassland ecology, the producer organism is grass. Filling the role of herbivore are grasshoppers which eat the grass. Mice, which eat the grasshoppers, are the first level of carnivores. Skunks, which eat the mice, are the second-level carnivores. And finally owls, which eat the skunks, are the top-level carnivores. Actually, the situation is more complicated than this, for besides grasshoppers the mice also eat grass, besides mice the skunks also eat grasshoppers, and besides skunks the owls also eat mice. But despite this their relative positions in the food chain remain the same.

From Academic English (Teacher's Manual) by Lee D. Rossi and Michael Gasser. Englewood Cliffs, New Jersey: Prentice-Hall, 1983, p. 6.

1. As used in paragraph five, the best definition of herbivores is

   A. producer organisms.
   B. plant life.
   C. animals.
   D. plant eaters.

2. The author develops the ideas in paragraph eight by

   A. comparison-contrast.
   B. problem-solution.
   C. illustration-example.
   D. cause-effect.

3. All of the following are non-living components of the environment except

A. fungi.
B. magnesium.
C. sunlight.
D. nitrogen.

4. The attitude of the author toward the subject is

A. favorable.
B. objective.
C. skeptical.
D. critical.

5. Based on the passage, the phrase food chain most likely means

A. feeding styles.
B. food producers.
C. food consumers.
D. feeding relationships.

6. Which of the following is not a carnivore?

A. organisms
B. grasshoppers
C. owls
D. skunks

7. Why does the author prefer the newer definition of ecology?

A. The older definition separates living things and the environment.
B. The older definition is outdated and false.
C. The newer definition seems more appropriate.
D. The newer definition focuses on reasons for natural occurrences.

8. In paragraph five, the primary focus is on

A. animal ecosystems.
B. primary consumers.
C. herbivores and carnivores.
D. types of carnivores.

9. In the ecology of the grassland, in which order does the food chain generally occur?

I. Owls eat skunks and mice.
II. Mice eat grasshoppers.
III. Grasshoppers consume grass.
IV. Skunks eat grasshoppers and mice.

A. I, II, III, IV
B. II, III, IV, I
C. III, II, IV, I
D. III, I, IV, II

10. The most likely conclusion we can draw from paragraph six is that decomposer organisms

A. help in recycling substances from the ecosystem.
B. play a major role in feeding producer organisms.
C. hinder the development of complex compounds in the ecosystem.
D. aid in the growth of living components of the ecosystem.

PASSAGE TWO

Red Sammy was lying on the bare ground outside The Tower with his head under a truck while a gray monkey about a foot high, chained to a small chinaberry tree, chattered nearby. The monkey sprang back into the tree and got on the highest limb as soon as he saw the children jump out of the car and run toward him.

Inside, The Tower was a long dark room with a counter at one end and tables at the other and dancing space in the middle. They all sat down at a broad table next to the nickelodeon and Red Sam's wife, a tall burnt-brown woman with hair and eyes lighter than her skin, came and took their order. The children's mother put a dime in the machine and played "The Tennessee Waltz," and the grandmother said the tune always made her want to dance. She asked Bailey if he would like to dance but he only glared at her. He didn't have a naturally sunny <u>disposition</u> like she did and trips made him nervous. The grandmother's brown eyes were very bright. She swayed her head from side to side and pretended she was dancing in her chair. June Star said play something she could tap to so the children's mother put in another dime and played a fast number and June Star stepped out onto the dance floor and did her tap routine.

"Ain't she cute?" Red Sam's wife said, leaning over the counter. "Would you like to come be my little girl?"

"No I certainly wouldn't," June Star said. "I wouldn't live in a broken-down place like this for a million bucks!" and she ran back to the table.

"Ain't she cute?" the woman repeated, stretching her mouth politely.

"Aren't you ashamed?" hissed her grandmother.

Red Sam came in and told his wife to quit <u>lounging on the counter</u> and hurry with these people's order. His khaki trousers reached just to his hip bones and his stomach hung over them like a sack of meal swaying under his shirt. He came over and sat down at a table nearby and let out a combination sigh and yodel. "You can't win," he said. "You can't win," and he wiped his sweating red face with a gray handkerchief. "These days you don't know who to trust," he said. "Ain't that the truth?"

"People are certainly not nice like they used to be," said the grandmother.

"Two fellers come in here last week," Red Sammy said, "driving a Chrysler. It was a old beat-up car but it was a good one and these boys looked all right to me. Said they worked at the mill and you know I let them fellers charge the gas they bought? Now why did I do that?"

From "A Good Man Is Hard To Find" by Flannery O'Connor in Literature: An Introduction to Reading and Writing. Edgar N. Roberts and Henry E. Jacobs, eds. Englewood Cliffs, New Jersey: Prentice Hall, 1989, p. 482.

11. The word <u>disposition</u> (paragraph two) most likely means

    A. face.
    B. personality.
    C. status.
    D. rhythm.

12. When Red Sam's wife responds to June Star (paragraph five), she expresses a feeling of

    A. delight and pride.
    B. sorrow and disappointment.
    C. irritation and annoyance.
    D. lethargy and indifference.

13. In the passage, June Star is

    A. the grandmother's daughter.
    B. the children's mother.
    C. the grandmother's sister.

D. the grandmother's grand-
child.

14. Based on the passage, which of
the following statements is an
opinion rather than a fact?

  A. The family chooses to play
  "The Tennessee Waltz."
  B. Red Sammy lets people
  charge their gas.
  C. The grandmother is eccen-
  tric and opinionated.
  D. Red Sammy owns a gray
  handkerchief.

15. The phrase <u>lounging on the
counter</u> (paragraph seven)
suggests that the wife was

  A. idle.
  B. leaving.
  C. busy.
  D. frightened.

16. Based on the passage, where
does the action occur?

  A. in a grocery store
  B. near a city
  C. at a shopping mall
  D. in a restaurant

17. According to the passage, why
does Red Sammy mistrust
people?

  A. He says that people are not
  as nice as they once were.
  B. He can't easily distinguish
  between honest and dishon-
  est persons.
  C. Two customers of his drove
  away without paying for
  their gas.
  D. Red Sammy does not have
  time to check people's credit
  rating.

18. The "broken-down place" June
Star mentions in paragraph four
is

  A. the nickelodeon.
  B. the Tower.
  C. the dance floor.
  D. the mill.

19. Which of the following phrases
best describes June Star?

  A. blunt and sassy
  B. talented and introverted
  C. sweet and courteous
  D. shy and obedient

20. What is most likely Red
Sammy's primary role at the
Tower?

  A. employee
  B. mechanic
  C. owner
  D. cook

PASSAGE THREE

The art of Antoine Watteau is typical of the carefree, aristocratic impulse of the Rococo. In Gersaint's Signboard Watteau gives us a picture of fashionable French society out for a day of shopping — shopping for pictures to decorate the opulent home. All is elegance, verging on the pretentious — the men in their powdered wigs, the women in their silks, everyone maintaining a pose of bored nonchalance. At right the gallery owner, Gersaint, displays a painting to prospective customers, while the adjacent group seem more taken with the charms of a lap dog. At left, paintings are being crated, presumably for shipment to purchasers. Watteau celebrates in painting a class of people whose most serious concern was maintaining a chic life style.

. . . Two painters in particular, also French, have become almost synonymous with the Rococo. To admirers their art is sumptuous and delightful; to detractors it is frivolous and decadent. The first is Jean-Honore Fragonard. The other is Francois Boucher. In Boucher's paintings all the people are pretty. The women are frequently nude and, if so, are very pink and voluptuous. (Fragonard's women are more often clothed but equally pink.) If the women are dressed, they are stunningly dressed. Everybody is in love.

Boucher's art suited perfectly the ideals of the French court presided over by Louis XV, great-grandson of the builder of Versailles. Form without substance, beauty without character, extravagance with little regard for paying the bills — such was the reign of Louis XV, and so it was chronicled by Boucher. In 1759 Boucher painted the Marquise de Pompadour, Louis's mistress and influential advisor. How beautiful she looks, how romantic — posed languidly in her lace-frilled dress, resting lightly against a classical statue. Boucher flattered her physically (she was a good deal fatter and less gifted with regular features), and he failed to record the steely political brain that lurked behind the soft face. During the reign of Louis XV, the government of France was on the brink of collapse. The king himself is reputed to have said, "Apres moi, le deluge" ("After me, the flood"). But for a little while — with Louis XV on the throne, the Marquise de Pompadour at his side, and Boucher at his easel — appearances were kept up.

The lower classes did not participate in this world. They could not afford to wear lace-frilled dresses and had no time to be charmingly in love. Many, in fact, were on the brink of starvation. Louis — if he really said it — was right. The flood was coming, and a mere thirty years after Boucher painted his so-lovely portrait of the Marquise de Pompadour, France was engulfed.

From Living With Art by William McCarter and Rita Gilbert. New York: Alfred A. Knopf, Inc., 1985, pp. 391-393.

21. The best meaning for kept up (paragraph three) is

    A. stopped.
    B. unimportant.
    C. disturbed.
    D. maintained.

22. Based on the passage, when was Rococo painting popular in France?

    A. 1500-1600
    B. 1600-1700
    C. 1700-1800
    D. 1800-1900

23. The artists mentioned in the passage painted in the Rococo style primarily to

    A. create a new kind of art.
    B. earn large sums of money.
    C. flatter their patrons.
    D. criticize the rich.

24. According to the passage, the French government was in danger of collapse because

A. the financial situation was worsening.
B. the king kept a mistress.
C. the women were frequently painted nude.
D. the lower classes became complacent.

25. The author explains the ideas in paragraph one through

A. description.
B. narration.
C. persuasion.
D. classification.

26. What is the best definition for Rococo (paragraphs one and two)?

A. mediocre, inferior style
B. extravagant, ornate art
C. plain, simple style
D. serious, solemn art

27. The author's attitude toward the lower classes is

A. critical.
B. neutral.
C. sympathetic.
D. disgusting.

28. If today's photographers followed the Rococo style, who would they tend to photograph?

A. factory workers
B. executives
C. store clerks
D. teachers

29. The passage implies that during the reign of Louis XV life was really

A. better than it appeared to be.
B. worse than it appeared to be.
C. about the same as it appeared to be.
D. neither better nor worse than it appeared to be.

30. Based on the passage, which of the following statements would the author most likely support?

A. Watteau preferred painting the wealthy whereas Boucher favored portraits of ordinary people.
B. The paintings of Watteau and Boucher were often critical of the French aristocracy.
C. Both Fragonard and Boucher preferred painting women of character and intelligence.
D. The paintings of Boucher and Fragonard are both admired and ridiculed today.

PASSAGE FOUR

The government itself has an influence on public opinion, for the most important opinion-shaper in our nation is the president. The president is the nation's leading spokesperson. As the representative of all the people, the chief executive is in a unique position to influence, persuade, and lead the public.

Although the opportunity to lead is unparalleled, however, not every president has a clear sense of direction on every issue. After reading public opinion polls during 1941, President Franklin D. Roosevelt <u>wavered</u> between detachment and involvement for the United States in World War II. "The president," concluded one of his advisors, "would rather follow public opinion than lead it."

Still, virtually all politicians do pay attention to public opinion. In order to create majorities and stay in office, elected officials must know what voters think. Of course, the most important public opinion poll of all is an election.

Since the 1930's, public opinion polling has also become a popular method for finding out how citizens feel about social issues. The news media regularly conduct polls on a wide variety of social, economic, and political issues. Reporting the public <u>pulse</u> has become an accepted practice, and many pollsters have become quite successful at measuring public opinion. By interviewing people who have just voted, for example, pollsters are often able to accurately project the winner of an election long before the voting itself has ended.

Many of the most popular politicians, however, are not those who measure public opinion. Instead, they are able to accurately sense what is important to their constituents. Other politicians capitalize on changes in public opinion before the changes are well-defined. For instance, in 1980 President Reagan took advantage of a conservative shift in the mood of the nation — a shift that was not evident until just before the election itself.

Forming educated opinions is important for citizens in a democracy, but it is not easy — even though Americans today have much better access to information than ever before. Prejudices and stereotypes often get in the way of reason. Other opinions sometimes scream loudly for attention, and conflicting claims can cloud or confuse understanding. Our opinions will have greater validity if we learn to distinguish truth from fiction, reason logically, and reflect critically on our own unique experiences.

From The Americans: The History of a People and a Nation by Winthrop D. Jordan, Miriam Greenblatt, and John S. Bowes. Evanston, Illinois: McDougal, Littell, and Company, 1985, pp. 334-335.

31. In paragraph two, the word <u>wavered</u> most likely means

    A. decided.
    B. sang.
    C. varied.
    D. stood firm.

32. The best definition for <u>pulse</u> (paragraph four) is

    A. feeling.
    B. support.
    C. news.
    D. confusion.

33. The main focus of the passage is on

    A. the president's influence on public opinion.
    B. the effect of opinion polls on Presidents Roosevelt and Reagan.
    C. voting in national and local elections.
    D. the role of public opinion in government and politics.

34. According to the passage, where does a public opinion poll become most important?

    A. in a social issue.
    B. in a world war.
    C. in an election.
    D. in a national emergency.

35. Public opinion is important in a democracy because

    A. the people will always agree with the president's views.
    B. the more information we have, the more likely we will understand the issues.
    C. politicians pay little attention to public opinion polls.
    D. pollsters create a better economy through their political projections.

36. Based on the passage, what opinion change led to the election of President Reagan?

    A. a need for strong leadership.
    B. a move toward conservatism.
    C. a shift in the economy.
    D. a change in public opinion.

(Turn to next page)

Read the following information and then answer the questions.

The Clark County Hospital Board wants to build a specialized facility for the growing number of senior citizens in the area. In order to increase public awareness on this issue, the Board is disseminating a series of health-related statistics in preparation for an upcoming referendum.

Selected Reported Chronic Conditions per 1,000 Persons by Sex and Age: United States, 1985

Number of Chronic Conditions per 1,000 Persons

Type of Chronic Condition	Male 65 Years and Over	Female 65 Years and Over
Arthritis	361.5	550.5
Disorders of Bone or Cartilage	*7.4	29.4
Visual Impairment	103.6	91.5
Cataracts	104.3	205.7
Glaucoma	33.5	41.1
Hearing Impairment	364.2	245.9
Deformity or Orthopedic Impairment	138.1	193.6
Ulcer	43.9	27.1
Gastritis or Duodenitis	•12.5	27.2
Frequent Constipation	31.7	75.4
Heart Disease	328.0	288.1
Hypertension	351.4	458.4
Cerebrovascular Disease	76.7	50.3
Emphysema	80.1	21.9

SOURCE: National Center for Health Statistics. Vital and Health Statistics. Series 10, No. 160

37. For which condition is the number of males and females nearly equal?

A. Cerebrovascular Disease.
B. Visual Impairment.
C. Ulcer.
D. Glaucoma.

38. Based on the chart, which of the following statements is not true?

A. Hearing impairment is more prevalent among men than it is among women.
B. Arthritis is more common among women than it is among men.
C. Men are more likely to die of heart disease than women are.
D. Men are more likely to contract emphysema than women are.

39. Which chronic conditions affect more than 40% of the females in the United States 65 years and over?

A. Arthritis, Hearing Impairment.
B. Glaucoma, Cerebrovascular Disease.
C. Hypertension, Arthritis.
D. Hypertension, Heart Disease.

40. From this data, we can probably infer that

A. the referendum will not pass.
B. the referendum will pass.
C. younger voters will more likely favor the referendum rather than older voters.
D. There is not enough information to determine an answer.

KEYS

MATH ANSWER KEYS

Diagnostic Test

1.	E	21.	A	41.	C
2.	D	22.	B	42.	E
3.	A	23.	A	43.	E
4.	A	24.	B	44.	B
5.	B	25.	B	45.	E
6.	E	26.	A	46.	E
7.	E	27.	D	47.	E
8.	C	28.	A	48.	E
9.	E	29.	E	49.	D
10.	E	30.	E	50.	E
11.	E	31.	E	51.	D
12.	C	32.	C	52.	C
13.	E	33.	D	53.	E
14.	A	34.	A	54.	E
15.	B	35.	D	55.	E
16.	D	36.	D	56.	B
17.	D	37.	A	57.	A
18.	C	38.	A	58.	A
19.	B	39.	B	59.	D
20.	B	40.	A	60.	D

Practice Test 1

1.	D	21.	B
2.	A	22.	E
3.	B	23.	E
4.	E	24.	C
5.	D	25.	B
6.	C	26.	A
7.	C	27.	A
8.	A	28.	E
9.	B	29.	A
10.	C	30.	A
11.	E	31.	C
12.	C	32.	A
13.	A	33.	D
14.	D	34.	B
15.	B	35.	E
16.	A	36.	C
17.	E	37.	E
18.	D	38.	E
19.	D	39.	D
20.	D	40.	C

Practice Test 2

1.	D	21.	D
2.	A	22.	A
3.	C	23.	B
4.	C	24.	B
5.	E	25.	A
6.	B	26.	E
7.	A	27.	D
8.	C	28.	A
9.	B	29.	B
10.	B	30.	B
11.	A	31.	A
12.	E	32.	E
13.	D	33.	D
14.	C	34.	D
15.	A	35.	C
16.	D	36.	E
17.	B	37.	C
18.	E	38.	B
19.	E	39.	D
20.	D	40.	E

Practice Test 3

1.	B	21.	D
2.	A	22.	B
3.	D	23.	C
4.	E	24.	E
5.	A	25.	A
6.	C	26.	B
7.	B	27.	A
8.	D	28.	E
9.	D	29.	A
10.	E	30.	B
11.	B	31.	C
12.	C	32.	E
13.	A	33.	C
14.	A	34.	D
15.	D	35.	D
16.	C	36.	E
17.	C	37.	A
18.	B	38.	E
19.	D	39.	C
20.	E	40.	A

Practice Test 4

1.	A	21.	D
2.	C	22.	C
3.	D	23.	D
4.	A	24.	B
5.	E	25.	A
6.	A	26.	C
7.	D	27.	C
8.	B	28.	E
9.	A	29.	A
10.	D	30.	E
11.	B	31.	B
12.	B	32.	E
13.	D	33.	C
14.	D	34.	C
15.	A	35.	E
16.	A	36.	E
17.	B	37.	A
18.	A	38.	E
19.	C	39.	C
20.	A	40.	B

Practice Test 5

1.	D	21.	E
2.	C	22.	C
3.	B	23.	D
4.	A	24.	A
5.	C	25.	E
6.	D	26.	E
7.	E	27.	E
8.	B	28.	B
9.	D	29.	A
10.	A	30.	C
11.	E	31.	D
12.	B	32.	B
13.	A	33.	D
14.	A	34.	D
15.	C	35.	C
16.	D	36.	A
17.	B	37.	B
18.	B	38.	E
19.	A	39.	B
20.	A	40.	B

ENGLISH ANSWER KEYS

The numbers in parentheses correspond to the types of errors in the English Error Log.

Diagnostic Test		Practice Test 1		Practice Test 2	
1. A	(7, 12)	1. A	(12, 1)	1. C	(6, 7)
2. D	(4, 10)	2. C	(4)	2. E	(7, 4)
3. C	(4)	3. D	(4, 12)	3. A	(4)
4. A	(4)	4. B	(12)	4. C	(1)
5. A	(7, 11)	5. A	(4)	5. B	(4)
6. B	(10)	6. B	(4)	6. E	(1)
7. A	(1)	7. C	(11, 12)	7. C	(7)
8. D	(8)	8. B	(9, 3)	8. B	(11)
9. A	(1)	9. D	(4)	9. A	(4)
10. D	(3)	10. D	(4, 12)	10. C	(4)
11. E	(12)	11. C	(4, 7)	11. D	(5, 11)
12. A	(12)	12. B	(8, 11)	12. B	(3,11)
13. B	(5, 12)	13. D	(10, 6)	13. B	(4)
14. D	(1, 13)	14. D	(9, 4)	14. E	(1)
15. A	(3, 4)	15. A	(7, 4)	15. A	(3, 9)
16. E	(11, 12)	16. A	(4)	16. B	(3)
17. A	(1, 12)	17. C	(5, 4)	17. A	(4, 8)
18. C	(7)	18. B	(12)	18. D	(10, 13)
19. D	(12)	19. B	(5, 12)	19. A	(12, 13)
20. E	(2)	20. D	(2)	20. E	(4, 10)
21. C	(4)	21. C	(1)	21. D	(12)
22. D	(11)	22. A	(7, 4)	22. E	(2)
23. B	(10, 12)	23. C	(4, 9)	23. D	(1)
24. A	(1)	24. A	(1, 4)	24. B	(4)
25. C	(4, 11)	25. B	(4, 12)	25. C	(4)
26. E	(4, 1)	26. C	(7)	26. A	(1)
27. A	(12)	27. D	(4, 7)	27. D	(4)
28. B	(3, 8)	28. C	(4, 12)	28. B	(6, 3)
29. C	(5, 12)	29. A	(1)	29. E	(7)
30. E	(1)	30. D	(2)	30. A	(4)
31. D	(9)	31. D	(7, 4)	31. C	(9)
32. C	(13)	32. D	(4)	32. E	(4)
33. B	(4)	33. A	(4)	33. B	(5, 3)
34. D	(5)	34. A	(7)	34. D	(7)
35. B	(8)	35. D	(7, 12)	35. A	(1, 12)
36. E	(7)	36. C	(3)	36. C	(8, 4)
37. A	(2)	37. C	(4)	37. B	(6)
38. D	(3)	38. A	(7)	38. E	(8, 4)
39. B	(5)	39. D	(4)	39. D	(7)
40. A	(11, 12)	40. B	(1)	40. A	(1)

ENGLISH ANSWER KEYS

Practice Test 3		Practice Test 4		Practice Test 5	
1. C	(4)	1. E	(4)	1. B	(3, 10)
2. A	(4, 1)	2. C	(12)	2. C	(1, 12)
3. C	(12)	3. B	(7, 12)	3. B	(4)
4. D	(7)	4. D	(11)	4. D	(10)
5. C	(8)	5. C	(3)	5. A	(4)
6. A	(13, 12)	6. E	(5, 12)	6. C	(7, 1)
7. A	(1)	7. A	(7)	7. B	(7, 9)
8. B	(12)	8. C	(4)	8. B	(12)
9. C	(4)	9. E	(2)	9. D	(4)
10. D	(1)	10. A	(4)	10. A	(8, 3)
11. A	(2)	11. D	(1)	11. C	(2)
12. C	(4)	12. B	(7)	12. D	(8, 4)
13. D	(2)	13. C	(7)	13. B	(12)
14. B	(4)	14. A	(1)	14. C	(4)
15. D	(4)	15. E	(4)	15. C	(3)
16. D	(6)	16. B	(6)	16. A	(8, 4)
17. A	(4)	17. D	(5, 12)	17. D	(2)
18. C	(3, 4)	18. A	(11)	18. B	(4, 12)
19. B	(6)	19. C	(4, 7)	19. D	(7)
20. A	(7)	20. E	(7)	20. C	(8)
21. D	(10)	21. A	(4)	21. D	(7, 12)
22. C	(3)	22. D	(1)	22. A	(1)
23. D	(1)	23. C	(4)	23. C	(2)
24. A	(3)	24. D	(1)	24. B	(5, 12)
25. D	(6, 1)	25. B	(7, 9)	25. D	(8, 3)
26. C	(11, 4)	26. E	(1)	26. C	(3)
27. A	(7)	27. D	(4, 7)	27. D	(4)
28. B	(7)	28. A	(7)	28. A	(4, 13)
29. D	(4)	29. D	(4, 12)	29. B	(12)
30. A	(2)	30. D	(4)	30. C	(11, 3)
31. A	(1, 2)	31. C	(11)	31. D	(3, 4)
32. C	(3)	32. E	(8, 4)	32. A	(11, 3)
33. C	(4)	33. B	(4)	33. D	(1)
34. B	(12)	34. B	(5)	34. D	(2)
35. D	(8)	35. A	(11, 4)	35. D	(4, 7)
36. A	(8, 4)	36. D	(5, 3)	36. B	(11, 12)
37. D	(3)	37. C	(13, 4)	37. C	(4)
38. B	(6, 4)	38. B	(4)	38. C	(4, 3)
39. C	(4)	39. C	(8)	39. D	(4)
40. D	(2)	40. A	(1, 2)	40. D	(1, 4)

ENGLISH ANSWER KEYS

Practice Test 6

1. D (8, 12)
2. C (4)
3. A (3)
4. D (5)
5. E (1)
6. E (6)
7. B (12)
8. A (4)
9. E (1)
10. A (1, 2)
11. E (7)
12. C (6)
13. E (8, 4)
14. B (12)
15. D (9, 3)
16. C (3)
17. A (7)
18. B (8)
19. E (5, 13)
20. A (4)
21. E (11, 4)
22. B (11)
23. E (2)
24. A (12)
25. C (12, 4)
26. E (2)
27. D (7, 9)
28. E (4)
29. A (4)
30. A (1, 2)
31. C (4, 12)
32. B (13, 12)
33. E (5)
34. A (3)
35. E (1)
36. D (4)
37. B (11, 4)
38. A (7)
39. C (7)
40. E (2)

Practice Test 7

1. D (5, 12)
2. C (4, 12)
3. A (12)
4. B (3, 4)
5. A (4, 3)
6. C (6)
7. D (12, 4)
8. B (9)
9. A (13)
10. D (12, 9)
11. B (4)
12. C (1, 12)
13. A (8, 10)
14. B (4, 8)
15. A (8, 4, 3)
16. B (4)
17. C (3)
18. D (12, 7)
19. B (1)
20. A (10, 12)
21. A (4)
22. A (4, 1)
23. B (8, 4)
24. D (12, 1)
25. D (3, 4)
26. B (7)
27. C (7, 12)
28. D (4)
29. B (4)
30. C (5)
31. B (4)
32. C (7)
33. B (11)
34. C (6)
35. C (8)
36. B (7, 4)
37. D (3)
38. D (4)
39. B (11)
40. D (4)

Answers — Reading Strategies

CHAPTER 10: VOCABULARY STRATEGIES

EXERCISE 1

1. monopoly – control by one person or group. The definition cue comes after the word. "Mono" is a prefix meaning "one" (see list of word parts).

2. fixed prices – one constant price. The previous sentence suggests that since only one company controls the production of a good, there would be one price.

3. oligopolies – several companies producing the same product. There is a definition cue in the previous sentence and a context cue in the sentence in which it appears.

4. variable cost – changing or fluctuating prices. In the list of word parts, "var" is the Latin root for "change."

5. mergers – combining of components into one large corporation. The key word "or" introduces the definition cue.

6. portend – suggest or warn of. The previous sentence implies a warning or a cautious feeling.

EXERCISE 2

1. reclamation – restoring (productivity). The contrast with waste disposal is a possible cue. "Re" is a prefix meaning "again"; therefore, we can claim wasted materials again.

2. recourse – choice or alternative. The words "simply no" and "but" suggest no other way. The prefix "re" (again) and the word "course" when placed together with "no" suggest no way or path to follow.

3. degraded – broken down or decomposed. The prefix "de" means to reverse or to do the opposite. The root "grad" means to improve; therefore, there is a reversal of progress.

4. feasibility – possibility. The verb "demonstrated" suggests something that can be shown or manifested.

5. Producer Players – the recycling systems made up of forests and agricultural lands. "Where" acts as a referent to recycling systems.

6. intrude – enter in an unwanted manner. The reference is to the "nutrients" in the same sentence.

7. free ride – something gained without any effort or responsibility. Precious metals and minerals will no longer be obtained without great effort.

8. exploiting – to take advantage of or use in a selfish way.

9. virgin – natural, raw, or unused. The contrast cue here is that since the recycling of used materials is more energy-efficient, then the continued exploitation of unused materials makes less sense.

10. amuck – in a confused manner.

11. paradox – a statement of contradiction that may in reality be true. The paradox arises from the fact that the increased use of natural resources like coal and oil will foster unnatural, destructive cycles in our environment.

CHAPTER 11: REFERRING STRATEGIES

EXERCISE 1

1. bun– hair pulled to the back of the head in a knot.

2. scribbled – written in a sloppy or careless manner. The cues are "phrase" which comes before and "letters" which follows the word. The Latin root "scrib" also means to write.

3. wary – careful, cautious. The shifting of Canice's eyes suggests fear and caution.

4. "20-cent" bags – small plastic bags of cocaine worth $20 apiece on the street. The definition cue comes after the term.

5. Canice is an indigent grandmother who sells drugs to support her grandchildren.

6. Canice is going to obtain cocaine from a dealer so she can sell it for needed cash.

7. In the second and third paragraphs, the author indicates that Canice sells drugs so that she can buy food for her grandchildren.

8. A Sunday morning (see first paragraph).

9. She will receive cash for Canice's groceries (end of paragraph 3).

10. Four. They are: 1) The Community Gospel Church, 2) Wood Street Apartments, 3) Fifth Street Elementary School, 4) The abandoned three story building.

11. Canice looks around so no one will see her when she scoots into the abandoned building.

12. Lack of food or poor food. At the end of paragraph 2, Canice recalls the "hungry eyes of her grandchildren."

EXERCISE 2

1. deterrents – obstacles or hindrances. Fear of something may discourage or hinder an action.

2. incidence – occurrence.

3. indiscretions – blunders or bad choices. Whether one contracts TD or not will depend on the right or wrong food choices one makes while traveling.

4. prudence – caution or foresight.

5. prophylactic – protective or preventive. The phrase "such as" points to examples of prophylactic measures — drugs and oral agents, thus providing clues to the word's meaning.

6. antimicrobial – capable of suppressing or destroying microorganisms such as bacteria, parasites, etc. "Anti" is a prefix meaning against. The roots for microbe derive from the Greek words for small (micro) and life (bio).

7. regimens – procedures or rules. The contexts where this word appears suggest ways to treat diarrhea or rules to follow while traveling.

8. They fear travelers' diarrhea or sickness in general. See paragraph 1.

9. Sixteen million persons. See paragraph 1.

10. False. Serious cases are rare. See paragraph 1.

11. All are equally liable to contract this illness. See paragraphs 1 and 4.

12. The effect is an economic one, the loss of 100 billion annually. See paragraph 1.

13. Intended destination, dietary choices, and style of travel. The presence of infectious agents may also be considered.

14. Neither is more useful. Scientists continue to debate this issue. See paragraph 4.

CHAPTER 12: REASONING STRATEGIES

EXERCISE 1

1. In the first paragraph, the main idea appears in the first sentence. In the third paragraph, part of the main idea is introduced in the first sentence and is completed in the last sentence.

2. Based on the losses after the fall of the Roman Empire, we could infer that Rome controlled and unified a large area of the world. Because of safe and efficient roads, the Roman economy was generally good, and the arts and literature flourished.

3. A president of the country. Like the king, the president holds the highest office in the land.

4. In the first paragraph, the author explains the causes or reasons for the uncertainty — the rise of feudalism. The author also classifies the various levels of society.

5. Based on the tone words in this chapter, the best choices would be serious, factual, objective or neutral.

6. The point of view seems to be that of a scholar or historian.

7. Feudalism came about because of chaotic conditions after the fall of the Roman Empire. People joined together in small groups for protection and mutual benefit.

8. Based on the number of times it is mentioned, social organization makes the best sense. The author discusses it frequently.

9. The lowest member is the serf and the highest member is God (see paragraph 3).

10. genius – talent or gift

11. factions – groups, parties. The word "political" suggests groups or parties.

12. hybrid – mixture, cross. "Mingling" in the previous sentence is the context cue.

13. hierarchical – organized into classes or ranks. The word "hierarchical" is explained in the sentence following .it.

EXERCISE 2

1. In the second paragraph, the main idea is in the first sentence. In the fourth paragraph, the main idea centers around the techniques and themes used to create oral tales.

2. Among possible conclusions are: 1) Language goes beyond the communication of information; 2) In rural Yugoslavia, language is used to preserve stories and traditions; 3) Oral poetry allows illiterate villagers to express and preserve their culture and traditions.

3. The best choices would be serious, factual, objective, or neutral.

4. In the fourth paragraph, the author uses process analysis and some general analysis as well. The fifth paragraph is an example of theorizing or hypothesizing.

5. Poetry written in isolation can be revised or refined whereas spoken poetry must be given spontaneously and shaped on the spot.

6. Rapid creation of metrical lines, use of familiar expressions, and patterned speech. See paragraph 4.

7. Among the reasons are: 1) The role of oral tradition in the creation of heroic epics; 2) The influence of storytelling on thinking and communicating in the native culture.

8. shaped – formed or adapted. The previous sentence provides a contrast cue.

9. feat – deed or action. The referent "this" points to the action of performing from the previous sentence.

10. guslari – Serbo-Croation epic singers. The definition cue precedes the word.

11. analog – resemblance or similarity.

12. recurrent – occurring or appearing again. The prefix "re" means again.

13. fixed – stationary or constant. The contrast cue "but" provides a clue as does the sentence that follows.

14. interdisciplinary – between or among disciplines or subject areas. "Inter" is a Latin prefix meaning between or among. Specialists forming a team also implies a working together among disciplines.

Answers and Explanations (CPE Diagnostic Reading Test)

1. (B) This answer makes the best sense compared to the other choices.

2. (E) The question asks for the order in which the events occurred. Laura passes the school children first. Her last activity will be the stop at Sears.

3. (B) Laura's reference to the "multi-colored leaves" suggests fall.

4. (A) "Forbade" is the past tense of forbid. In the context, it implies limits.

5. (D) Though the main idea is not stated directly, the author suggests this idea through Laura's characterization.

6. (E) In the flashbacks to Laura's childhood (paragraph 3), she recalls feeding chickens and cleaning the water trough.

7. (C) Laura's relationship with her husband comes through her thoughts. He tells her where to go and what to do (paragraph 1). She is not able to ask questions (paragraph 3).

8. (A) Laura has a husband and works (paragraph 1). She also has children (paragraph 2).

9. (E) In paragraph 3, the purpose of Laura's drive is made clear.

10. (D) In the beginning of the first paragraph, the author describes Laura driving "just ahead of the bus."

11. (C) This detail is stated in the first paragraph.

12. (A) In the context, ended makes sense since it appears to be the final event of the festival after dancing and singing.

13. (D) The author explains both similarities and differences between tragedy and comedy.

14. (B) The author does not criticize or make fun of the subject. The passage is objective and factual.

15. (E) One can determine the meaning of the phrase through analysis of the Latin origins. "Deus" means "god" and "machina" is "machine"or "structure." There is also a context clue. The preceding sentence defines it.

16. (E) This question required you to apply what you read to a different situation. An auditorium most resembles the theater described in paragraph 3.

17. (C) The last sentence of the final paragraph provides the answer.

18. (B) The author states this fact in the first sentence of the passage.

19. (D) All of the statements are true except for one answer. The description in paragraph 3 indicates that the audience sat in front of and on either side of the stage.

20. (A) This question requires the reader to identify the main idea of the passage. Each passage contains part of the main idea. The first and second paragraphs deal with the development of Greek drama. The third paragraph focuses on the way it was presented.

21. (D) "Laissez-faire" comes from the French expression (to let people do as they please). From the sentence following the expression, we can infer that since the government needed to be more involved in helping the workers, a "laissez-faire" non-involved policy was not working.

22. (A) This answer requires the drawing of a conclusion. Though the passage is about post-Civil War problems, there are hints that before the Civil War the United States was largely agricultural. See the third sentence of paragraph 1 and the second paragraph.

23. (C) Historical analysis consists of an author's comments and opinions about a series of past events. This passage has historical examples and reveals the author examining the causes and effects of the events.

24. (C) In the first paragraph, the author says that the business boom excluded the lower classes while the upper class became rich.

25. (E) This statement includes the important ideas discussed in each paragraph. The other answers focus on only part of the passage.

26. (B) The sentence preceding the word provides the clue. "Starvation wages" suggests poverty.

27. (E) The passage does not directly state the time period discussed.

28. (E) This fact is discussed in paragraph 4.

29. (A) The answer to this question requires an interpretation of a bar graph. The middle bar represents immigrants from Northern and western Europe in millions of persons. Because each interval equals two million persons, the best estimate would be 10.5 million.

30. (D) The Populists clearly identify themselves with the farmers (see second paragraph).

31. (E) This answer derives from a hypothetical question; that is, the situation is imaginary. Questions of this type are sometimes asked on the CPE Reading Test. Basically, you should apply the facts of the passage to this new situation. Determining the cause of the girl's reaction first by visiting an allergist would make the best sense.

32. (C) This statement is the only one that can be verified (see paragraph 2). The others are not stated in the passage.

33. (A) Because of the technical nature of the discussion, the viewpoint is most likely that of a person with a medical background.

34. (D) The context of "suspect foods" and "molds and dusts" suggests something bad.

35. (B) The context of husband and wife from the previous sentence is the tipoff. "However" is a key word, suggesting a shift in thought after the phrase is defined. The Latin roots con (together) and jugum (to join) are also clues.

36. (D) This reason is paraphrased from the second paragraph.

37. (A) In the first sentence of paragraph 3, the author introduces the two categories of allergy medicine and then defines them.

38. (B) This fact is directly stated in the last paragraph.

39. (D) Wheezing is the only side effect not mentioned in the explanation of side effects related to allergy medications (paragraph 4).

40. (C) Correct diagnosis and proper medication are the best conclusion one can draw since they are both fully described in the passage. There is no factual basis in the passage for the other conclusions.

READING ANSWER KEYS

Practice Test 1

1.	B	21.	D
2.	D	22.	E
3.	E	23.	D
4.	D	24.	A
5.	A	25.	D
6.	E	26.	A
7.	D	27.	B
8.	B	28.	D
9.	A	29.	B
10.	C	30.	D
11.	E	31.	A
12.	B	32.	B
13.	B	33.	D
14.	D	34.	E
15.	C	35.	C
16.	A	36.	C
17.	E	37.	A
18.	E	38.	E
19.	D	39.	C
20.	C	40.	B

Practice Test 2

1.	C	21.	C
2.	A	22.	D
3.	C	23.	C
4.	E	24.	A
5.	B	25.	D
6.	D	26.	B
7.	B	27.	E
8.	A	28.	C
9.	E	29.	D
10.	D	30.	A
11.	D	31.	A
12.	C	32.	C
13.	A	33.	E
14.	B	34.	D
15.	C	35.	B
16.	A	36.	D
17.	D	37.	C
18.	C	38.	E
19.	E	39.	E
20.	B	40.	B

Practice Test 3

1.	A	21.	A
2.	B	22.	D
3.	D	23.	C
4.	D	24.	D
5.	C	25.	B
6.	D	26.	B
7.	B	27.	D
8.	C	28.	C
9.	B	29.	C
10.	A	30.	B
11.	A	31.	D
12.	B	32.	B
13.	B	33.	D
14.	A	34.	D
15.	C	35.	A
16.	D	36.	C
17.	C	37.	D
18.	D	38.	D
19.	B	39.	C
20.	B	40.	C

Practice Test 4

1.	B	21.	C
2.	A	22.	D
3.	D	23.	B
4.	C	24.	D
5.	B	25.	A
6.	C	26.	B
7.	D	27.	C
8.	D	28.	A
9.	A	29.	A
10.	C	30.	C
11.	A	31.	C
12.	B	32.	A
13.	D	33.	D
14.	B	34.	C
15.	C	35.	D
16.	D	36.	B
17.	A	37.	A
18.	B	38.	B
19.	C	39.	A
20.	A	40.	C

Practice Test 5

1.	D	21.	D
2.	C	22.	C
3.	A	23.	C
4.	B	24.	A
5.	D	25.	A
6.	B	26.	B
7.	A	27.	C
8.	C	28.	B
9.	C	29.	B
10.	A	30.	D
11.	B	31.	C
12.	C	32.	A
13.	D	33.	D
14.	C	34.	C
15.	A	35.	B
16.	D	36.	B
17.	B	37.	D
18.	B	38.	C
19.	A	39.	C
20.	C	40.	D

A SELECTED BIBLIOGRAPHY

The following titles are merely a sampling of additional books that may help you prepare for the CPE. For additional titles and recommendations, see an instructor in the appropriate subject area.

MATHEMATICS

Keedy, Mervin L., and Marvin L. Bittinger. *A Problem-Solving Approach to Introductory Algebra.* 2nd ed. Reading, Mass.: Addison-Wesley, 1986.

Rich, Barnett. *Modern Elementary Algebra.* New York: McGraw-Hill, 1971.

_____. *Plane Geometry with Coordinate Geometry.* New York: McGraw-Hill, 1963.

_____. *Review of Elementary Mathematics.* New York: McGraw-Hill, 1977.

ENGLISH

Fawcett, Susan, and Alvin Sandberg. *Grassroots: The Writer's Workbook.* 3rd ed. Boston: Houghton Mifflin, 1987.

Gefvert, Constance J. *The Confident Writer.* 2nd ed. New York: Norton, 1988.

Howell, James F. and Dean Memering. *Brief Handbook for Writers.* 2nd Ed. Englewood Cliffs, N.J.: Prentice Hall, 1989.

Kirszner, Laurie G., and Stephen R. Mandell. *The Holt Handbook.* Fort Worth: Holt, Rinehart and Winston, 1989.

Perrin, Robert. *The Beacon Handbook.* Boston: Houghton Mifflin, 1987.

READING

Funk, Wilfred, and Norman Lewis. *30 Days to a More Powerful Vocabulary.* New rev. ed. New York: Pocket Books, 1970.

Nist, Sherrie L., and William Diehl. *Developing Textbook Thinking.* Lexington, Mass.: D.C. Heath, 1985.

Smith, Brenda D. *Bridging the Gap: College Reading.* 2nd ed. Glenview, Ill.: Scott, Foresman, 1985.